CAMBRIDGE LIBRARY COLLECTION

Books of enduring scholarly value

Women's Writing

The later twentieth century saw a huge wave of academic interest in women's writing, which led to the rediscovery of neglected works from a wide range of genres, periods and languages. Many books that were immensely popular and influential in their own day are now studied again, both for their own sake and for what they reveal about the social, political and cultural conditions of their time. A pioneering resource in this area is Orlando: Women's Writing in the British Isles from the Beginnings to the Present (http://orlando.cambridge.org), which provides entries on authors' lives and writing careers, contextual material, timelines, sets of internal links, and bibliographies. Its editors have made a major contribution to the selection of the works reissued in this series within the Cambridge Library Collection, which focuses on non-fiction publications by women on a wide range of subjects from astronomy to biography, music to political economy, and education to prison reform.

The Bacon–Shakspere Question Answered

Charlotte Carmichael Stopes (1840–29) is best known as the mother of birth control advocate Marie Stopes. Like her daughter, Stopes forged the way for women seeking academic careers: she was the first woman in Scotland to graduate from university, and was later elected a fellow of the Royal Society of Literature. In this monograph Stopes resolves to settle once and for all whether or not Francis Bacon wrote the plays attributed to William Shakespeare, concluding that the Baconian theory is wholly without foundation. Over nearly 300 pages of erudite argument, Stopes examines the numerous distinctions between the lives and experiences of the two Renaissance writers, their differing styles of writing, and the evidence provided by Shakespeare's playwright contemporaries themselves. Stopes' book also includes extensive appendices providing background information on Shakespeare, Warwickshire and the early modern theatre in London.

For more information on this author, see http://orlando.cambridge.org/public/svPeople?person_id=stopch

Cambridge University Press has long been a pioneer in the reissuing of out-of-print titles from its own backlist, producing digital reprints of books that are still sought after by scholars and students but could not be reprinted economically using traditional technology. The Cambridge Library Collection extends this activity to a wider range of books which are still of importance to researchers and professionals, either for the source material they contain, or as landmarks in the history of their academic discipline.

Drawing from the world-renowned collections in the Cambridge University Library, and guided by the advice of experts in each subject area, Cambridge University Press is using state-of-the-art scanning machines in its own Printing House to capture the content of each book selected for inclusion. The files are processed to give a consistently clear, crisp image, and the books finished to the high quality standard for which the Press is recognised around the world. The latest print-on-demand technology ensures that the books will remain available indefinitely, and that orders for single or multiple copies can quickly be supplied.

The Cambridge Library Collection will bring back to life books of enduring scholarly value (including out-of-copyright works originally issued by other publishers) across a wide range of disciplines in the humanities and social sciences and in science and technology.

The Bacon–Shakspere Question Answered

Charlotte Carmichael Stopes

CAMBRIDGE
UNIVERSITY PRESS

CAMBRIDGE UNIVERSITY PRESS

Cambridge, New York, Melbourne, Madrid, Cape Town, Singapore,
São Paolo, Delhi, Dubai, Tokyo, Mexico City

Published in the United States of America by Cambridge University Press, New York

www.cambridge.org
Information on this title: www.cambridge.org/9781108021906

© in this compilation Cambridge University Press 2010

This edition first published 1889
This digitally printed version 2010

ISBN 978-1-108-02190-6 Paperback

THE

BACON-SHAKSPERE
QUESTION

ANSWERED.

THE

BACON-SHAKSPERE

QUESTION

ANSWERED.

BY

C. STOPES.

" *Non sans droict.*"

Second Edition, Corrected and Enlarged.

LONDON:

TRÜBNER & CO., LUDGATE HILL.

1889.

𝔅allantyne 𝔓ress
BALLANTYNE, HANSON AND CO.
EDINBURGH AND LONDON

PREFACE TO FIRST EDITION.

—◆—

THE great Shaksperean scholars have considered it beneath their dignity to answer the assertions of the Baconians. "Silence" may be "golden" in regard to the character of the living, but in defence of the character of the dead, I think that speech is golden when it answers speech; and proof, when it contests proof. Hence I thought it not in vain to put together the main results of the studies I had undertaken on my own account during the past two years. These may help to turn the balance of opinion in some wavering minds, or to aid some warm Shakspereans (that are too busy to go through original work on their own account) to reconsider the subject justly, and "give a reason for the faith that is in them."

C. STOPES.

PREFACE TO SECOND EDITION.

——◆——

DURING the four months that have elapsed since the publication of my little book comparing Bacon and Shakspere, I have continued my studies at the British Museum and elsewhere, so as to be able somewhat to correct its errors and expand its materials in a second edition. The enormous mass of matter at our disposal makes it impossible to do this either thoroughly or fully. What I have aimed at is, first, to *suggest* the lines of greatest distinction in Life, Character, and Writing, without attempting to exhaust them (except in the one new illustration), so that all may be tempted to read for themselves and "see if these things be so." All may or ought to be possessors of the works of Shakspere and Bacon, and should be able to read them at home. Second, to put before all, in a concise form, the most important information to be derived from antecedent, contemporary, and later literature, as only those who live near some great treasure-house of books like the British Museum are able to do, by seeing and comparing them together. I have seen the originals of all I quote, except four or five, in which case I quote my authority. Third, to show from these the weaknesses of the Baconian theory.

Some few have thought my work in vain. It certainly has not been so in regard to my own education, at least. In regard to my subjects, I can only say that most men would rather be tried in open court on a clear charge than to have rumours gather around them affecting the multitude. To allow statements to appear unanswered seems, at best, too like accepting the Scotch verdict of "not proven." This argues only weakness in the arguments of the accusers, and not innocence on the part of the accused; the accusation haunts men's minds long after, and may, at any time, be revived. But a clear case, openly tried, arguments fairly sifted on both sides, can result in a unanimous verdict, boldly given, of "not guilty," whereby the accused is freed from all the consequence and reproach of the accusation, and men forget it. If I am trespassing on the sphere of Senior Counsel I regret it; but I trust my action will not prejudice the case. I have done the best I could under the circumstances. My desire is that the motto Shakspere chose to bear through life, his works should also bear as his—

"*Non sans droict.*"

CHARLOTTE CARMICHAEL STOPES.

KENWYN, NORWOOD, LONDON,
December 1888.

CONTENTS.

—◆◆—

SOME INTRODUCTORY DATES.

—◆◆—

1558–1603. Elizabeth's Reign.

1575. The Lord Mayor expelled players from London. They settled outside the liberty.

1576. Theatres built :—
1st. The Theatre ⎱ outside the liberty.
2nd. The Curtain ⎰
3rd. Blackfriars, by Burbage, within.
A great controversy arose as to morality of plays.

1576. Gosson writes for the stage.

1579. He alters his views, and brings out *The Schoole of Abuse*, censuring plays, &c. ; dedicated to Sir Philip Sydney.

1583. Philip Stubbes, in his *Anatomy of Abuses*, exposed and denounced *Stage Plays and their Evils*.

1586. Sydney died. Shakspere came to London.

1592. Greene, Chettle, Nash, and Harvey commenced a literary controversy.

1593. The Globe on Bankside built.

1593. *Venus and Adonis* published and dedicated by the author to Lord Southampton.

1594. *Lucrece* published.

1595. Sydney's *Apology for Poetry*, in which he took the opposite view to Stubbes, published.

1595. Clarke's *Polimanteia* gave first printed reference to *Venus and Adonis* and *Lucrece* as Shakspere's.

1597. Bacon's *Essays* published by the author. Shakspere's *Richard II.*, *Richard III.*, and *Romeo and Juliet* published by the printers as Shakspere's.

1598. Francis Meres, M.A., a graduate of both Universities, noticed Shakspere with praise in *Palladis Tamia.*

1599. John Rainoldes published his *Overthrow of Stage Plays.*

1601. John Shakspere died.

1601-2 (Jan. 18). *Merry Wives of Windsor,* as originally written, licensed for the press ; printed 4to, 1602.

1606. *The Return from Pernassus,* acted about 1602, printed with a highly eulogistic account and flattering estimate of Shakspere.

1607. Shakspere's daughter Susanna married Dr. Hall.

1608. Mary Shakspere died.

1609. Sonnets published.

1610. Histrio mastix ; or, the Player Whipt.

1612. *Apology for Actors,* by Thomas Heywood, is printed.

1613. Globe Theatre burnt during performance of *Henry VIII.*

1614. Shakspere, according to contemporary testimony, expressed a strong repugnance to the enclosure of common lands near Stratford.

1614. Great fire at Stratford.

1615. Greene's *Refutation of the "Apology for Actors."*

1616. Shakspere's daughter Judith married Richard Quiney.

1616. Jonson at Stratford. Shakspere died.

1616. All Jonson's papers burned, and probably some of Shakspere's, in London. Fire at Stratford.

1623. Shakspere's wife, Anne Hathaway, died. Heming and Condell brought out his collected works.

1642. Edict against plays.

1660. Restoration.

CONTEMPORARY BIOGRAPHICAL DATES.

1536-1608. Thomas Sackville, Lord Buckhurst, and Earl of Dorset (dramatic poet).

1552-1596. George Peele (dramatic poet).

1552-1618. Sir Walter Raleigh (poet and historian).

1553–1599. Edmund Spenser (poet).

1554–1601. John Lyly (dramatic poet, and author of *Euphues' Anatomy of Wit*, 1569 ; *Euphues, his England*, 1582).

1554–1586. Sir Philip Sydney (soldier, poet, and author of the *Arcadia* and *Sonnets and Apologie for Poetrie*).

1554–1628. Fulke Greville, Lord Brooke (philosophic poet).

1556–1625. Thomas Lodge (dramatist and prose-writer).

1557–1634. George Chapman (dramatic poet, translator).

1558–1609. William Warner (author of *Albion's England*, historical poem).

1560–1592. Robert Greene (dramatist and pamphleteer).

1561–1612. Sir John Harrington : his translation of *Ariosto* published 1591.

1561–1626. Francis Bacon, Lord Verulam, Viscount St. Alban (philosopher, historian, &c.).

1562–1619. Samuel Daniel (poet).

1562–1593. Christopher Marlowe (dramatist and poet).

1563–1618. John Davies of Hereford (poet).

1563–1631. Michael Drayton (poet, author of *Polyolbion*).

1563–1618. Joshua Sylvester (translator of Du Bartas' *Divine Weeks and Works*).

1564–1616. William Shakspere.

1567–1600. Thomas Nash (dramatist and pamphleteer).

1568–1639. Sir Henry Wotton (essayist and poet).

1569–1640. John Webster (dramatic poet).

1569–1626. Sir John Davies (philosophic poet).

1570–1632. Edward Fairfax : published his version of *Tasso*, 1600.

1573–1631. Dr. John Donne (poet and preacher).

1574–1626. Richard Barnefield (poet).

1574–1637. Ben Jonson (dramatist, poet, and critic).

1575–1634. John Marston (dramatist).

1576–1625. John Fletcher (dramatist and poet).

1586–1615. Francis Beaumont (dramatist and poet).

CONTEMPORARY MINOR DRAMATISTS.

Henry Chettle.	Thomas Nabbes.
Thomas Dekker.	William Rowley.
John Day.	Robert Taylor.
Thomas Middleton.	Cyril Tourneur.

William Haughton.

THE

BACON-SHAKSPERE QUESTION

ANSWERED.

—◆—

INTRODUCTORY CHAPTER.

THE Bacon-Shakspere theory in one way benefits literary
students. The opportunity of studying, on parallel lines of
date and action, the lives of the two greatest writers of the
greatest period of English literature is too good to be lost.
The Baconian theory acts as a *filum labyrinthi* in the mass
of materials of the period, and much matter that might
otherwise be passed as unimportant is carefully sifted in
reviewing what has come down to us from a Past that was
once a Present.

The proceedings of the Bacon Society tell us, "The contention of the Baconians is that William Shakspere had
no hand whatever in the production of either the plays or
the poems—that he was an uneducated man, who could
just manage to write his own name; that there is not a
particle of evidence that he ever wrote, or could write, anything else." They also accuse him of every sin and crime,
short of murder, to take away his character, and thus argue
from his want of character an incapacity to have produced
his poems. It is reasoning in a circle with a vengeance,
when the *argumentum ad hominem* is thus made to contra-
dict the *argumentum ad rem*. The personal animus shown
in the way their proofs are presented, discounts from the

validity of their conclusions. The Baconians are unwise, they try to prove too much. They say Shakspere was utterly illiterate and unable to write any of his works. If I can only prove he wrote "some," or even that he was *capable* of writing "any," I can prove their universal assertion *false* by a particular.

I cannot imagine any literary student asserting Bacon's claim. I cannot imagine a psychologic student believing in its possibility. As Dr. Furnivall said, "Some men are born colour-blind, and cannot distinguish tints; those must be born character-blind that cannot distinguish Bacon from Shakspere."

I may divide my answers into four groups.

1st. The probabilities from known character and education of the writer of the plays.

2nd. Internal evidence, gained by comparing Shakspere's plays and the works of Bacon, and referring each to the character of the ascribed author and supposed author.

3rd. The external evidence of most of the poems and plays being at some time claimed by Shakspere, and *never* by Bacon.

4th. The external evidence of the writings of contemporaries, some of whom personally knew both these great men.

The question is too large to be discussed fully in these pages, yet I must briefly consider each of these four divisions, introducing specially as a novel illustration the differing views of the two writers regarding stimulants. Afterwards I shall notice briefly the history of the heresy, and one or two particular contradictions.

CHAPTER I.

THE PROBABILITIES FROM KNOWN CHARACTER AND EDUCATION OF THE WRITER OF THE PLAYS.

THE probabilities from character and education are those that the Baconians specially present to us in favour of their theory; so it is well to consider this point first.

The psychologic aspect is of prime importance in such a discussion, but the historical is a part of the psychological. All minds live and learn through environments; all are, to a certain extent, moulded by circumstances.

The first question naturally to be considered is the birth-place of an individual. William Shakspere was not born in London, it is true, but probably he was born in a more favourable nursery for poets than York House, Strand.

Warwickshire belonged to the province Flavia Cæsariensis. It is a central county; the great Roman roads from Dover to Chester and from Totnes to Lincoln met there, so that much traffic and interchange of ideas must have sharpened the natives, from the times of the Romans on into the sixteenth century. In Saxon times it was the district of Mercia, whither King Alfred sent for scholars, and which gave the literary language to later England. This pre-eminence it had not lost. Bacon, in his *Jewel of Joy*, dedicated in 1549 to the Princess Elizabeth, speaks of it as the most intellectual of the English counties.[1]

---

[1] See Appendix, Note 1.

Drayton speaks of it as "warlike Warwickshire." It
was the border-land between the Celtic and Teutonic races.
Shakspere is the type Englishman who has, as Green says,
"combined the mobility and fancy of the Celt with the
depth and energy of the Teuton," and the place of his birth
must not be ignored. By the River Avon it was divided
into "Arden," a part of the primeval forest in the north-
west, and Felldon in the south-east, where hills, dales, clear-
ings, woods, and fields alternated. The whole neighbourhood
was haunted by suggestions; subjects for romance floated
in the very atmosphere.[1]

Guy of Warwick [2] and Heraud of Arden formerly roamed
there. Evesham and Bosworth were fought on the borders
of the shire. Layamon and Piers Ploughman and Wycliffe
were writers of the district. Henry VII. had slept in
Coventry, where the old "Mysteries" lingered until Shakspere's youth, and the pageants of Kenilworth (1575) were
among the most magnificent in Elizabeth's royal pro-
gresses.

The address presented to Elizabeth on coming to Warwick
in 1572 gives the history of the shire under the Britons
and Saxons. The Black Book of Warwick contains an
account of the celebration of the Order of St. Michael (1571)
by Robert Dudley, Earl of Leicester, at St. Mary's Church
in Warwick; and an account of the magnificent funeral of
the Earl of Northampton in 1571 at Warwick. Though
the young Shakspere may not have seen these pageants,
he must have heard of them.

[1] John Rous, our earliest antiquary, in the reign of Edward IV. writes
the Antiquities of Warwick, of which Dugdale makes much use in his
Warwickshire, 1644.

[2] In the *Gesta Romanorum* is the story of Guy of Warwick return-
ing from Palestine to a hermit's cell near Warwick, and receiving alms
for three days from his lady without her recognising him.
"Guy of Warwick, I understand,
Slew a dragon in Northumberland."
He also fought Collbrun, the Danish giant.—*Legend of Guy of Warwick.*

Jean Paul Richter said that every poet ought to choose to have himself born in a small town, so as to grow up having the advantages of town and country life. This happened in Shakspere's case, and every other condition known of his life is essentially congruous with the idea of a poet's development. Stratford was no inconsiderable town. It was of old foundation, having a history that led back to Roman times. In Shakspere's early life it was prospering, in common with the rest of the kingdom, under Elizabeth. Camden calls it "emporiolum non inelegans." In Speede's county map of England, 1610,[1] we find it marked as of the same size and importance as Warwick, and second only to Coventry in the county. It possessed the first highway bridge over the Avon below Warwick, and much traffic must therefore have passed through it. It had a handsome church ; liberal feast-days ; an annual fair ; frequent visits from the Earl of Leicester's and other companies of players ; a good grammar-school, and a town-council intelligent enough to know the value of written records, and to preserve them.

The scenery was sweet rather than majestic, yet varied sufficiently, within the stretches of a young man's ride, for all the inland suggestions of the scenery of the plays ; for the foliage, the flowers, the heaths. For the town lay just by the fair Forest of Arden,[2] placed on the sweet Avon, whose banks, with their "hoar willows," their "footpath way," their stiles, their merry knaves, are often suggested in his plays.

---

[1] See Appendix, Note 2.
[2] " Where nightingales in Arden sit and sing
    Amongst the dainty dew-empearlèd flowers."—DRAYTON.
" Muse, first of Arden tell, whose footsteps yet are found
In her rough woodlands more than any other ground,
That mighty Arden held, even in her height of pride,
Her one hand touching Trent, the other Severn's side."
— DRAYTON'S *Polyolbion.*

Shakspere was born of one of the best families within that town.[1] His father had passed through the various grades of municipal dignity, having been successively Ale-taster, one of the four Constables, one of the four Affeerors, then High Alderman or Bailiff of Stratford, and that more than once, until 1586; and a sense of importance and general interest must have risen in his house. He was evidently much respected; even the old records give witness of that; and he must have met the best society to be had.[2] His wife, an heiress of the neighbouring old family of Arden, of good connections, was a great "gift from God" to him. Well-endowed and capable; probably handsome,[3] and certainly affectionate; she gave her husband a chance in life such as few of his townsfolk had. No doubt she cherished the memories of her old family, that went back into warlike Saxon times; even though her branch of it had ended among seven distaffs.[4]

On many winter nights she would doubtless pour into the youthful ears of her children the family and local legends (for tradition in those days took the place of much of our modern education), and would connect the present with the past. A sense of the romance of war and a dream of the pomp of courts would thus arise in young Shakspere's heart. We can see how he would appreciate the martial suggestion in his patronymic, so much made of by his contemporaries.[5]

[1] See Appendix, Note 3.   [2] See Appendix, Note 4.
[3] Oldys says Mary Arden was beautiful.
[4] There is an old superstition about the seventh child of the same sex having a "seer's eye." Mayhap, Mary had just enough of it to transfer it to her heir.
[5] A record of the name appears in Kent in 1279: "Some are named from that they carried, as Palmer, . . . Long-sword, Broad-spear, and, in some respect, Shakespeare."—*Camden's Remaines*, ed. 1605.
"Breakspear, Shakspear, and the like, have bin surnames imposed

Though his father seems to have had at least little skill with the pen, William would certainly get the best opportunities of education the place could afford. Nine years before his birth, King Edward VI. specially interested himself in the re-establishment by royal charter of the Free Grammar-School of Stratford, which had been suppressed at the dissolution of the religious houses in his father's reign. The head-master had £20 a year at the time the master of Eton had but £10 a year. It may be supposed that he was at least rather above the average, and that his school was relatively a good one. Mr. Baynes[1] gives a list of the books used there. But I imagine that to this list should be added Thomas Wilson's *Art of Rhetoric*, which was dedicated in 1557 to the Earl of Warwick, to whom Stratford belonged, and would very naturally be introduced here. Not only does he explain how "three things are required of an orator, to teache, to delight, and to persuade;" but the foundation of Iago's speech, which the Baconians insist is from untranslated Berni, is found therein. Herein also is an epistle devised by Erasmus in behalf of his friend, to persuade a young gentleman to marry, that suggests passages in the Sonnets. William must have learned something at school. No doubt he often was dreaming and indolent, he had so many interests. He might remember himself when he wrote of the "school-boy creeping unwillingly to school," or playing truant, from facts to weave his fancies, "of imagination all compact." The old chap-books and romances must have floated many a time between the pages of his Latin Grammar and his eyes. The river, the stile-paths, the woods, the wild

---

upon the first bearers of them for valour and feates of armes."—*Verstegen's Restitution of Decayed Intelligence*, ed. 1605.

In Polydoron (undated) : " Names were first questionlesse given for distinction, facultie, consanguinity, desert, quality, . . . as Armstrong, Shakspeare of high quality."

[1] Appendix, Note 2.

flowers, the clouds, and the birds must have been an early attraction to the natural poet-soul.

Doubtless the temptations of beautiful Mother Nature were often too much for him, and he would rush off from the chattering town to the sweet solemn silences of the Forest of Arden, thinking, " I know a bank whereon the wild thyme blows ; " and perhaps he would dream there till he *saw* the Fairy Queen as evening fell, and was sworn into her service like Thomas of Ercildoune.

It was all so natural, further, for one like him to have merry times with young fellows as he grew older, and to play big schoolboy pranks on Sir Thomas Lucy and his keepers. We cannot but think there must have been some foundation for the legend of deer-stealing. It was a part of the romance of youth to re-enact the legends of the past. The old literature of the time shows that "to have a buck" was to win a feather in one's cap. The law of the time [1] proves that no dreadful consequences would have ensued on such a deed, even if Lucy had wished to enforce them, which would not have been likely had the culprit been a child of his old neighbour, Mary Arden, and of his old fellow Justice of the Peace, John Shakspere. Besides, a conclusive evidence of its haziness lies in the fact that Lucy was preparing to be member of Parliament for the county of Warwick, for which he was returned in 1584.

I do not think that Shakspere meant all the satire in Justice Shallow for Lucy. There must have been many another "Justice of the Peace" familiar to him, whose peculiarities would be more original than those of a culti-

[1] The "penalties" were only attached to poaching on the royal parks. For taking a deer from an "enclosed park," a man was liable to pay three times its price, or, in default, to remain in prison for three months. But the park from which Shakspere was said to have taken the deer, Fulbrooke, was not enclosed. It was sequestrated, and lay next to that of Sir Thomas Lucy, whose park also had not been "licensed" at the date necessary to make penalties legal.

vated man like Sir Thomas.[1] But a little irritation is displayed. My own opinion is that Lucy had withdrawn from intimacy with the family at the time of its waning fortunes, and roused a bitter feeling thus in the eldest son's heart, which afterwards expressed itself in *Timon*. But it was not Sir Thomas Lucy that drove Shakspere from Stratford.

His over-early and impetuous love, suddenly sobered by a hasty marriage, suggests many a poetic thought in his love scenes. But it was his too rapid awakening to the responsibilities of paternity that changed the current of his life. His father had a large family to support upon the lands, and the trade slipping from him; and more than enough domestic help to perform the various employments that farmers combined in those days before the division-of-labour system had arisen. Times or people had changed, and the fortunes of the family had grown darkest just before a new dawn.[2] Its eldest-born son rose to the emergency. His mother's inheritance, that should have been his own, had gone at great disadvantage in times of sore pressure. The Henley Street house was retained, but anxious thoughts must have often darkened it, how to keep the wolf from the door. There is no doubt that the money difficulties of that period acted as a peculiar, and perhaps necessary, training for the free poet-soul, and were the real cause of his after industry and worldly success. When, in the midst of his father's money anxieties (that he evidently sympathised in), he compli-

---

[1] Mr. Halliwell has unearthed the strange fact that Sir Thomas Lucy himself, supposed to be so Puritanic, was a patron of players, as he found in a record of the Chamberlain's accounts in Coventry, 1584 : " To Sir Thomas Lucy's plaiers, x. s." If so different in one respect from his received character, he may also be in another.

[2] There is a complaint that "for want of such trade as heretofore they had by clothing and making of yarn," the town had become less prosperous than formerly at this time.

cated matters by marrying Anne Hathaway before he
could support her, he had met the crisis of his life.

> "Love is too young to know what conscience is :
> Yet who knows not conscience is born of love."

After that he certainly felt that he must *give up* his future
life to duty. That he had power to combine two dissimilar aims, and succeed in both, showed no common
mind. In choosing a career, he allowed his inclinations
some play ; buckled on his knapsack, and, like many
another man, went to seek his fortune in London, and
found it. He went not unknown. His mother had good
friends, his father many acquaintances ; there were many
Stratford men in London ; I find about a dozen in the
Stationers' records ; but it is more than likely he went
straight to his old school-fellow Field, who was a printer
in Blackfriars. In Blackfriars also were the players that
had been often down in Stratford, Warwickshire men also,
Burbage among them. To them would he go, possibly with
the rough scroll of *Venus and Adonis,* the "first heir of his
invention," in his pocket. If he went to London in 1586,
as some think, it may only have been as a visit, for he
must have returned to Stratford in 1587, as he then concurred with his parents in giving up his right to inheritance in Asbies, that they might mortgage it further to
Lambert, for an additional sum of £20.[1]

Several companies of players were in Stratford in 1587,
and it is more than likely he went to London along with
them, and engaged to them. His father had always been
fond of spectacle, had been kind to the players in the day
of his power, and they, more than likely, had a kindly feeling towards the young Benedict of their own neighbourhood,
on whom the cares of domestic life were now pressing so
heavily. For there is no doubt his parents and younger

---

[1] See Appendix, Note 5.

brethren leaned on him, as well as Anne and his three children. His player-friends could not help him outside of their own circle ; but they did what they could for him, and took him into their company to train. This training would necessitate a thorough understanding of all the various responsibilities in the theatre, from the taking of the money at the door to arranging the seats and dresses.

He was young, handsome, healthy, and ambitious, a charming companion, a versatile genius. They very soon discovered his gifts, and taught him to act. Burbage wanted a young leading actor, and he filled the post awhile, acting Romeos. Seeing his power in impromptu, they set him to alter and freshen up some of their old stock of plays. His success in that department kindled him to spend his powers on original work, and in a few years he was famous ; how few relatively may be calculated, by comparing with his, the number of years it generally takes a poet to get written about by other poets or by professors of literature. The universality of his genius, his range of thought, his congruity of diction and sweetness of versification, must have been fed by a wonderful power of observation and retentive force of memory. His mind seemed like a magnet, that drew all grains of iron to itself, and impressed its power on what it drew.

Just think how rapidly he would develope then. Transplanted from the centre of a small town, where every one knew him, to the fringes of a great city unknown to him, the unknown ; how small the unit to him would seem before the mass of humanity. Instead of the Coventry Mysteries of his boyhood, and the travelling players of his youth, he would see in the best theatres the best plays of the time.[1] At first a critical spectator, he entered behind the scenes. The stage becomes a different thing when one treads it ; life is a different thing when seen from behind the foot-

[1] See Appendix, Note 6.

lights. The *people* would become the actors to him, and
he learned their ways by heart. He was endowed with a
determination to make the best possible of every opportunity. Among the stage-properties would be a large stock
of manuscript and printed plays, accepted and rejected. We
must remember that the Drama was but a modern revival.
It was then about fifty years old. Dr. Palsgrave's play of
Acolastus was printed 1529. Heywood's Plays appeared in
1533. Sackville's *Ferrex and Porrex*, 1554, had initiated
Tragedy and blank verse; and Nicholas Udall's *Ralph
Roister Doister*[1] had led off true Comedy (1553) in a rapid
transition from the old Mysteries, and *Gammer Gurton's
Needle* had followed it in 1575. By 1580 the form of art
had taken shape. Every writer was bound to be original
then, for the very form of art was original to the period.
How eagerly he would pore over the ripening powers of
Lily, Greene, Peele, Marlowe, Kyd, and Lodge, with a pre-
liminary rapture that kindled his own soul!

Marlowe was the one that most affected him, the only
one he definitely quoted, after his death saying—

> " Dead Shepherd, now we know thy spell of night :
> Who ever loved that loved not at first sight ? "—

the one who finally introduced blank verse, and wrote to
free the stage

> " From jigging veins of rhyming mother wits,
> And such conceits as clownage keeps in pay."

Shakspere absorbed " Marlowe's mighty line," while

---

[1] *Roister Doister,* written and probably acted before 1553 by Nicholas
Udall, Master of Eton (with a salary of £10), afterwards Rector of
Braintree, Prebend of Windsor, Rector of Calborne, and Master of
Westminster Grammar-School. The two first lines, spoken by Matthew
Merygreeke, remind one of Autolycus :—

> " As long lyveth the mery man (they say)
> As doth the sory man, and longer by a day."

Nash called *Tamburlaine* "the swelling bombast of a bragging blank verse." Thus the determination of his poetic form he owed to his worldly success as well as his worldly misfortunes. The *Venus and Adonis* and *Lucrece* showed what he would have done had he been free to develope his poetic nature in what was then considered the higher forms of pure poetry. But he was not free. He would neither beg nor starve. He had to make money for his family, and support them decently. He threw the whole of his energy into his present duty, so as to benefit his partners as well as himself. Doubtless, also, dreams of redeeming his lost inheritance of Asbies glorified his then unhonoured toil, and the proud consciousness of making the best of a life that had its difficulties. And he succeeded in it, from every aspect.

The litigation [1] between Burbage's sons and other intending partners shows the true meanings of Greene's jealousy of him, and of the ruling power he had acquired in the short space of five years.

We must not imagine the young rustic hemmed in the heart of London as it is now. Gerard was at this time pre-

---

[1] 1635. A collection of papers relating to shares and sharers in the Globe and Blackfriars Theatres, preserved among the official manuscripts of the Lord Chamberlain at St. James's Palace. Benefield, Swanstown, and Pollard appealed to be allowed to buy a share in these: Cuthbert Burbage, and Winifred, his brother's wife, and William, his son, petitioned "not to be disabled of our livelihoods by men so soon shot up, since it hath been the custom that they should come to it by far more antiquity and desert than these can justly attribute to themselves. . . . The father of us, Cuthbert and Richard Burbage, was the first builder of playhouses, and was himself in his younger years a player. The theatre he built with many hundred pounds taken up at interest . . . and at like expense built the Globe, with more summes taken up at interest : and to ourselves we joined those *deserving* men, Shakspere, Hemings, Condell, Philipps, and others, partners in the profittes of that they called the house. . . . Now for the Blackfriars, that is our inheritance ; our father purchased it at extreme rates, and made it into a playhouse with great charge and trouble, . . . and placed men players, which were Hemings, Condell, Shakspere, &c."

paring his *Historie of Plants*,[1] and we can there learn how easily a strong-limbed youth could reach fields and bushes, heaths and ditches, flowers and trees. No doubt he had many a lonely walk to solace and inspire him.

But that was his relaxation. There was other work to do. He had much to read. Many have asked where is Shakspere's library? I think that beyond the books of his boyhood and the "properties" of the theatre, there is so strange a connection between his knowledge and the publications of Vautrollier and Field, that we must consider a probability that he derived his information direct from them. A bookseller's shop of the period would supply the place of the library of to-day. It would be so natural that Shakspere should have the "freedom of the press" there. We can well imagine his first period in London, spent in sharing even the same room with Field, eagerly reading the books thus naturally brought within his reach, and filling up the gaps in his education with an interest that no scholastic method could have done. Perhaps even, as Mr. Blades suggests, with arguments more forcible than are brought forward to prove Shakspere belonging to any other profession, he might have learned type-setting and proof-correcting then, as there are in his works so many phrases that, to a printer's eye, intimate special knowledge of his trade. Mr. Halliwell-Phillips suggests that he must, at least, have gone carefully over his dedicated poems, as the title-page and the typography are so superior to anything else of the time. At least it was certain Shakspere knew Field, and he could not know any man without learning something from him. I give a list and some particulars in the notes [2] for our special purpose. The titles even of their books are most suggestive. Greene's Novels, Lyly's *Euphues*, Sydney's *Arcadia*, Spenser's *Faery Queene*, were of course in every one's hands, as well as Chaucer and Gower.

---

[1] See Appendix, Note 7.   [2] See Appendix, Note 8.

I believe that he also had the volume of Montaigne's Essays that contains his name.[1] This was translated by Florio, who taught the French and Italian languages, and lived in the pay of the Earl of Southampton, whom he called the " pearl of peers." From this connection he probably knew Shakspere, and might have himself given him this copy of Montaigne's Essays. It is evident he had read them, as he frankly borrows much from them, especially in the *Tempest*. Other books in existence are said to have belonged to Shakspere, but one cannot prove anything by tradition alone.

But the plays are not the work of a *mere* student.

His only son died in 1596, and for his sake the heart-wrung father calls boys always " sweet." As the years pass on, and young sisters and brothers, and old grandfather, father and uncles die, he is impressed with the certainties and uncertainties of that " undiscovered bourne, from which no traveller ever returns."

His company meanwhile had their annual tours, and probably he went with them over the face of the country.[2] Mr. Halliwell's superhuman industry has already unearthed from various registers the dates of payments to them for playing in Coventry, Dover, Faversham, Barnstaple, Bath, Bristol, Oxford, Rye, Saffron-Walden, Shrewsbury, Folkestone, Leicester, Marlborough, New Romney; and many

---

[1] Montaigne's Essays, written 1580, were translated by Florio, and published 1603. He dedicated each of its three parts to two noble ladies, the second part to Lady Rich—Sidney's Stella and the " Dark Ladye " of the Sonnets.

The authenticity of the autograph of Shakspere has been disputed, though not disproved. But the writing might have been Southampton's or Florio's, or his publishers on giving the book to Shakspere. The signature was extant before the forging suggestions of Ireland, having in 1780 belonged to the Rev. Edward Patteson of Smethwick in Staffordshire, about three miles from Birmingham and near Stratford, and was shown as a great curiosity by his father to his literary friends.

[2] See Halliwell's *Shakespeare's Tours*.

other places, Edinburgh among them, are shown to have been visited by them. How many an incident of the road do we owe to these excursions !

Between these tours he learned old London life, from the poet's schools at the taverns, which meant then clubs, newspapers, discussions, literary criticism, and literary inspiration. We hear later of his wit-combats at the "Mermaid," where amid all wits he was the chief. Hence may we trace the origin not only of many a tavern-scene in his plays, but of many a bright thought and lively conversation. In these haunts of the Muses he probably became acquainted with many of the best wits of the age—noble, or fighting, like himself, in the battle of life for bread ; and he became the poet of them all, feeling, thinking, expressing for all. He would meet no one without learning something from him ; so there would be suggestions from Tarleton, Kemp, Burbage, and all the players ; from the poets of the "Mermaid" and the "Apollo" suppers; the lawyers that he met at the cheap tavern[1] dinners ; from the street demagogue of the Jack Cade type ; from Elizabeth and all her nobles, Southampton and Pembroke among the chief, mingling with memories of the sweet women and children he had left in his home, and the rustic, homely souls he knew in Stratford, modifying *himself*, the underlying substratum of all.

It was from the breadth of his experiences and the depth of his intuitions that arose his special power of moving as of painting men. Hence in a period when the dicta of

[1] "There is another ordinary, to which your London Usurer, your stale Batchelor, and your thrifty Atturney do resort, the price threepence ; the roomes as full of company as a jaile, and indeed divided into severall wards, like the beds of an Hospitall. The Complement betweene these is not much, their words few : . . . if they chance to discourse, it is of nothing but of Statutes, Bonds, Recognizances, Fines, Recoveries, Audits, Rents, Subfidies, Sureties, Inclosures, Liveries, Inditements, Outlawries, Feoffments, Judgments, Commissions, Bankerouts, Amercements, and of such horrible matter."—*Gul's Hornbook*, chap. i. Deckar, 1609.

Pastoral Poetry had been pushed to an absurdity, when every poet was a "Shepherd," even on the sea or the battle-field, there arose a new and unexpected vision. A real Shepherd, or at least a man, sprung from a real inland farm, appeared and conquered the whole realm of poetry; and the masks of the mock-shepherd poets were cast away for ever. But the chivalric romance, the Arcadianism and the Euphuism; the Mystery and the Morality; the Tragedy and the Comedy; the History of the nation and the Life of the people, that had been rising like the four sides of a pyramid up to its apex, ended there in him. No one has ever risen higher. After him could only come a necessary descent.

Many poets have been great in one direction or another; but to none was it given to *be the man*, and to *have the hour*, in which it was possible, even to a genius, to concentrate the whole art possibilities of a people in one form. Other poets since have only resembled him in parts. Wordsworth had his love of Nature and exactitude in description; Burns his ecstatic naturalness; Walter Scott his humour, his chivalric and antiquarian interests, his money successes, and his desire of re-establishing his name, family, and estate.

The first proceeds of his success went in purchasing property in Stratford; relieving his father from pressure; settling his Anne in the best house of the town; gratifying his father's desire by applying for a coat of arms for him; possible only now, when he had "finally retired"[1]

---

[1] Freeman's *Epigrams*, 1614, asks:—

> "Why hath our age such new-found 'gentles' made
> To give the Master to the farmer's son?"

This was answered previously by Sir Thomas Smith in his *Commonwealth of England and Maner of Government thereof*, London, 1589, 1594, chap. xx., Of Gentlemen: "As for gentlemen, they be good cheape in England. For whosoever studieth the laws of the realm; who studieth in the universities; who possesseth liberal sciences; and, to be short, who can live idly, and without manual labour; and will

from business.[1] Buying, improving, lending, giving ; acting as the head of the whole family, the benefactor of the
whole town.

A letter from Abraham Sturley to his brother-in-law
Richard Quiney has been preserved :—"It seemeth by your
father that our countryman Mr. Shakespeare is willing to
disburse some money. . . . Move him to deal in the matter
of our tithes. By the instructions you can give him thereof, and by the friends he can make therefore. . . . It
obtained would advance him indeed, and would *do us much
good.*" "Moved" by this friend, he did buy the half of
the great tithes and the small tithes. He looked ever
towards the home of his youth as the retreat of his age.
With poets his friends to the last, loved by his relatives,
honoured by his native city, he died, when he had "*lived
long enough.*"

How different was Bacon, full of ambitions, with no immediate personal duty to others to raise or purify them.
Essentially a city youth, a University student, a classic
critic, an observant traveller, a man of the world, a statesman born and bred, a lawyer, a member of Parliament, an
Attorney-General, a Lord Chancellor, an essayist, a scientist,
a philosopher—above all, the author of "The greatest birth
of Time." [2]

That was his secret work, the idea of his life, his happiness, his hope, his Alpha and Omega. All other work has
meaning only in relation to this. His virtue was centred
in it. It was a great idea, greatly planned, and some of it
greatly performed. Probably for the sake of his experiments, he was continually in debt, and thought it no dis-

---

beare the port, charge, and countenance of a gentleman, he shall be
called Master, for that is the title men give to Esquires and other
gentlemen ; and shall be taken for a *gentleman.*"

This appears before Shakspere's application for arms, but illustrates it.

[1] Appendix, Note 9.   [2] Appendix, Note 10.

grace to allow his mother and brother to pinch themselves
for him. Yet it was not a poetic conception. His faults
were essentially unpoetic. His character was selfish and
self-centred; he never did an impulsive thing in his life.
He fell in love at forty-three, and married at forty-six
a young and eligible maiden; did not make her happy, and
was not very happy with her himself. A hunter for place
and reward all his life, he plied his sovereign with petitions,
and beside his sovereign, all his sovereign's favourites. He
might have loved Essex in his own way, but he deserted
him; he could not have honoured James and Villiers, but
he loaded them with adulation. When charged with the
interrogatory of Peacham before, during, and after torture,
he did not appeal to the King's heart with "the quality
of mercy," but took it quite easily.

During the time of the Plague in 1592, flying to Twick-
enham, at the time the *Venus and Adonis* must have
been in preparation, he wrote *Mr. Bacon in Praise of
Knowledge*, and *Mr. Bacon in Praise of his Sovereign*, parts
of the device of the Earl of Essex, called the *Conference of
Pleasure*. This was was his "invention." For solid work
that year he was writing his *Observations on a Libel*.

In 1593, when *Lucrece* must have been in process of
development, he was in Parliament, speaking eloquently
on the question of supplies, and in one way offending the
Queen, while he amused her with his sharp retorts on the
other. He was thirty-three then, and he had settled to
nothing. His tastes and desires were at war. Thomas
à Kempis says, "The more a man is united within himself
and interiorly simple, the more he will succeed in his aim."
Bacon was not united within himself; he was interiorly
complex.

In 1594, the year of the publication of *Lucrece*, appeared
his first political production, *A Declaration of the Causes
of the Great Troubles*. He also wrote a letter to Essex
when discouraged by the Queen's delays: "My nature can

B

take no evil ply, but I will by God's assistance with this disgrace of my fortune, and yet with that comfort of the good opinion of so many honourable and worthy persons, retire myself with a couple of men to Cambridge, and there spend my life in my studies, without looking back." It is a pity he did not. The great scheme might have been completed then, and possibly an autobiography produced that would have set this and many other knotty questions at rest.

In 1597, in the same year as *Romeo and Juliet*, the quintessence of Love apart from circumstance, appeared his *Essays*, among which is his essay on "Love." "A man must be of a very serious nature to think love a serious matter." He can analyse the elements of love; neither in life nor in writing did he acknowledge its power. "Great spirits and great business do keep out this weak passion." Much sympathy has been felt for him by some on account of his refusal by Lady Hatton, and his mortification that his rival should win her. It is probable she had wisely compared his professions with his publications, and had decided accordingly. He evidently suffered more from the loss of her money than of her affection. I cannot imagine him much regretting his single state. In his essay on *Marriage and a Single Life* he says, "Certainly the best works, and of greatest merit for the public, have proceeded from the unmarried or childless man." He approves of the saying of Thales, who, when asked when a man should marry, answered, "A young man not yet; an elder man not at all."

His *Wisdom of the Ancients* appeared in the year of *Troilus and Cressida;* and he was preparing his great work for the press in the year of the folio edition of the Plays, in 1623, about which so much has been said, and in the year following (1624) his metrical translation of the Psalms.

Meanwhile, as his life showed no passion, no self-sacrifice, no devotion of any kind, neither did it show the manly pride of the poet. Begging, praying, petitioning, he can have had no time for content or happiness. Though lavish, he was not generous; though magnificent, he was not virtuous. His genius is that of a man of science. He distinctly states what he would do if left to himself : " The call for me, it is book-learning." I confess I have as vast contemplative ends as I have moderate civil ones." " I am like ground fresh. If I be left to myself, I will grow and bear *natural philosophy ;* but if the King will plow me up again and sow me on, I hope to give him some yield. . . . If active, I should write—

1. The Reconciling of Laws.
2. The Disposing of Wards.
3. Limiting the Jurisdiction of Courts.

If contemplative, I would write—

1. Going on with the story of Henry VIII.
2. General treatise of De Legibus et Justitia.
3. The Holy War."

Writing to Sir Thomas Bodley, he says : " Therefore calling myself home, I have now for a time enjoyed myself, whereof likewise I desire to make the world partake. My labours, if I may so term that which was the comfort of my other labours, I have dedicated to the King." And this was *Cogitata et Visa—i.e.,* philosophical writings—no claim for poetry.

His tremendous energy and perseverance are worthy of note. From sixteen to sixty he kept making experiments and inventions, studying philosophy, noting facts, writing and rewriting his marvellous collection of philosophic works —some of them even twelve times ; attending to his health, diet, and medicines in a very special way ; besides the work of Parliament, of office, of society, of gaiety, of masquewriting, with occasional acting and shows to make him like the other gay men of the period. He advised this accomplishment to young men : " Though the thing itself be disreputable in the profession of it, yet it is excellent as a discipline, we mean the action of the theatre "stage-playing, which strengthens the memory, regulates the tone and effect of the voice and pronunciation, teaches a decent carriage of the countenance and gesture, gives not a little assurance, and accustoms young men to bear being looked at."

The amount of disappointment he received through life showed that he had not understood his men any more than his men understood him. His undoubted superiority gave him rivals; his eagerness to please made him enemies; his speeches in Parliament offended Elizabeth, who thought him more showy than deep; his secret experiments and "speculations" disgusted his relative, Burleigh. Writing poetry would have been a venial offence compared to this of "speculation." Buckhurst, Raleigh, Davies, Spenser, and many others were known poets and in office. Doubtless Elizabeth's shrewd eye read his inner character better than he thought—better than her successor did. Under James his efforts to rise were crowned with success, and he fell a victim rather to his vanity and his rivals than to his crimes.[1] Still the forms of bribery and corruption, of which he was accused, and which *he acknowledged*, are of a most unromantic nature. Much was done by his contemporaries to lighten his fall; but he left his memory to the calmer and more dispassionate reasoning of the next ages.

We must remember he was before his times. The practical nature of his science was considered degrading; his language too plain or too obscure; and his philosophy confusing. It did not develope so naturally as that of Bruno,[2] writing at the same period. The *Instauratio Magna* was presented to Sir Edward Coke in 1620, who wrote on the title-page—

---

[1] See Appendix, Note 11.

[2] Giordano Bruno was in Cambridge from 1583 to 1585, lecturing against Aristotle and in favour of the Copernican theory of the rotation of the earth. Bacon believed it to be fixed.

Edw. C., ex dono Auctoris,

"Auctori Consilium,
Instaurare paras veterum documenta sophorum,
Instaurare Leges Justitiamque prius."

And over the device of the ship passing between Hercules'
Pillars, Sir Edward wrote—

"It deserveth not to be read in Schooles,
But to be freighted in the 'Ship of Fooles.'"

Mr. Henry Cuffe said that "a fool could not have written
this work, and a wise man would not." And King James
used to say the book was "like the peace of God, that
passeth all understanding." Yet while in advance of many,
he was behind some. He did not agree with Galileo and
did not accept the theory of Copernicus. His *Thema Cœli*
gives extraordinary astronomy : "Flamy and sidereal nature
produces the starry heavens. Between earth and heaven
are three regions—1st, extinction of flame ; 2nd, union of
flame ; 3rd, dispersion of flame." He denies the moon to
be solid, but flamy. The earth is stationary, the heaven
revolves with the exterior of the earth in twenty-four hours,
not on movable poles, but cosmical. Some of the planets go
slower than others. He affirms spiral motion and denies
perfect circles : "These then are the things I see, standing
on the threshold of natural history and philosophy ; and
it may be, the deeper a man has gone into it, the more
he will approve them." Sir Thomas Bodley, while praising, criticised sharply both his style and works, and said
that "it was only averments without force of argument."
Harvey would not allow him to be a great scholar, saying,
"He writes philosophy like a Lord Chancellor." Sir Toby
Matthew seemed his most faithful admirer through life
and death. He was his Boswell.

The women he knew, his mother, wife, and queen, suggested no poetic types, and he seemed to have imagined
none. There is no love in his *New Atlantis :* his women
are silent there.

He was constantly occupied either in his professional or his literary and scientific ambitions. How the Baconians imagine he could find *time* to write the plays, even if he had the inspiration, I know not. The question of time taken, even for his acknowledged writings, occurs to his own mind. In his Epistle Dedicatory to the King prefacing his great work, he says : " Your Majesty may perhaps accuse me of larceny, having stolen from your affairs so much time as was *required* for this work. I know not what to say for myself. For of time there can be no restitution, unless it be that what has been abstracted from your business may, perhaps, go to the memory of your name and the honour of your age."

Yet he found time to write a little verse, *always in rhyme* when he did try it. His acknowledged poems are scarcely third rate : his masques, such as the *Conference of Pleasure*, pompous speeches, with flattery in them, as a means to display magnificent robes to give others pleasure, and thereby further his own advancement.

In his later years he gave a translation of the Psalms of commonplace type, occasionally even with crude rhymes, such as—

"The huge Leviathan
Doth make the sea to seethe as boiling pan."

Maurice calls him "this enemy of poets and poetry," because his very definitions of poetry are defective. He considers the drama far from what it ought to be ; " it is not good to remain long in the theatre."

The real discord in Bacon's life is illustrated in the *Geschichte der Philosophie* of Dr. Heinrich Ritter, vol. x. p. 318 : "There can be no doubt about the duplicity and weakness of the character of Bacon. In a letter to Thomas Bodley, he confesses the great mistake of his life, that, though drawn by inward inclination to the sciences, he devoted himself to the employments of public life, whilst his heart was not there. It is sad to remark that he should thus have made confession to a friend of this his unfaithfulness to his destined sphere, and yet should not have found in himself the strength to apply the remedy. It was a confession of the lip rather than the heart."

This is the secret that lay hid behind his mask of statesmanship; the longing for a life of science, simple, methodical, apart from the fret and shows of city life, and not the longing to write poems; these he never dreamed of, never honoured, probably never *read.* He might have heard them acted; he would not think them worthy of the leisure of his closet.

We have no information regarding Bacon and Shakspere's acquaintanceship. It is certain they must have heard of each other; it is more than probable they must have met. Possibly characters so different repelled each other, and opportunities of friendship were purposely ignored. On one occasion, when it is almost certain they were in the same hall together, we cannot but think of the two in contrast. At Gray's Inn, December 28, 1594, there were to be high times; Bacon and others were going to uphold the honour of the old institution, and had invited a goodly company. But the crowd was too large, and proceeded to great uproar and disorders; and so, in default of those "very good inventions and conceptions," which had been intended for their delectation, the guests had to "content themselves with ordinary dancing and revelling, and when that was over with a comedy of errors (like to Plautus his *Menæchmus* [1]), which was played by the players. This performance seems to have been considered the crowning misfortune of the evening. A "conjurer" was

---

[1] Entered at Stationers' Hall, 10th June 1594. "A book entitled 'Menœchmi,' being a pleasant and fine conceited comedie taken out of the most excellent wittie poet Plautus, chosen purposely from out the rest as being least harmfull and most delightful. Thomas Creed entered for his book."

arraigned on several charges, of which the last was "that he had foisted a company of base and common fellows, to make up our disorders with a play of errors and confusions." The members held a consultation "to recover their lost honour by some graver conceipts." Probably Bacon aided them, for on the 3rd January a very superior one appeared, *Divers Plots and Devices*, to symbolise the reconciliation between the Gray's Inn and the Temple, which had been disturbed by the *Night of Errors*. These treated of the laws of knights and the enrolment thereof. Speeches on the glory of war; the study of philosophy; on procuring eternizement and fame by buildings and foundations; on virtue and a gracious government. A sixth councillor appeared, advising pastimes and sports. "What! nothing but tasks, nothing but working days? No feasting, no music, no dancing, no triumphs, no comedies, no love, no ladies? Sweet sovereign, dismiss your other five councillors and take counsel of your five senses!" Which the Prince of Purpoole answered and then set to dancing.

"The performance of which night's work, being very carefully and orderly handled, did so delight and please the nobles and the other auditory, that thereby Gray's Inn did not only recover their lost credit, quite take away all the disgrace that the former Night of Errors had incurred, but got instead thereof so great honour and applause, as either the good reports of our honourable friends that were present could yield, or we ourselves desire." Spedding considers the speeches of the councillors "evidently by Bacon; they carry his signature in every sentence."

I like to picture that evening; Shakspere and his fellows called in, in hot haste, to try to quell the tumult of the crowd by distracting attention; and bravely acting through the uproar until interest arose and silence fell, one of *their new conceipts;* while Bacon, ashamed, mortified, and perplexed, with the rest of his company, went home brooding how to retrieve the lost honour of Gray's Inn, when base fellows had acted a "mean piece" instead of theirs. I like to imagine Southampton among the nobles; an appreciative youth, who preferred Shakspere's "Errors" to Bacon's "Councillors."

"The Gesta Grayorum, or the History of the High and Mighty Prince Henry of Purpoole, who reigned and died 1594," reports all this, printed by W. Canning, 1685.[1]

Bacon was always among the upper classes. He attained all the desires of his life; and having attained all, he fell. *Bacon lived too long;* had he died at Shakspere's age, he too might have left an unstained name, a mourning wife, and friends who missed him sorely. The sad picture of his later years is one that haunts us; yet it gives the truth of the man's nature. The pursuit of science lay nearest to his heart; the ruling passion was strong in death; and in prosecuting a scientific discovery, he was chilled to the heart, and died in a stranger's house, alone.

I close here the "probabilities" of these lives. The plan I have proposed to myself is more general than verbally critical. It is not to save people from reading, but to induce them to do so for themselves, that I suggest these points.

When we have well studied the contrasts of the lives of the writers, we must see what each of these writers has to say for himself in relation to the plays.

---

[1] See Spedding's *Bacon*, vols. i. and ii.

CHAPTER II.

THE INTERNAL EVIDENCE OF SHAKSPERE'S PLAYS AND BACON'S BOOKS.

DISTINCTIONS of internal evidence can be drawn from the subjects of the writings, the treatment, the accessories, and the style in relation to the lives of the two men we are considering. Now, though it is too much to say that Bacon would not have chosen any of Shakspere's subjects, it is certainly permissible to assert he could not have chosen *all* of them ; because Bacon never wrote without some intention, either didactic or practical. Therefore, while some of the histories might have been written as warnings, and others as glorifications of the reigning sovereign, nothing in his life or writings suggests a possibility of his having treated pure poetry for art's sake. There seems no cause likely to have tempted him to select subjects like *Midsummer's Night's Dream, Romeo and Juliet, As You Like It.* The same remark may be applied to the poems. One cannot imagine Bacon selecting either *Venus* or *Lucrece* as " inventions " worthy the devotion of his pen. A few masques, a *New Atlantis*, a few sonnets, a few psalms, are all he has acknowledged.

But the difference is more strongly exemplified when we turn to the treatment of the subjects. Bacon's criticisms of poetry, *De Augmentis*, book ii. chap. xiii., shows that he considers it has a right to go beyond Nature in treating life, and to introduce a moral and physical order higher than is found compatible with truth. In fact, poetry ought to show things as they ought to be, rather than as they are. This arises from his definition of poetry as feigned. Shakspere never writes thus. He does not make the poet the Providence of the play, but follows Nature and life in his delineations. Where his imaginations act, it is on the same lines as true, not feigned history. Hence Cordelia and Lear are not saved, to live happily ever after, nor are Romeo and Juliet resuscitated to heal the hearts of their parents. Be sure Bacon would have arranged his series so as to make virtue triumphant, as it ought to be. Further he says : " Dramatic poetry would be of excellent use if well directed ; for the stage is capable of no small in- fluence both of discipline and corruption. Now of corrup- tions of this kind we have enough, but the discipline in our times has been plainly neglected. And though in modern states play-acting is esteemed but as a toy, except when it is too satirical and biting, yet among the ancients it was used as a means of educating men's minds to virtue. Nay, it has been regarded by learned men and great philo- sophers as a kind of musician's bow, by which men's minds could be played upon. And certainly it is most true, and one of the great secrets of Nature, that the minds of men are more open to impressions of affections when many are gathered together than when they are alone."

There is no doubt that by " discipline " he partly meant the rules of the ancient stage, the unities of time, place, and action. The utter regardlessness of the Romantic school of the drama as to the first two of these canons at least, must have ruffled his orderly and cultured soul. That he could so have infringed the forms of dramatic thought was a natural impossibility. It was Aristotle, not Æschylus, he revolted from.

Bacon did not consider the drama of his time education ; it was only, if more than a toy, satirical and biting ; in connection with which he must have remembered the scene in which one of his kindly *bon mots* did good service.

When Elizabeth asked him, as a lawyer, if there was not treason in Dr. Hayward's *Richard II.*, "Not treason, madam, but much felony ; . . . he hath stolen much from Tacitus."

But the writer of the plays could not have esteemed them a "toy ;" neither were they "satirical and biting ;" neither were they "without discipline," though after other laws than Bacon's. They were treated with a solemn purpose throughout; men's minds were by them attuned to patience, fortitude, justice, truth, and the other cardinal virtues ; while they forgot not the cardinal needs of men —faith, hope, love, joy, laughter, sympathy, and variety. Bacon was no sympathetic student of psychology ; he did not understand the nature of man otherwise than in natures like his own. He could not project himself, and see the needs of others. He could live without love himself. "The stage is more beholden to love than the life of man." But how could such a man write so as to incur censure for saying too much of "love's lazy languishment," and receive advice to content himself with graver studies ? If he understood the nature of men little, he understood the nature of women not at all. He might have grasped some superficial character, or some strong strange nature like his mother ; but he could not even *imagine* such female characters as Juliet, Imogen, Hermione ; any woman with *abandon, naiveté,* purity, faithfulness, gentle strength, would have been a sphinx to him. To imagine love a moving power of life and action, yet subordinate to duty, was beyond his conception.

Bacon was also almost destitute of the sense of humour, in which the plays are so super-eminently rich. The notices of his contemporaries as to his "wit" need not confuse our ideas. "Wit" with them meant wisdom, and a wealth of allusion, with an antithetic arrangement of ideas, and epigrammatic terseness of expression. His was a form laboured, chiselled, often *réchauffé ;* there was no sense of spontaneity, there was electric light, not sunshine in it.

His was a kind of wit men remembered, but never laughed at, nor laughed with. We could not imagine him seeing any "humour" in Dogberry, Verges, Autolycus, Bottom, Quince, and his fellows, or even in Sir John Falstaff himself. There was no discipline in these.

His utter want of sympathy, as shown in his life, is reflected in all his writings. His correspondence with Burleigh showed that he did not grasp that astute relative's ideas; his connection with Essex proved how incapable he was of measuring that impulsive, generous, rash nature, or of acting on it for good (see his *Advice to Lord Essex*, with its mean subterfuges and low aims). He was always trying to impress men with himself, instead of allowing them to impress him, as Shakspere did. Hence he did not thrive with Elizabeth; but the younger, weaker James accepted him at his own terms, and proved that Elizabeth's measurement of him was the wiser. The friendly though hazy and ill-proportioned allusions to Shakspere show how well he had gauged his contemporaries, and how little he either astonished or ruffled them. Everything about him seemed so *natural*. There is a dangerous opinion abroad, seriously affecting men's judgments, that one must expect the "eccentricities of genius." Now, far from eccentricities being necessary to genius, they are not even natural. They only occur in natures in which an abnormal development of genius in one direction warps all the other powers. The true universal genius, the man in whom all the powers are developed, not irregularly, but regularly, not in abnormal partial growth, but in a gracious all-round, well-balanced proportion, becomes not *eccentric* but *concentric*. The circles that should lie farthest from his heart do so, and the nearer you reach to *him*, there is the more intensity in his feeling. Such a man wrote these plays. All the natural powers of a human mind were broadly and genially developed. To

him it was a great and living truth, afterwards enunciated
by Pope as an antithetic proposition, "The proper study of
mankind is *man.*" Hence man and his surroundings, and
his surroundings only in relation to man, is the under-current
of Shakspere's works. One cannot even *suppose* Bacon felt
this, and only failed in expressing it. He was a natural
philosopher, not a moral philosopher; not a metaphysic
philosopher, which Shakspere was, ever looking at the
roots of things.

Hence in the relative triviality of the outer circle of mere
nature, mere history, mere dates, mere facts, Shakspere
often erred, but his errors never affected his meaning.
Bacon would not have erred thus, because he was nearer
the external circle of Nature on one side than to the heart
of things. He too was a genius, but an eccentric one.

But even more distinctive than either subjects or
methods of treatment were the "accessories." Shakspere was a man who had been "educated;" and the form
he chose for himself was peculiarly his own. Bacon was
first of all "instructed." He had been a sickly youth.
It was all brain with him and no body. Only after
his period of instruction did he begin his period of self-
evolution or education. This was essentially characterised
by patient, methodical, exact research, with every opportunity accepted and exhausted, with a disposition to
combat contemporary ideas, and with a wide grasp of
coming possibilities.

The learning of Shakspere is just such as might have
been commenced, amid varied interruptions, at a good
grammar-school, and finished by later reading and conversation. Though, like Keats, he was keenly sympathetic
with ancient story and literature, his classics were eclectic
and uncertain; his linguistic education fragmentary; his
science undeveloped; his reading limited, and unguided by
more than opportunity and inclination.

The learning of Bacon ranged over all that was known

and had been known to man, in history, philosophy, and science, and he supplemented this by continual experiments, observations, and correspondence. He knew several languages, read largely in all, and wrote much in Latin.

Just as one can say it is impossible that Shakspere could have written Bacon without a learning he did not possess, so we can say it was impossible for Bacon to have written Shakspere without putting into the poems some of the learning he did possess.

The heterogeneous nature of Shakspere's interests have been taken to show his knowledge. In one way it does so, but not in another. The child who has only just learned that each twinkling star in the midnight sky is a sun and the centre of a system of worlds like his own, is more impressed with the magnitude and poetry of the idea than many an astronomer who has swept the sky for fifty years. He is also more likely to talk of his discovery. Even so was Shakspere like the child; Bacon, the astronomer. Shakspere brought in all he knew, sometimes deficient in fact, never in thought or feeling. Bacon, inclined to do the same, would have had much more matter to introduce; more true to fact, more exact in method, but deficient in philosophic unity and devoid of human feeling.

To go through all the works of either man and print all the contrasts is beyond my task. The result would make this little book a tome, and would perhaps help to prevent my readers from going to the originals thoughtfully for themselves. A host of inaccuracies in history and science, that would have been impossible to Bacon, appear in the plays; and these inaccuracies do not always occur in positions where, to interest the groundlings, some contemporary incident might have been innocently introduced into ancient tales. As Mrs. Cowden Clarke says: "Had Shakspere attended to the history and manners of Britain in the days of King Lear, he would not have grown what Douce calls 'so plentiful a crop of blunders.'

He would not have talked of 'Turks;' of 'Bedlam Beggars;' of 'Childe Roland;' nor of 'Nero.'" He speaks
of the Turks as in possession of Constantinople in King
Henry V.'s reign, though they did not take it until 1453.

Bacon would not have had courage or rashness enough
to have so combined and falsified the story of Macbeth by
basing it on two tales of different dates in Scottish history;
nor would he have introduced "cannon" into it, "as can-
nons overcharged with double cracks," Act i. sc. 1; also,
"The thunder of my cannon shall be heard," *John*, Act i.
sc. 1. John commenced to reign in 1199, and the first
cannon were heard at Crecy in 1346.

Even in earlier dates, "If I can get him within my
pistol's length, I'll make him sure," *Pericles*, Act i. sc. 1.
And in 1 *Henry IV.*, Act ii. sc. 4, he speaks again of
pistols. "That sprightly Scot of Scots, Douglas, that runs up
a hill perpendicular : he that rides at high speed, and with
his pistol kills a sparrow flying." Jonson criticises this.

"A piece many years in doing, and now newly performed,
by that rare Italian, Master Julio Romano," Act v. sc. 2,
Winter's Tale, introduces a compliment to the greatest
artist of his time in conjunction with an oracle of Apollo.
An allusion in the same play is made to " Judas Iscariot."

He speaks of Hamlet " going back to school in Witten-
berg," though the University there was not founded until
1502, five hundred years after Hamlet's death.

" And set the murderous Macchiavel to school," 3 *Henry
VI.*, Act iii. sc. 2, before Macchiavelli was born.

In *Troilus and Cressida*, Act ii. sc. 2, " Unlike young
men, whom Aristotle thought unfit to hear moral[1] philosophy," says Hector. Also, " Bull-bearing Milo his addition yield to sinewy Ajax." Both Aristotle and Milo lived
long after Hector.

---

[1] It is brought forward on the Baconian side the fact that both
Bacon and Shakspere quote Aristotle as saying " moral " while he said
" political philosophy." Both, however, followed Baudwin in this.

"Thou wert a soldier even to Cato's wish," *Coriolanus*, Act i. sc. 4, though Coriolanus preceded Cato.

Also in the same play, "The most sovereign prescription in Galen is but empirieutic," involves an error of six and a half centuries.

Bacon had written a work on Horology, and understood clocks. He knew they were unknown to the Romans. Yet we find—

> "Peace, count the clock :—
> The clock hath stricken three."
> (*Julius Cæsar*, Act ii. sc. 1.)

They appear also in *Cymbeline* and in *Winter's Tale*.

The geography of the plays is as un-Baconian as the chronology. They speak of sailing from Verona to Milan, when only a carriage could connect these cities. "Our ship hath touched upon the desert of Bohemia," *Winter's Tale*, Act iii. sc. 3. Jonson is severe upon this.

Foreign natural history is also distinctly hazy. It is different with local natural history.

The name of Stratford does not appear in the plays, and the name of St. Albans does; but that does not prove the plays written by a St. Albans man. It only shows that the writer knew English history and geography better than he knew Continental affairs. On the other hand, the words and phrases are much more suggestive of Stratford and Warwickshire than of any other place. The "proper names" applied to subordinate characters in the plays are many of them Stratfordian, such as Bardolph, Fluellen, Peto, Curtis, Travers, Gower, Gregory, Clement, Perkes o' the Hill, Barton, Wincot. Some have supposed that Wincot was a contraction for Wilmecote, the place of Mary Arden's birth. But it is not so. There is a "Wincot" pure and simple within a mile or two of Stratford, and there was a Wincot in the days of Shakspere; and what is more striking, Mr. Savage of Stratford has only just discovered from the local registers that "Hackets"

C

lived there. Were any of that family "the fat alewife of Wincot"?—Induction to *Taming of the Shrew.*
We see in Sir Aston Cokaine's address "to Mr. Fisher
of Wincot," quoted chapter v., that there was then an
established connection between Wincot and its ale. Mr.
Savage says the old *Hall* measured thirty-four feet in
length; that the nearest house in the neighbouring village,
a few hundred yards from the gate, is still left outlined in
its foundations, and much resembles the design of an inn;
and that the "Hackets" lived in that house. The want of
artistic connection between the Induction and the *Taming
of the Shrew* may very naturally be explained, if, at the
time that the town-council of Stratford shut its guild-hall
to the Lord Chamberlain's players, they should have been
invited to act by the owner of Wincot, and embodied some
practical joke of their host with local allusions, that always
interest the company, before they began the play proper to
their tour, for which they had dresses and parts prepared.
It shows the value in criticism of trifling detail; when
little things are pieced together wisely, they make a tessel-
lated pavement with a meaning in it. "Old Sly's son of
Barton-Heath" is a true name. "Cotsall" evidently means
Cotswold. "Ford" and "Page" are Stratford as well as
Windsor names. "Roland de Boys," an extinct family of
Weston-in-Arden. "Thomas Jakes of Wonersh," a gentleman of *Henry VI.*, was a Warwickshire man; some of the
name still live near Stratford. "William Visor of Wincot against Clement Perkes of the Hill." Is this a local
pronunciation of Fisher of Wincot, a misspelling, or a
misprint? (2 *King Henry IV.*) Many of the Stratford
records earlier than Shakspere have the name of Hamlet
and Hamelot, as well as Hamnet. Allusions also to the
characters of the Coventry Mysteries appear in the plays,
"Herod and Pilate," "Cain and Judas," "Termagant,"
"Turbaned Turks and Infidels."

It is, however, the absence of many things that speak

more strongly against the claim for Bacon than the presence of others.

As the genius of the two differs throughout, so does the life of their work. There is a want of free air in Bacon's works, a want of horizon, perspective, light and shade; there is a want of youth, health, and happiness, freedom and space. One cannot imagine Bacon going forth to the chase on the lusty charger of Adonis, or careering post-haste over the country as the bearer of news. Mr. Flower of Stratford-on-Avon wrote a little pamphlet called *Shakspere on Horseback*, showing how well he knew every point in a good horse; how well he understood the joy of a wild career; and the sympathy that grows between a master and a well-treated horse.[1] We have only, on the other side, to turn to Bacon's works to see the forms of interest he took in horses. "Every tenant by knight's service is obliged to keep one horse for the king's use." "English horses for strength and swiftness are not excelled by those of any other country." "Horses' flesh is eaten by some nations." "Horses' teeth give the mark of age." "The tooth of the sea-horse made into a ring is good for the cramp." "I leave my wife my four horses for the caroache" (Bacon's will).

This is all he has about this noble animal. It is evident he knew little of the pleasures of horses and riding, and a free leap and a firm seat; little of the deep-baying hounds,

---

[1] " Look, when a painter would surpass the life
In limning out a well-proportioned steed,
His art with Nature's workmanship at strife,
As if the dead the living should exceed ;
So did this horse excel a common one
In shape, in courage, colour, pace, and bone.
Round-hoofed, short-jointed, fetlocks shag and long,
Broad breast, full eye, small head, and nostril wide,
High crest, short ears, straight legs, and passing strong,
Thick mane, thick tail, broad buttock, tender hide ;
Look, what a horse should have he did not lack,
Save a proud rider on so proud a back."—*Venus and Adonis.*

the hunt and the hare.   But Bacon knew "how to stunt
the growth of dogs and make them little;" and Bacon
thought that "if a dog bit in anger, a stone thrown at him,
he communicated a choleric quality to the powder of it."

Similes constantly occur in the Plays that could only
have been suggested by a man of exercise from bowling,
archery, wrestling.   Bacon's physical frame forbade this.

Much has been made of the law in Shakspere.   This
might easily have been acquired in his experience in
Stratford, from his father and Thomas Greene; from
attending the law-courts (a favourite habit of writers of
the period); or from attending the lawyers' taverns.   (See
chap. i.)   It is only just such law the Plays can show.   A
Bacon *could not* have imagined the law in the *Merchant of
Venice.*

Much also is made of his medical knowledge.   But in
those days of quackery, many men knew more of medicine
than they do in these division-of-labour days.   He had a
friend, afterwards son-in-law, a skilful and famous physician; and among Vautrollier and Field's publications
were medical books of note.   It is strange that the forms
of medical knowledge displayed in Shakspere's plays are
not those that most rivet Bacon's attention in his works.
But there is more than learning in the making of a man,
especially of a poet.

The Plays are evidently the work of an *actor* of the very
modern English school of dramatic art, and not of a listener.
Only a *player* could have recognised and introduced the
various trifles, so telling to contemporaries of the period he
lived in; the alterations of the scenes, not only to relieve
the feelings of the audience, but to give the actors time to
dress; the stage directions in the play-scene in *Hamlet*
and in *Midsummer's Night's Dream.*   The whole series were
created by a player for the people.   Bacon would have
scorned their scholarship, despised their neglect of the
unities, denied their passion, and ignored their wit.   Ben

Jonson was more near to him in every way, and it would have been much more natural to say that he had written Ben Jonson's plays to teach Shakspere how to do it.

Bacon was no player, though he spent some time in preparing gorgeous masques, where expenditure showed a gentlemanly superiority to profit.

The Sonnets expressly say the writer was a *player*, and was at mental discord with his profession; they say he was a poet, whose lofty rhymes should live, and that his name was *Will*. They harmonise with expressions elsewhere, and with the general tone of feeling in the Plays; and whoever wrote the one might be treated as able to write the other.

SONNET CX.

" Alas, 'tis true, I have gone here and there,
    And made myself a motley to the view,
Gored mine own thoughts, sold cheap what is most dear,
    Made old offences of affections new:
Most true it is, that I have looked on truth
    Askance and strangely ; . . ."

SONNET CXI.

"Oh, for my sake do you with fortune chide,
    The guilty goddess of my harmful deeds,
That did not better for my life provide
    Than public means, which public manners breeds."

SONNET CXXXVI.

"If thy soul check thee, that I come so near,
    Swear to thy blind soul that I was thy *Will*." . . .
Make but my name thy love, and love that still,
    And then thou lov'st me—for my name is *Will*."

Though considering that the Sonnets would live, he evidently considered himself able for higher work. I rather fancy that in this *one* instance his feeling and Bacon's coincided, and that he would have named them "toys," even if he did not really mean them as a satire on the romantic sonnets of the period, as Mr. Brown suggests. If he did so, then in them, as in the character of Falstaff, he was a fellow-worker with his famous contemporary Cervantes, in killing with ridicule the last outbursts of mediæval chivalry, then dead at heart and root.

The whole structure of language in the two writers is as characteristic, and therefore as different, as is possible in the case of two great men living at the same time, in the same city, serving the same sovereign, rubbing shoulders with the same men, conversing with the same wits, hoping the same national thoughts. Shakspere's was of an older date, a more simple, homely, national use than Bacon's. The style also is distinct ; and this not altogether dependent on the different forms of verse and prose, as Bacon has just owned enough poetry, and Shakspere enough prose, to mark their varieties.

Bacon's and Shakspere's prose are perfectly different. Bacon's verse, when he writes it, is always rhymed ; Shakspere's generally in blank verse. Bacon's style is antithetic, epigrammatic. Shakspere's, though varied with the passion of the speaker, has a gradual growth, tending rather to end in a climax when fervours are on him, or to break abruptly, suggesting the inexpressible. Shakspere often mixes his metaphors and crowds his allusions, in a way Bacon would not have done.

One very striking point of contrast has not been sufficiently noted elsewhere. Bacon is essentially a subjective writer—*subjective* to an extraordinary degree, even when he is scientific. He writes much in the first person ; his very experiments are narrated as "singular" or "in consort ;" his great *Idea* is an invitation to mankind to work with *him*. The hundreds of his letters which have been preserved also show this peculiarity, which at times developed into vanity ; and he was aware of it ; for he says, "I know I am censured of some conceit of mine ability."

Shakspere, on the other hand, is *objective* to as extraordinary a degree. He never writes in the first person, except in the Sonnets, and even there we can notice an objective dominating power, and a suggestion that they too might have been written dramatically, or as a natural expression or voice *for* the friends to whom he gave them to express their feelings to their friends. In all other writings, the man Shakspere never brings *himself* forward by word or suggestion. The actor element in him throws him so intensely into the real life of the being he delineates, that he becomes, as it were, simply a vehicle to carry the thoughts of a Romeo, a Hamlet, a Cæsar, a Lear, where even the use of the first and second persons are practically the third to him.

The unobtrusiveness of Shakspere's life reflected itself in his writings. His dramatic form veiled him, as he intended it should. It could not have veiled Bacon. You would at once have been able to pick out which character he meant most nearly to represent himself, as you can do in Byron. When Bacon writes for the stage, he writes masques, utterly unlike Shakspere, and just like himself—thoughtful, heavy, and adulatory. "They answer very well to the general description in Bacon's Essays of what a masque should be, with its loud and cheerful music, abundance of light and colour, graceful motions and forms, and such things as do naturally take the sense" (Spedding's *Bacon*).

With the same exception of the Sonnets, Shakspere also writes little *to* the *second person.* Bacon is always intensifying its use, and is full of flattery as well as dedication. Not only does he lavish it on Elizabeth and James, but *on* every one who could in any way help him. That it was the position and not the man he honoured, may be seen by the way he forgot the warm, helpful cordiality of Essex; and prepared adulation and advice for succeeding royal favourites, however unworthy. This, though partly a part of character, is also an element of style, only to be discovered now in the literary works of each.

The simple, manly character of Shakspere prevented him ever writing " Panegyrics," " Elegies," " Dedications," of the fulsome type in which Bacon constantly indulged. He never mentions Elizabeth openly, except in Cranmer's speech in *Henry VIII.* and in the *Merry Wives of Windsor.* He never alludes to James except in *Macbeth.* The simple dedication of his two poems to Southampton by Shakspere may be compared to Bacon's dedication of his *Advancement of Learning* to James; and the thought must be impressed upon every reader that the same mind could not have used such differing forms.

Even in the treatment of the third person they are very different. The progress of their development also is different, Shakspere's style begins profuse and ends terse; Bacon begins terse and somewhat bald, and ends with greater freedom, variety, and richness.

No author more often repeats similar phrases and ideas, sometimes identical, than Bacon, because he was a scientist; while the recurrences of Shakspere are few, and are modified by the mood and the circumstance, as becomes a poet and a seer.

Shakspere writes as if he forgets everything he had written before. Bacon's good things are always cropping up again, in new combinations and connections, as if Bacon the writer never forgets Bacon the author.

One *resemblance* the Baconians do not notice, though it is a likeness with a difference. They both *borrow* largely, and they *do not acknowledge* it. Shakspere, however, borrows to illustrate his subject, and under conditions in which he could not acknowledge his debts. Bacon borrows, but it is to increase his own glory, and in circumstances under which he could have very well acknowledged his authorities. In his *Anatomy of Melancholy,* Robert Burton does so, and says, " I have wronged no man; I have given every man his own;" and where it would be inartistic to mention the authors' names in the text, he puts them in a series of side-notes, most impressive to every reader. This book has been also said to be Bacon's by some of the Baconians; but this peculiar literary honesty of Burton's is quite sufficient to disprove any such claim. We find Bacon borrowing his Essays, not only from classic sources,[1] but wholesale from Montaigne, and a small volume of Essays by J. S., published in 1596, altogether unacknowledged. We find his *New Atlantis* not only suggested in idea from Plato, but in plan from Sir Thomas More's *Utopia*, and in title and circumstance borrowed from Burton himself. The *Anatomy of Melancholy*, published in 1621 and signed by Burton, contained this passage: "I will yet, to satisfy myself, make a Utopia of mine own, a New Atlantis, a poetical commonwealth of mine own, in which I will freely domineer, build cities, make laws and statues as I list myself;" and then goes on to sketch his ideas, which marvellously resemble Bacon's *New Atlantis*, appearing in 1627.

Christian Paradoxes he never claimed, so that it is no discredit to him that the Rev. Alexander Grosart should have found they were the work of Herbert Palmer, B.D. They were published anonymously on the 24*th July* 1645, in a pirated edition, spoken of in the author's works; and the very next day, 25*th July* 1645, they were published in full, as Part II. of the *Memorials of Godliness and Christianity*, by Herbert Palmer, B.D., Master of Queen's Coll., Cambridge. They were printed as Bacon's first in 1648, after the death of Palmer. This is only here introduced because much of the reasoning on his religious feeling was based on this little work.

But Bacon did most essentially claim the whole and sole glory of his "great work." Yet his great namesake, Roger Bacon, who died in 1292, had also written an *Opus Majus*,

[1] See Appendix, note 12.

Opus Minus, and *Opus Tertium ;* had also fought against the adoration of Aristotle, the power of authority and appearances, the neglect of experiment. Some of his ideas wonderfully suggest the *Novum Organum ;* for instance, " Appearances alone rule men, and they care not what they know, so they are thought to know by a senseless multitude. There are four principal stumbling-blocks in the way of arriving at knowledge—authority, habit, appearances as they present themselves to the vulgar eye, and concealment of ignorance combined with the ostentation of knowledge. We must prefer reason to custom. Though the whole world be possessed by these causes of error, let us freely hear opinions contrary to established usage " (*Opus Majus,* Roger Bacon). Not only great ideas, but many rich phrases are borrowed from various authors, such as Heywood, Baudwin, Greene, Erasmus, Lyly, and even Shakspere himself, without any acknowledgment. I am not touching this as a moral question, but as a question of style common to Shakspere and Bacon in a certain degree. But the process and result of the amalgamation differs in each case entirely. What Shakspere borrows is always the inferior part of what he creates ; with Bacon it is not always so. Shakspere's finished work is a chemical combination ; Bacon's a physical mixture. Hence, through the seer's inspiration, Shakspere is often far ahead of the commonplace " advancement of the sciences " in Bacon's schemes, and sometimes far behind. In the observational, experimental sciences, Bacon is at his best. He attends to each point, however vulgar ; he expresses each step with an exactitude at that time unknown ; and he tells whether each experiment had been performed by him alone, or in concert with some other person (not named), or whether he had only taken them on hearsay. It is in a point of science then that we must look for the crucial test for the distinction of the two writers—a point of science, however, that has another aspect in a philosophic and social relation.

CHAPTER III.

SPECIAL ILLUSTRATION.

THERE is only one manufacture, treated both by Bacon and Shakspere, that gives an opportunity of revealing their scientific and psychologic methods of treatment. This I have worked out exhaustively, as I believe the distinction is critically valuable as well as original.

The relation each holds to wine, spirits, and beer is peculiar. Bacon considers no experiment too vulgar to be regarded. Trade facts and habits had been collected and criticised by his thoughtful mind. He notices wine more than beer ; cyder with much interest ; perry and mead a little ; spirits, in any separate modern form, not at all. He gives advice as to the process of wine-making—methods of grafting vines, of training and manuring them, of ripening and preserving grapes; of the must, clarification, maturation, and methods of treatment, such as burying, heating, cooling. He tests the relative weights of wine and water. He treats of barley as seed, as growing corn, drying corn, as malt, as mash, as beer, and of other forms of grain that might be used as malt. He writes of hops, of finings, of casking, of bottling, of preserving, of doctoring. He gives valuable historical information as to the taxes on ale-houses, and the monopoly of sweet wines ; legal information regarding felony, pardonable when a man is mad, but not when he is drunk. He writes the natural history of drunkenness and its effects. He gives some preventives against inebriety—i.e., by burning wine, taking sugar with it—taking large draughts rather than small ones—and recommends oil or milk as an antidote to its after-effects.

The moral question never touches him ; not even in his *Colours of Good and Evil* does he consider drink in relation to character. The psychological effect is treated only physiologically. Man, to him, is but a means of experimenting upon the various effects of spirit in wine.

We do not hear of Bacon mingling with the "people," or indulging in their "small ales," though he uses beer chiefly with medicine. Being a gentleman, and moving only among gentlemen, he chiefly affected wine, probably of expensive sorts, as he was a connoisseur.

Shakspere, in his non-dramatic poems—*i.e.,* *Venus and Adonis, Lucrece, Passionate Pilgrim, Sonnets*, &c., never mentions wine or strong drink, as if it did not play so large a part in his life as the Baconians think. But it is different when we turn from the poems that shadow forth his own thoughts, to those that represent the thoughts of others. He knows that stimulants form an important element, not only of action, but also of character. The author of Shakspere was always ready to suggest what knowledge he had gleaned on every subject. Had he been Bacon, he could not have avoided some allusions to his knowledge and experiments on this point. Among the many trades and professions, the critics have "proved" that Shakspere "must have practised," no one suggested his being a brewer, distiller, wine-maker, maltster, or lecturer on the art of manufacturing liquors, as one might well have said of Bacon. Indeed, Mrs. Pott gives as one reason that he could not have written the Plays, that he did *not* allude to a brewing, &c. Now, we see that this test acts quite on the other side. Mr. Donnelly now says that Shakspere *was a brewer*, but he gives no proof of this. I am not going to contest this affirmation now, only this is just the profession in which he would require most help from Bacon. Shakspere, in his plays, at least receives and knows only the "finished product," and treats it only in relation to man. He was acquainted with the use of stimulants as known in a house, an inn, or an ale-house, as he had proved in many a parish between Stratford and London. We find he knew the value of "froth and lime" and "sugar" to the tapster, probably learned when, in some holiday, he enacted the part he gave to Prince Henry. He knew that tapsters sometimes put water in their beer; that brewing was one of the duties of a good housewife; that ale and beer were the drinks of the people, and where they could best be got. He was aware that wine was the drink of some foreign nations, who considered themselves on that account superior to the "ale-drinking Englishmen;" that wine was the drink of the upper classes in this country, probably from its greater cost and its higher and more subtle effects. There were no temperance drinks invented at that time, and a man had then only to choose between water and beer or wine when he wished to drink. The habit of drinking healths was in full fashion in his day; and the "heavy drinking" had begun amongst Englishmen which had previously prevailed among the Germans and Dutch.[1] A number of interesting phrases are preserved to us in relation to this special subject. One little geographical notice tells powerfully in favour of Shakspere, if not against Bacon. In the Induction to the *Taming of the Shrew*, he praises the power of the "Wincot ale," which sent Christopher Sly to sleep. Now, Wincot was a village at a walking distance from Stratford, famed for its ale, which no doubt Shakspere had often tasted on his youthful wanderings; but we have no record of Bacon having tried that decoction.

Cyder, perry, and mead are never mentioned. No allusion appears in any drinking scene to spirits by any modern name, except *aqua vitæ*, which appears twice—once in connection with an Irishman, hence not meaning brandy.

[1] See Dekkar, Gascoigne, Sir John Smith, Nash, Stubbs, Earle.

When Juliet's nurse calls out, "Some aqua vitæ, ho !" it is supposed to be simply a restorative.   But while giving thus comparatively little information on the objective nature of these drinks, Shakspere has given us a masterly analysis of the subjective effects of stimulants in various degrees on different minds, and the views they have of it. The simple honest Adam, in *As You Like It*, considers his abstinence in youth the cause of his health and strength in age. Falstaff is always requiring a reinforcement of Dutch courage in "an intolerable deal of sack to a halfpenny-worth of bread;" and he gives us the reason of Prince Henry's superiority over his father, his free use of wine.   Lady Macbeth is made "bold" by what had made her attendants drunk. The degradation of a higher nature is shown in Mark Antony; but the most masterly description of the effects on an imaginative, sensitive, and hot-blooded man is shown in Cassio.   He knows he cannot stand much wine; he has already suffered in the past; he has resolved to have no more than one cup; tempted to his destruction by the cold-blooded villain Iago, by specious pretexts, he feels the full shame of his broken resolve to himself, of his broken faith to Othello, as a moral death.

In several of his plays, Shakspere makes no mention of any stimulant; these are the *Midsummer's Night's Dream, Love's Labour's Lost, Winter's Tale, All's Well That Ends Well, Comedy of Errors, Richard II.,* Part 3, *Henry VI.,* and *Titus Andronicus.* The only allusion in *Much Ado About Nothing* is Leonato's invitation to Dogberry, "Drink some wine ere you go;" and in *King John* the only suggestion lies in Faulconbridge's exclamation :—

> "St. George, that swinged the dragon, and ere since
> Sits on his horseback at mine hostess' door,
> Teach us some fence !"

It is interesting to note the different kinds of stimulant and the names of the vessels and accessories in different plays :—

"Cup of Charneco," "Sack," "Pot of double beer," "Three-hooped pot," "Claret," "Wine," and "Beer." (*Henry VI.*, Part 2.)

"Butt of Malmsey," "Sop," "Wine." (*King Richard III.*)

"Pot of small ale," "Pot of the smallest ale," "Stone jugs and sealed quarts," "Fat alewife," "Sheer ale," "On the score." (Ind. to *Taming of the Shrew.*)

"Muscadel and sops." (*Taming of the Shrew.*)

"Wine and wassail," "Drink." (*Macbeth.*)

"Drunken spilth of wine," "Subtle juice o' the grape," "Honest water." (*Timon of Athens.*)

"Cup us," "Vats," "Tippling," "Wine." (*Antony and Cleopatra.*)

"Stoops of wine," "Measure," "Potations pottle-deep," "Flowing cups," "Old fond paradoxes to make fools laugh in the alehouse," "Chronicle small-beer," "The wine she drinks is made of grapes," "Cup," "Canakin," "Potent in potting," "Pottle," "Pint," "Dead drunk." (*Othello.*)

"Stoops [or, as in first folio, stopes] of wine," "Flagon of Rhenish," "The Queen carouses," "Throw a union in the cup," "A stoup of liquor." (*Hamlet.*)

"Can," "Canary," "Cakes and ale," "Stoop of wine." (*Twelfth Night.*)

"Aqua vitæ," "Healths five fathom deep." (*Romeo and Juliet.*)

"Pot of ale," "Cups of ales." (*Henry V.*)

"Quart of sack," "Toast," "Spigot," "Canary," "Pipe-wine," "Wine and sugar," "Pottle of burnt sack," "Toast," "Aqua vitæ bottle," "Fap." (*Merry Wives of Windsor.*)

"Ale and cakes," "Baiting of bumbards [ale-barrels]." (*King Henry VIII.*)

"Sack," "Bottle," "Wine." (*Tempest.*)

"Bowl of wine" (in *Julius Cæsar, Pericles*, and *Richard III.*)

"Bottle brandished," "Sherris," "Sherris sack," "The

poor creature, small-beer," "Canaries," "Crack a quart," "Pottlepot." (*Henry IV.*, Part 5.)

"These mad, mustachio, purple-hued malt worms," "Bombard of sack," "A brewer's horse," "Madeira," "Pint," "Cup of wine," "Brown bastard," "Tavern," "Bottle." (*Henry IV.*, Part 1.)

"Glasses is your only drinking," says Falstaff when his landlady complains she must sell her silver if he will not pay her bill. But "glass," to hold liquor, was then an innovation, as shown in contemporary literature, and it is only mentioned elsewhere once—*i.e.*, in *Merchant of Venice.*

Shakspere also shows many of the habits prevailing in the country at his time. While alluding to "brewers" and to "brewers' horses," he shows the prevalence of private brewing, chiefly by women, and the habits of drinking beer in those days, before the importation of tea, coffee, and cocoa.

In the *Two Gentlemen of Verona*, Speed, in giving a "catelog" of a maiden's conditions, says :—

She brews good ale.
Launce. And thereof comes the proverb, "Blessing o' your heart, you brew good ale."
Speed. She will often praise her liquor.
Launce. If her liquor be good, she shall ; if she will not, I will ; for good things should be praised. (Act ii. sc. 1.)

Also Doctor Caius has for his housekeeper Mrs. Quickly (*Merry Wives of Windsor*) :—

Quickly. I keep his house ; and I wash, wring, brew, bake, scour, dress meat and drink, make the beds, and do all myself.
Simple. 'Tis a great charge to come under one body's hands.

(Act i. sc. 4.)

In Act iii. sc. 3, Mrs. Ford says to her men-servants, "Be ready here, hard by in the brewhouse."

He tells us that "Good wine needs no bush. . . . Yet

to good wine they do use good bushes." (Epilogue to *As You Like It.*)

We find a general use of "sops in wine."

In the *Taming of the Shrew*, Act iii. sc. 2 :—

> After many ceremonies done,
> He calls for wine : " A health," quoth he, as if
> He had been aboard, carousing to his mates
> After a storm ; quaffed off the muscadel.
> And threw the sops all in the sexton's face,
> Having no other reason,
> But that his beard grew thin and gingerly,
> And seemed to ask him sops, as he was drinking.[1]

Sir John Falstaff was much attracted by "sops" in wine and "toasts" in his sack; and an allusion to the habit is given in *Richard III.*, when the 1st Murderer says :—

> Throw him [Clarence] in the Malmsey butt in the next room.
> *2nd Murderer.* Oh ! excellent device, and make a sop of him.
> (Act i. sc. 4.)

"Cakes and ale" seemed to have been given at christenings; for at Westminster the porter beats back the crowd at the christening of the infant, afterwards Queen Elizabeth :—

> You must be seeing christenings ?
> Do you look for ale and cakes here, you rude rascals ?
> (*King Henry VIII.*, Act v. sc. 3.)

In the *Merry Wives of Windsor* and *King Henry IV.* we have an example of the jolly side of tavern-life—not the lowest, and one often redeemed with touches of humour,

---

[1] We find in Laneham's Letter (1575), Leland's *Collectanea*, that it was the custom then, at the marriage of the humblest as well as of the highest, for a "bride-cup," sometimes called a "knitting-cup," to be quaffed in church. At the marriage of Philip and Mary in Winchester Cathedral in 1554, after mass was done, wine and sops were hallowed and delivered to them both. And there is another description of a real rustic wedding, when the sweet "bride-cup" attracted the flies around.

D

wit, and wisdom. Act i. scene 1, *Merry Wives*, Slender says :—

> Though I cannot remember what I did when you made me drunk, yet I am not altogether an ass.
>
> *Falst.* What say you, Scarlet and John?
>
> *Bard.* Why, sir, for my part, I say the gentleman had drunk himself out of his five sentences.
>
> *Evans.* It is his five senses : fie, what the ignorance is !
>
> *Bard.* And being fap, sir, was, as they say, cashiered ; and so conclusions passed the careers.
>
> *Slender.* Ay, you spake in Latin then too ; but 'tis no matter : I'll ne'er be drunk whilst I live again, but in honest, civil, godly company, for this trick : if I be drunk, I'll be drunk with those that have the fear of God, and not with drunken knaves.
>
> *Evans.* So Got judge me, that is a virtuous mind.

Ford promises them a "pottle of burnt sack," and as Mrs. Quickly said—

> In such wine and sugar of the best and fairest, as would have won any woman's heart. . . .
>
> *Bard.* Sir John, there's one Master Brook below would fain speak with you, and be acquainted with you ; and hath sent your worship a morning draught of sack.
>
> *Falst.* Call him in. Such Brooks are welcome to me, that o'erflow such liquor. . . .
>
> *Ford.* I will rather trust an Irishman with my aqua vitæ bottle.
>
> (Act ii. sc. 2.)
>
> *Host.* I will to my honest Knight Falstaff, and drink canary with him.
>
> *Ford (aside).* I think I shall drink in pipe-wine first with him.
>
> (Act iii. sc. 2.)
>
> *Falst.* Go fetch me a quart of sack : put a toast in it. Have I lived to be carried in a basket ? . . . Come, let me pour in some sack to the Thames water. . . . Take away these chalices : Go brew me a pottle of sack finely.
>
> *Bard.* With eggs, sir ?
>
> *Falst.* Simple of itself ; I'll no pullet-sperm in my brewage.
>
> (Act iii. sc. 5.)

In *King Henry IV.*, Part 1 :—

> *Falst.* Now, Hal, what time o' day is it, lad?

P. Henry. Thou art so fat-witted, with drinking of old sack, and unbuttoning thee after supper, and sleeping upon benches after noon, that thou hast forgotten to demand that truly which thou wouldst truly know. What a devil hast thou to do with the time of day? unless hours were cups of sack.

Poins. What says Sir John Sack-and-sugar? Jack, how agrees the devil and thee about thy soul, that thou soldest him on Good Friday last, for a cup of Madeira and a cold capon's leg? . . .

Falst. Rare words, brave world! Hostess, my breakfast come? O, I could wish this tavern were my drum! (Act i. sc. 2.)

In Part II. Silence sings :—

> A cup of wine that's brisk and fine,
> And drink unto the leman mine ;
> And a merry heart lives long-a. . . .

Shal. You'll crack a quart together. Ha! will you not, Master Bardolph?

Bard. Yes, sir, in a pottle-pot. (Act v. sc. 3.)

The payment for these pleasures puzzled many, as it did Falstaff :—

Bardolph, get thee before to Coventry ; fill me a bottle of sack.

Bard. Will you give me the money, captain?

Falst. Lay out, lay out.

Bard. This bottle makes an angel.

Falst. An' if it do, take it for thy labour ; if it make twenty, take them all, I'll answer the coinage. (Part I. Act iv. sc. 2.)

This aspect is also suggested in *Cymbeline.* The Gaoler says to Posthumus :—

A heavy reckoning for you, sir : But the comfort is, you shall be called to no more payments, fear no more tavern-bills, which are often the sadness of parting, as the procuring of mirth : you come in faint for want of meat, depart reeling with too much drink ; sorry that you have paid too much, and sorry that you are paid too much ; purse and brain both empty,—the brain the heavier for being too light, the purse too light, being drawn of heaviness. (Act v. sc. 4.)

This light way of considering death is illustrated in *Measure for Measure*, when the Gaoler says :—

Look you, the warrant's come.

Barnard. You rogue, I have been drinking all night, I am not fitted for it.

Clown. O, the better, sir ; for he that drinks all night, and is hanged betimes in the morning, may sleep the sounder all the next day.   (Act iv. sc. 3.)

The *Merry Wives of Windsor* illustrates the Elizabethan tapster :—

Host. I will entertain Bardolph ; he shall draw, he shall tap ; said I well, bully Hector ?

Fals. Do so, mine host.

Host. I have spoke ; let him follow. Let me see thee froth and lime ; I am at a word ; follow !

Fals. Bardolph, follow him ; a tapster is a good trade ; an old cloak makes a new jerkin ; a withered serving-man a fresh tapster : Go, adieu.

Bar. It is a life I have desired : I will thrive.

Pistol. O, base Hungarian wight ! Wilt thou the spigot wield ?
                                                     (Act i. sc. 3.)

Steevens explains the above phrase by saying, "The beer was frothed by putting soap in the tankard, and the sack sparkling by lime in the glass." He does not give his authority for this very peculiar recipe of the tapster's craft. Shakspere, however, alludes to the habit elsewhere.

In *King Henry IV.*, Part I., for instance, Poins asks :—

Where hast been, Hal ?

P. Henry. With three or four loggerheads, with three or four score hogsheads. I am sworn brother to a leash of drawers. . . . They call drinking deep, dyeing scarlet. . . . To conclude, I am so good a pro-ficient in one quarter of an hour, that I can drink with any tinker in his own language during my life. . . . But, sweet Ned, to sweeten which name of Ned I give thee this pennyworth of sugar . . . clapped even now into my hand by an under-skinker ; one that never spake other English in his life than "eight shillings and sixpence," and "You are welcome," with this shrill addition, "Anon, anon, sir ! Score a pint of Bastard in the Half-moon," or so. But, Ned, to drive away time till Falstaff come, I prithee do thou stand in some by-room, while I question my puny drawer to what end he gave me the sugar. . . . How long have you to serve, Francis ?

Fran. Forsooth, five years. . . .

P. Henry. Five years ! by'r Lady, a long lease for the clinking of pewter. . . . Your brown bastard is your only drink : for, look you, Francis, your white doublet will sully : in Barbary, sir, it cannot come to so much. . . .

Fals. A plague of all cowards ! Give me a cup of sack. . . . You rogue, here's lime in this sack too. . . . Yet a coward is worse than a cup of sack with lime in it. . . . (Act ii. sc. 4.)

In *Measure for Measure* also :—

Escal. Come hither to me, Master Froth. Master Froth, I would not have you acquainted with tapsters ; they will draw you, Master Froth, and you will hang them. Get you gone, and let me hear no more of you.

Froth. I thank your worship : For mine own part, I never come into any room in a taphouse, but I am drawn in. (Act iii. sc. 1.)

In relation to the heavy drinking said to have been lately imported from the Flemings and Germans by the English soldiers who campaigned abroad, we may note that Mrs. Page calls Sir John Falstaff "the Flemish drunkard."

Also in the *Merchant of Venice* Nerissa asks :—

How like you the young German, the Duke of Saxony's nephew ?

Por. Very vilely in the morning, when he is sober ; and most vilely in the afternoon, when he is drunk ; when he is best, he is a little worse than a man : and when he is worst, he is little better than a beast ; an the worst fall that ever fell, I hope I shall make shift to go without him.

Ner. If he should offer to choose, and choose the right casket, you should refuse to perform your father's will, if you should refuse to accept him.

Por. Therefore, for fear of the worst, I pray thee set a deep glass of Rhenish wine on the contrary casket ; for, if the devil be within, and that temptation without, I know he will choose it. I will do anything, Nerissa, ere I will be married to a sponge. (Act i. sc. 2.)

But the habit seems to have been widely spread by Shakspere's time, and coupled with that of "drinking healths," as we see in Stubb's *Anatomy of Abuses* and Nash's *Pierce Penilesse's Supplication to the Devil*, and in Dekkar's works.

For instance, in *Romeo and Juliet* Mercutio says Queen
Mab makes a soldier dream of "healths five fathom deep."
We may also refer to the carousals in *Twelfth Night* :—

Sir Toby. These clothes are good enough to drink in, and so be these
boots too ! an they be not, let them hang themselves in their own
straps.

Mar. That quaffing and drinking will undo you : I heard my lady
talk of it yesterday. . . . They add, moreover, Sir Andrew's drunk
nightly in your company.

Sir Toby. With drinking healths to my niece. I'll drink to her as
long as there is a passage in my throat, and drink in Illyria. He's a
coward and a coystril that will not drink to my niece till his brains
turn o' the toe like a parish-top. . . .

Sir Toby. O Knight, thou lack'st a cup of canary; when did I see
thee so put down ?

Sir Andrew. Never in your life, I think, unless you see canary put
me down : Methinks sometimes I have no more wit than a Christian
or an ordinary man has ; but I am a great eater of beef, and that does
harm to my wit.　　　　　　　　　　　　　　　(Act i. sc. 2.)

Olivia. What's a drunken man like, fool ?

Clown. Like a drowned man, a fool, and a madman ; one draught
above heat makes him a fool : the second mads him : and a third
drowns him.

Olivia. Go thou and seek the crowner, and let him sit o' my coz ; for
he's in the third stage of drink, he's drowned : go look after him.

Clown. He is but mad yet, and the fool shall look to the madman.

　　　　　　　　　　　　　　　　　　　　(Act i. sc. 5.)

Sir Toby. A false conclusion, and I hate it as an unfilled can. . . .
Do not our lives consist of the four elements ?

Sir And. 'Faith, so they say ; but I think it consists rather of eat-
ing and drinking.

Sir Toby. Thou art a scholar : let us therefore eat and drink.
Marian, I say, a stoop of wine. . . .

Clown. . . . The Myrmidons are no bottle-ale houses. . . .

Mal. Do you make an alehouse of my lady's house, that ye squeak
out your cozier's catches without any instigation or remorse of
voice ? . . .

Sir Toby. Out o' time ? Sir, ye lie. Art any more than a steward ?
Dost thou think because thou art virtuous there shall be no more
cakes and ale ? . . . A stoop of wine, Maria ! . . . (Act ii. sc. 2.)

Sir Toby. Sot, didst see Dick Surgeon, sot?

Clown. Ah, he's drunk, Sir Toby, an hour agone; his eyes were set at eight this morning.

Sir Toby. Then he's a rogue and a passy-measures pavin. I hate a drunken rogue. . . .

Clown's Song.

> But when I came unto my bed,
>   With hey, ho, the wind and the rain,
> With toss-pots still had drunken head,
>   For the rain it raineth every day.

(Act v. sc. 1.)

Shakspere does not often prophesy into a future beyond his own time; but one of these cases occurs when in *King Lear*, Act iii. sc. 3, the Fool says :—

> I'll speak a prophecy ere I go . . .
> When brewers mar their malt with water . . .
> Then shall the realm of Albion
> Come to great confusion.

He makes Cranmer prophesy of Elizabeth at her christening in Westminster—

> In her days every man shall eat in safety,
> Under his own vine, what he plants :
> (*Henry VIII.*)

which suggests a more general cultivation of the vine than might have been supposed.

He notices " the vines of France " in *King Lear ;* also in *Henry V.*, Burgundy groans that the war should hurt France :

> Her vine, the merry cheerer of the heart, unpruned dies . . .
> And as our vineyards, fallows, meads, and hedges,
> Defective in their natures, grow to wildness.

Wine is the drink of France, the trade of France. Hence the French cannot appreciate ale.

> *Constable.*   Can sodden water,
> A drench for sur-rein'd jades, their barley broth,
> Decoct their cold blood to such violent heat ?
> And shall our quick blood, spirited with wine,
> Seem frosty ?   (*Henry V.*, Act iii. sc. 5.)

Wine also is a drink of the upper classes and of those who ape them.

> *Menenius.* I am known to be a humorous patrician, and one that loves a cup of hot wine with not a drop of allaying Tiber in't. . . If the drink you give me touch my palate adversely, I make a crooked face at it.
>
> (*Coriolanus*, Act ii. sc. i.)

This distinction between ale and wine is noted in the socialistic creed propounded 300 years ago by Shakspere as Jack Cade. The expressions in some points are very much like the present ideas of socialism among the masses, though Jack Cade meant to be " KING " of these masses—a good king, however, who should bring in a millennium.

> *Cade.* There shall be in England seven halfpenny loaves sold for a penny : the three-hooped pot shall have ten hoops ; and I shall make it felony to drink small-beer : all the realm shall be in common ; and in Cheapside shall my palfrey go to grass. . . . . There shall be no money ; all shall eat and drink on my score. . . . [*Henry VI.*, Part II. Act iv. sc. 2.)
>
> And here, sitting upon London-stone, I charge and command that, at the city's cost, the conduit run nothing but claret wine this first year of our reign. (Act iv. sc. 6.)

It is also illustrated in the Induction to the *Taming of the Shrew*, where the " Wincot ale " was too much for Christopher Sly :—

> *Sly.* For God's sake, a pot of small ale.
> *1st Servant.* Will't please your lordship drink a cup of sack ? . . .
> *Sly.* I never drank sack in my life. . . .
> *Lord.* Heaven cease this idle humour in your honour. . . .
> *Sly.* Am not I Christopher Sly,[1] old Sly's son of Burton Heath, by birth a pedlar, by education a cardmaker, by transmutation a bear-herd, and now, by present profession, a tinker. Ask Marian Hacket, the fat ale-wife of Wincot, if she know me not : if she say I am not fourteen-pence on the score for sheer ale, score me up for the lyingest knave in Christendom.
> *Lord.* Thou art a lord, and nothing but a lord. . . .

---

[1] Sly and Burton Heath, as well as Hacket and Wincot, are real local names.

Sly. I do not sleep ; I see, I hear, I speak.
Upon my life, I am a lord indeed.
And once again, a pot o' the smallest ale. . . .
    Serv. These fifteen years you have been in a dream,
Or when thou waked, so waked as if you slept.
    Sly. These fifteen years ? By my fay, a goodly nap—
But did I never speak of all that time ?
    Serv. Ah yes, my lord, but very idle words—
For though you lay here in this goodly chamber,
Yet would ye say ye were beaten out of doors,
And rail upon the hostess of the house,
And say you would present her at the leet [1]
Because she brought stone jugs and no sealed quarts.

We also see the social distinction of the quality of the drink noted in *King Henry IV.*, Part II. Act ii. sc. 2 :—

P. Henry. Doth it not show vilely in me to desire small-beer ?
Poins. Why, a prince should not be so loosely studied as to remember so weak a composition.
P. Henry. Belike, then, my appetite was not princely got, for in truth I do remember the poor creature, small-beer. . . .

As Shakspere makes the beer-drinking English beat the wine-drinking French, so he makes the beer-drinking English beat the wine-drinking English in the judicial combat :—

1st Neigh. Here, Neighbour Horner, I drink to you in a cup of sack ; and fear not, neighbour, you shall do well enough.
2nd Neigh. And here, neighbour, here's a cup of charneco.
3rd Neigh. And here's a pot of good double beer, neighbour : and fear not your man.
Horner. Let it come, i'faith, and I'll pledge you all : and a fig for Peter ! . . .
1st Prent. Here, Peter, I drink to thee, and be not afraid.
2nd Prent. Be merry, Peter, and fear not thy master ; fight for the credit of apprentices.

---

[1] At the leet or court-leet of a manor, the jury presented those who used false weights and measures, and amongst others, those who, like the " fat alewife of Wincot," used jugs of irregular capacity instead of the sealed and licensed quarts.

Peter. I thank you all : drink and pray for me, I pray you ; for, I think I have taken my last draught in this world. . . . .

York. Take away his weapon : Fellow ! thank God and the good wine in thy master's way. (*King Henry VI.*, Part II. Act ii. sc. 4.)

The only two characters who emphatically drink water instead of wine are Adam in *As You Like It :*—

> Though I look old, yet am I strong and lusty,
> For in my youth I never did apply
> Hot and rebellious liquors in my blood (Act ii. sc. 3),

And Apemantus in *Timon :*—

> Ay, to see meat fill knaves and wine heat fools. . . .
> If I were a huge man, I should fear to drink at meals
> Lest they should spy my windpipe's dangerous notes :
> Great men should drink with harness on their throats.
>   *Tim.* My lord, in heart : and let the health go round.
>   *Lord.* Let it flow this way, my good lord.
>   *Apem.* Flow this way ?
> A brave fellow ! He keeps his tides well.
> Those healths will make thee and thy state look ill, Timon.
> Here's that which is too weak to be a sinner,
> Honest water, which ne'er left man i' the mire ;
> This and my food are equals ; there's no odds,
> Feasts are too proud to give thanks to the gods.
>   (Act i. sc. 1, 2.)

The only real " praise of wine " he puts in the mouth of Falstaff :—

This same young sober-blooded boy doth not love me : nor a man cannot make him laugh ; but that's no marvel, he drinks no wine. There's never any of these demure boys come to any proof ; for their drink doth so over-cool their blood. . . . A good sherris-sack hath a twofold operation in it. It ascends me into the brain ; dries me there all the foolish, and dull and crudy vapours which environ it, makes it apprehensive, quick, forgetive, full of nimble, fiery, delectable shapes ; which, delivered o'er to the voice (the tongue), which is the birth, becomes excellent wit. The second property of your excellent sherris is the warming of the blood, which, before cold and settled, left the liver white and pale, which is the badge of pusillanimity and cowardice ;

but the sherris warms it, and makes it course from the inwards to the parts extreme. It illumineth the face, which as a beacon gives warning to the rest of this little kingdom, man, to arm : and then the vital commoners, and inland petty spirits, muster me all to their captain, the heart ; who, great and puffed up with this retinue, doth any deed of courage ; and this valour comes of sherris: so that skill in the weapon is nothing without sack ; for that sets it awork ; and learning a mere hoard of gold kept by a devil ; till sack commences it, and sets it in act and use. Hereof comes it that Prince Henry is valiant, for the cold blood he did naturally inherit of his father, he hath, like lean, sterile, and bare land, manured, husbanded, and tilled, with excellent endeavour of drinking good, and good store of fertile sherris ; that he is become very hot and valiant. If I had a thousand sons, the principle I would teach them should be to forswear thin potations, and to addict themselves to sack.   (*Henry IV.*, Part II. Act iv. sc. 3.)

He certainly lived up to his creed in the use of wine, but the wine lived not up to his ideas of the making a man of him, and his cowardice gives a whole "Morality" in his one character. Prince Henry, when imitating his father in giving his opinion of Falstaff, said :—

Why dost thou converse with that huge trunk of humours. . . . That bombard of sack. . . . Wherein is he good but to taste sack and drink it ? . . .

Then in the scene where Prince Henry picks his pockets :—

Let's see what they be—read his papers.
Poins. Item, a capon, 2s. 2d. ; Item, sauce, 4d. ; Item, sack, two gallons, 5s. 8d. ; anchovies and sack after supper, 2s. 6d. ; Item, bread a halfpenny. Ob.
P. Henry. O monstrous ! But one halfpenny-worth of bread to this intolerable deal of sack !   (*Henry IV.*, Part I. Act ii. sc. 4.)

The general impression given is, that people thought that *wine*, in the first instance, *filled the veins with blood*, as in *Pericles* Thaisa says to her suitor :—

The King, my father, sir, hath drunk to you . . .
Wishing it so much blood unto your life.

Per. I thank both him and you, and pledge him freely.
(Pericles, Act ii. sc. 3.)

Menenius. He was not taken well, he had not dined,
The veins unfilled, our blood is cold, and then
We pout upon the morning, are unapt
To give or to forgive ; but when we have stuffed
These pipes and these conveyances of our blood,
With wine and feeding, we have suppler souls
Than in our priest-like fasts.   (*Coriolanus*, Act v. sc. 1.)

That it acts medicinally; see the *Tempest*, when Stephano
finds Caliban :—

If he have never drunk wine afore, it will go near to remove his fit,
if I can recover him, and keep him tame . . . Here is that which will
give language to you.   (Act ii. sc. 2.)

I am weary—yea, my memory is tired ;
Have we no wine here ?   (*Coriolanus*, Act i. sc. 9.)

I will see what physic the tavern affords.
(*Henry VI.*, Act ii. sc. 3.)

That it heats the blood, as in *King Henry VIII.* :—

Sands. The red wine first must rise
In their fair cheeks, my lord, then we shall have them
Talk us to silence.   (Act i. sc. 4.)

In *Troilus and Cressida* Achilles says :—

I'll heat his blood with Greekish wine to-night,
Which with my scimitar I'll cool to-morrow.
Patroclus, let us feast him to the height.   (Act v. sc. 1.) .

*That it fires the face ; the effect on Bardolph's complexion
illustrates this :—*

P. Henry. O villain, thou stolest a cup of sack eighteen years ago,
and wert taken with the manner, and ever since thou hast blushed
extempore.   (*Henry IV.*, Part I. Act ii. sc. 4.)
Fal. The fiend hath pricked down Bardolph[1] irrecoverably, and his
fate is Lucifer's private kitchen, where he doth nothing but roast malt
worms.   (Part II. Act ii. sc. 4.)

---

[1] Bardolph and Fluellen are names found in Stratford records.

'Tis in the nose of thee, Bardolph. Thou art the knight of the burning lamp. . . . Thou art a perpetual triumph, an everlasting bonfire light. Thou hast saved me a thousand marks in links and torches walking with thee in the night between tavern and tavern: but the sack that thou hast drunk me would have bought me lights as good cheap at the dearest chandler's in Europe.[1]

(Part I. Act iii. sc. 3.)

That it fevers the heart :—

> *Charm.* I had rather heat my liver with drinking.
> *(Ant. and Cleo.*, Act i. sc. 2.)

Timon says :—

> Go suck the subtle juice o' the grape
> Till the high fever seethe your blood to froth,
> And so 'scape hanging. (Act iv. sc. 3.)

Thus it makes some natures bold, like Lady Macbeth's; and by just a turn in the scale this courage develops into quarrelsomeness and murderousness :—

Fluellen. Alexander in his rages, and his furies, and his cholers, and his moods, and his displeasures, and his indignations, and also being a little intoxicated in his prains, did, in his ales and his angers, look you, kill his pest friend, Clytus.

(King Henry V., Act iv. sc. 7.)

That it drowns the reason.—Macbeth's grooms sink in " swinish sleep."

> *Lady M.* . . . His two chamberlains
> Will I with wine and wassail so convince,
> That memory, the warder of the brain,
> Shall be a fume, and the receipt of reason
> A limbeck only. *(Macbeth*, Act i. sc. 7.)

A senator says of his friend to Alcibiades :—

> He's a sworn rioter ; he has a sin
> That often drowns him and takes his valour prisoner.
> If there were no foes, that were enough
> To overcome him : in that beastly fury

---

[1] See Deckar's *Wonderful Year,* 1603.

> He has been known to commit outrages
> And cherish factions ; 'tis inferred to us
> His days are foul and his drink dangerous.
>
> (*Timon,* Act iii. sc. 5.)

Macbeth's porter considers "drink is a great provoker of
three evil things ; " and though "drink gave him the lie
last night," " he requited him for his lie, and made a shift
to cast him."

And finally degrades the man.—The play of *Antony and
Cleopatra* shows the degrading power of habitual intoxi-
cation on noble natures. Enobarbus says the fortunes of
all shall be "drunk to bed." Cæsar says of Antony :—

> He fishes, drinks, and wastes the lamps of night in revel. . . . He
> sits and keeps the turn of tippling with a slave, and reels the streets at
> noon. . . . Antony, leave thy lascivious wassails.
> *Eno.* Ay, sir, we did sleep day out of countenance, and made the
> night light with drinking.   (Act ii. sc. 2.)

Even Cleopatra shows her scorn :—

> And next morn
> Ere the ninth hour I drunk him to his bed,
> Then put my tires and mantles on him, whilst
> I wore his sword Philippan.

The banquet in Act ii. scene 7, is a sermon on temperance, with the moral of the fates of the guests. Menas
tells Pompey, " Thou art, if thou darest be, the earthly
Jove."

> *Men.* For my part, I am sorry it is turned to a drinking. Pompey
> doth this day laugh away his fortune.
> *Pompey.*   . . . Desist and drink.
> *Eno.*   . . . Here's to thee, Menas. . . .
> *Pompey.* Fill till the cup be hid.
> *Eno.* There's a strong fellow, Menas.
> *Men.* Why ?
> *Eno.* 'A bears the third part of the world. Man, seest not ?
> *Men.* The third part then is drunk. Would it were all, that it
> might go on wheels.
> *Eno.* Drink thou, increase the reels.

Pomp. This is not yet an Alexandrian feast.
Ant. It ripens towards it. Strike the vessels, ho !
Here is to Cæsar.
Cæsar.   I could well forbear it.
It is monstrous labour, when I wash my brain
And it grows fouler. . . . I had rather fast
From all, four days, than drink so much in one. . . .
           . . . Gentle lords, let's part.
You see we have burnt our cheeks : strong Enobarbus
Is weaker than the wine ; and mine own tongue
Splits what it speaks ; the wild disguise hath almost
Anticked us all.
Eno. Shall we dance now the Egyptian Bacchanals
And celebrate our drink ?
Pomp. Let's ha't, good soldier !
Ant. Come, let us all take hands ;
Till that the conquering wine hath steeped our sense
In soft and delicate Lethe.
Eno.   All take hands ;
Make battery to our ears with the loud music
The while I'll place you.   Then the boy shall sing.
The holding every man shall bear, as loud
As his strong sides can volley.

           Come, thou monarch of the vine,
           Plumpy Bacchus with pink eyne.
           In thy vats our cares are drowned ;
           With thy grapes our hairs are crowned ;
           Cup us, till the world go round ;
           Cup us, till the world go round !

Pompey dropped out; Antony still followed the same
life.   In Act iv. scene 9, Antony cried :—

                    Come,
    Let's have one other gaudy night ; call to me
    All my sad captains ; fill our bowls ; once more
    Let's mock the midnight bell. . . .
    Scant not my cups, and make as much of me
    As when mine empire was your fellow, too,
    And suffered my command. . . . Let's to supper come,
    And drown consideration.

And so the end was wrought, and hence came Cleo's
prophecy :—

> The quick comedians
> Extemporally will stage us, and present
> Our Alexandrian revels : Antony
> Shall be brought drunken forth. . . . Now no more
> The juice of Egypt's grape shall moist this lip.
>
> (Act v. sc. 2.)

And thus these great lives ended. The metaphysic tendency of Shakspere's mind leads him to sad and solemn thoughts of the carelessness of man, of the shortness of life, the evanescence of glory, the dominance of the Unseen. Man perceives not the real and the permanent; he drops the reality to pursue shadows; after all, all men are like drinkers at a banquet. Sad as he leaves us in the sunset of the earthly glory of Antony, there is even a greater sadness written in *Othello* in the fate of Cassio. For with him it was not a frequent habit, nor even a natural inclination, but an insidious temptation; he suffered, not for a course of riotous living, but for one false step, and he dragged down with him other good and pure lives. In *Othello* there is another " revel," a Cyprian banquet (Act ii. sc. 3) :—

Iago. Come, lieutenant, I have a stoop of wine ; and here without are a brace of Cyprus gallants, that would fain have a measure to the health of black Othello.

Cassio. Not to-night, good Iago; I have very poor and unhappy brains for drinking. I could well wish courtesy would invent some other custom of entertainment.

Iago. O ! they are our friends ; but one cup. I'll drink for you.

Cassio. I have drunk but one cup to-night, and that was craftily qualified, too, and behold what innovation it makes here : I am unfortunate in the infirmity, and dare not tax my weakness with any more. . . .

Iago. If I can fasten but one cup upon him,
With that which he hath drunk to-night already,
He'll be as full of quarrel and offence
As my young mistress' dog. Now, my sick fool Roderigo,
Whom love has turned almost the wrong side out,
To Desdemona has to-night caroused
Potations pottle-deep ; and he's to watch :

Three lads of Cyprus—noble swelling spirits—
Have I to-night flustered with flowing cups ;
And they watch too. Now, 'mongst this flock of drunkards
Am I to put my Cassio.

 Cassio. 'Fore heaven, they have given me a rouse already.

 Mon. Good faith, a little one ; not past a pint, as I am a soldier.

 Iago. Some wine, hoa !

     And let the canakin clink, clink,
      And let the canakin clink ;
    A soldier's a man, a man's life's but a span,
     Why, then, let a soldier drink.

Some wine, boys.

 Cassio. 'Fore heaven, an excellent song.

 Iago. I learned it in England, where, indeed, they are most potent in potting ; your Dane, your German, and your swag-bellied Hollander —Drink, hoa !—are nothing to your English.

 Cas. Is your Englishman so exquisite in his drinking ?

 Iago. . . . . Why, he drinks you, with facility, your Dane dead drunk ; he sweats not to overthrow your Almain ; he gives your Hollander a vomit ere the next pottle can be filled.

 Cassio. To the health of our general.

 Iago. Some wine, hoa ! . . .

 Cassio. Do not think, gentlemen, I am drunk ; this is my ancient— I can stand well enough, I can speak well enough. . . .

 Iago. You see this fellow that is gone before,
He is a soldier fit to stand by Cæsar
And give direction : and do but see his vice ;
'Tis to his virtue a just equinox,
The one as long as the other ; 'tis a pity of him.
I fear the trust Othello puts him in
On some odd time of his infirmity,
Will shake this island. . . .

Then, after tempting him, Iago leads the excited Cassio to quarrel with the excited Roderigo, taking care that witnesses are prepared to carry the news to Othello. Meanwhile, Cassio is sobered, and horrified by being told he is " drunk," and by seeing Othello approach :—

 Iago. What, are you hurt, lieutenant ?

 Cassio. Ay, past all surgery.

 Iago. Marry, Heaven forbid !

E

Cassio. Reputation, reputation, reputation ! O, I have lost my reputation ! I have lost the immortal part, sir, of myself, and what remains is bestial. My reputation, Iago, my reputation !

Iago. As I am an honest man, I thought you had received some bodily wound ; there is more offence in that than in reputation. . . .

Cassio. I will rather sue to be despised than to deceive· so good a commander with so slight, so drunken, so indiscreet an officer. Drunk ? and speak parrot, and squabble ? swagger ? and swear ? and discourse fustian with one's own shadow ? O, thou invisible spirit of wine, if thou hast no name to be known by, let us call thee devil ! . . .

Iago. What had he done to you ?

Cassio. I remember a mass of things, but nothing distinctly : a quarrel, but nothing wherefore. O, that men should put an enemy in their mouths to steal away their brains ; that we should, with joy, pleasure, revel, and applause, transform ourselves into beasts.

Iago. Why, but you are now well enough : How came you to be recovered ?

Cassio. It hath pleased the devil drunkenness, to give place to the devil wrath : one imperfectness shows me another, to make me frankly despise myself.

Iago. Come, you are too severe a moraler : As the time, the place, and the condition of this country stands, I could heartily wish this had not befallen ; but since it is as it is, mend it for your own good.

Cassio. I will ask him for my place again ; he shall tell me I am a drunkard ! Had I as many mouths as Hydra, such an answer would stop them all. To be now a sensible man, by and by a fool, presently a beast ! O strange !—Every inordinate cup is unblessed, and the in-gredient is a devil.

Iago. Come, come, good wine is a good familiar creature, if it be well used ; exclaim no more against it. And, good lieutenant, I think you think I love you ?

Cassio. I have well approved it, sir. I ? drunk ?

Iago. You, or any man living, may be drunk at a time, man. . . .

Iago, like Mephistopheles, attempts to harden his con-science. Desdemona, like the angels, pardoning his fault, would remove his penalty :—

> And yet his trespass, in our common reason
> (Save that, they say, the wars must make examples
> Out of their best), is not almost a fault
> To incur a private check.   (Act iii. sc. 3.)

Though there is a good deal said about wine in the

Tempest, it illustrates no great question. And in the Masque, Ceres is addressed as the bounteous lady who spreads the rich leas with wheat, rye, barley, and pole-clipped vineyards.

Trinculo echoes Falstaff, "Was there ever a man a coward that drank so much sack as I to-day ?"

The death-scene in *Hamlet* represents his uncle following the classic usage of throwing a pearl into the cup to honour a special guest, to conceal the poison :—

> Set me the stoups of wine upon that table.
> The king shall drink to Hamlet's better breath ;
> And in the cup an union shall he throw. . . .
> Stay, give me drink : Hamlet, this pearl is thine ;
> Here's to thy health. Give him the cup.
>   *Queen.* The queen carouses to thy fortune, Hamlet.

The result of my reading is to make me believe that Shakspere approved of stimulant in exceeding moderation ; that he preferred beer to wine; and that, even when drinking immoderately, it was better to drink beer than wine. In spite of Falstaff's praise, the series of quotations I have given show that the evils of excessive drinking chiefly came through the use of "wine"—the Irishman's *aqua vitæ* being little known. All his characters that came to evil through drink (like Edgar in *King Lear*), "Wine loved they dearly." He never blames that "poor creature, small-beer."

Another important consideration beyond the psychological in regard to the discussion is, that in treating the drinking-customs of different peoples or ancient times—for instance, in *King Lear, Antony and Cleopatra, Hamlet,* &c.—Shakspere commits anachronisms and incongruities impossible to such a thorough student of history and literature as was Bacon, and yet these very errors were in keeping with the canons of dramatic art at the time, of which Bacon *disapproved.*

The reading of Bacon's works gives very different results.

I will first notice the differing lists of phrases in regard to various stimulants that Bacon uses. Of course there are some similar ones. Contemporaries must always retain a partial identity in language. But we have only to compare the list at the head of this chapter with the present one, to see the distinction. *Nat. Hist.* :—" Hippocras liquor," "Claret wine," "Quart of vinegar," "Must of wine," "Wort of beer," "Wine burnt," "Infusions," "Kernels of grapes," "Capon-beer," "Kilderkin," "Bung-hole," "Beer-carding," "Flowering," "Mantling," "The like brew," "Acceleration of germination," "More splendour in the liquor," "More lustre," "Turbid," "Refined," "Racked," "Unracked," "New beer," "Stale beer," "Lees," "Malt infusion," "Hops," "Maturation," "Bottling of beer and ale," "Goodness of waters for brewing," "Strong waters," "Steeped wines and beers are very medicinal," "The dulcoration of malt," "Potable drinks," "Mead," "Cyder," "Perry," "Verjuice," "Malmsey," "Greek wine," "Canary wine," "Sweet wines," "In September grapes," "Wine-press," "Harsh-wine, tasting of the grape-stone," "Distillations," "Hot water," "Alehouse glass," "English drinking-glass."

In Bacon's *Medical Remains*, in which the "advice" seems to have been more practised on himself than on others, we can notice his notion of the value of mixtures in his "Wine for the spirits," "Wine against melancholy," "Wine with swine's flesh or hart's flesh," "Ale of the second infusion of the vine of the oak," "Ale of raisins, dactyles, potatoes, pistachios, honey, tragacanth, mastic," "To use ale with enula campana, carduus, germander, sage, angelica seed, cresses," "Vino odorato," "Wine in which gold has been quenched," "Rhubarb in white wine or beer."

From his position, as well as from his *mission*, he was able to learn much of this subject, and he was, in several peculiar ways, connected with "the trade." His friend Essex, according to Queen Elizabeth's own profession, fell through his urgency in desiring a renewal of the farm of sweet wines. In James's reign, Bacon arranged the settlement of this monopoly on the Lady Arabella. At his own fall, the twenty-seventh charge brought against him was that he had been bribed by the French merchants to force their wines upon unwilling London vintners, by putting their persons illegally in prison. Another charge was that he had accepted bribes from three parties, when the Company of Apothecaries separated from the Grocers. Previously to this, he had not been considered free of blame in allowing Christopher Villiers, the brother of the Duke of Buckingham, to oppress the keepers of alehouses by extortions and fines, in his monopoly of licensing powers.

In his purely intellectual relations to the subject he is more honourably known. In his " Advice to Sir George Villiers," regarding home industries, he notes : " First, for the home trade, I first commend unto your consideration the encouragement of tillage, which will enable the kingdom to bring forth corn for the natives. . . . Third, planting of orchards, in a soil and air fit for them, is very profitable as well as pleasurable; cyder and perry are notable beverages in sea-voyages. . . . Fifth, the planting of hop-yards are found very profitable for the planters." Not only did he give political counsel to those in power, but he gave scientific counsel to those in practice, which, though occasionally confused by superstition and credulity, was wonderfully sound and suggestive, considering the state of advancement in his time. He first showed the dignity of *dietetics*. " Among the particular arts, those are to be preferred which exhibit, alter, and prepare natural bodies and materials of things, such as agriculture, cooking, and chemistry " (*Parasceve*, v., and elsewhere).

He notices the paucity of technical literature, and suggests " A Catalogue of Particular Histories that ought to be Written." 55. " History of the Food of Man, and of all Things Eatable and Drinkable, and of all Diet; and of the variety of the same according to nations and smaller differences. 83. History of Wine. 84. History of the Cellar and of different Kinds of Drinks. 128. Miscellaneous History of Common Experiments that have not yet been raised into an Art." These histories many are now helping this great suggestor to complete; these experiments that he begun many have kept working out. In his *Advancement of Learning*, Book ii., he says: "For history of Nature, wrought or mechanical, I find some collections made of agriculture, and likewise of manual arts, but commonly with a rejection of experiments familiar and vulgar. For it is esteemed a kind of dishonour unto learning to descend to inquiry or meditation upon matters mechanical, except they be such as may be thought secrets, rarities, and special subtilties." Bacon thereupon, by example as well as by precept, went on to show the value of "experiments familiar and vulgar." We may consider a few of these in relation to our subjects. He suggests the soaking of corn seeds in various liquids before planting (*Nat. Hist.*, c. v. 402), and gives the experiments he performed himself. After the corn has grown, "winds are injurious to the corn crops at three seasons— namely, on the opening of the flower, at the shedding of the flower, and near the time of ripening;" and he gives the reasons of this (*Hist. of Winds*, 24). He advises men to inquire more into the diseases of corn (*Nat. Hist.*, c. vii. 669, 696, 670). He notices the importance of "waters" in making malt, &c., in *Nat. Hist.*, c. iv. 391, 392, 393; and in 394 he adds: "Fourthly, try them by making drinks stronger or smaller with the same quantity of malt; and you may conclude that that water which maketh the stronger drink is the more concocted and nourishing, though perhaps it be not so good for medicinal use. Such water is commonly the water of large and navigable rivers, or of large and clean ponds of standing water, for upon both them the sun hath more power than upon fountains and small rivers. And I conceive that chalk water is next them, the best for going furthest in drink, for that also helpeth concoction." *Nat. Hist.*, c. vii. 647, he notes that " Barley, as appeareth in the malting, being steeped in water three days, and afterwards the water drained from it, and the barley turned upon a dry floor, will sprout half an inch long at least, and if it be let alone and not turned, much more, until the heart be out." 648. " Malt in the drenching will swell, and that in such a manner as, after the putting forth in sprouts and the drying upon the kiln, there will be gained at least a bushel in eight; and yet the sprouts are rubbed off; and there will be a bushel of dust besides the malt, which I suppose to be not only by the loose and open lying of the parts, but by some addition of substance from the water." In *Nat. Hist.*, c. ix. 857, he tells us " Barley in the boiling swelleth not much, wheat swelleth more, rice extremely," and gives the reasons. 649. " Malt gathereth a sweetness to the taste, which appeareth yet more in the wort. The dulcoration of things is worthy to be tried to the full; for that dulcoration importeth a degree to the nourishment, and the making of things inalimental to become alimental, may be an experiment of great profit for making new victual."

In *Nat. Hist.*, c. i. 49 : " Indian maize hath of certain an excellent spirit of nourishment; I judge the same of rice." 24. " In the same way, if beer were to be brewed not only of the grains of wheat, barley, oats or peas, but should likewise have about a third part of roots or fat pulps, as potato roots, the pith of artichokes, burdocks, or any other sweet and esculent roots, I conceive it would be a drink much more conducive to longevity than beer made of grain." It is evident that the modern definition of "pure beer" had not then arisen as a standard on a battle-field.

In the *History of Dense and Rare* he treats of must : " New beer, and the like, when casked, swell and rise exceedingly, so that, unless they obtain a vent, they will burst the cask ; but if this be given them, they rise and froth up, and, as it were, boil over." He gives a whole series of experiments on beer.

In the same way he treats of wine from the beginning. *Nat. Hist.*, c. vii. 668 : "The grafting of vines upon vines, as I take it, is not now in use; the ancients had it, and had three ways; the first was incision, which is the ordinary manner of grafting; the second was terebration through the middle of the stock, and putting in the scions there; and the third was paring of two vines that grew together to the marrow, and binding them close."

Nat. Hist., c. i. 35, is "On making vines fruitful. It is reported of credit, that if you lay good store of kernels of grapes about the root of a vine, it will make the vine come earlier and prosper better. The cause may be, for that the kernels draw out of the earth juice fit to nourish the tree, as those that would be trees of themselves, though there were no root ; but the root, being of greater strength, robbeth and devoureth the nourishment when they have drawn it." And in c. v. 457 : "It is reported that trees will grow greater and bear better fruit if you put lees of wine to the root."

In *Nat. Hist.*, c. vii. 638 : "As for the vine, it is noted that it beareth more grapes when it is young, but grapes that make better wine when it is old ; for that the juice is better concocted, and we see that some wine is inflammable, so as it hath a kind of oiliness."

664. "Showers, if they come a little before the ripening of fruits, do good to vines, but it is rather for plenty than for goodness, for the best vines are in the driest vintages." 666. "It is strange which is observed by some of the ancients, that dust keepeth the fruitfulness of vines, insomuch as they cast dust upon them of purpose. It should seem that that powdering, when a shower cometh, maketh a kind of soiling to the tree, being earth and water finely

laid on. And they note that countries where the fields and ways are dusty bear the best wines."

Next after his favourite scents of violets and musk-roses and decaying strawberry leaves, he prefers the scent of the vine-flower, and suggests utilising it in wine.

He notices in his essay *Of Judicature* (L. vi.), " Where the wine-press is hard wrought, it yields a harsh wine, that tastes of the grape-stone."

In *De Augmentis Scientiarum* (L. v.) he speaks of cider, &c., " According to the Roman adage, ' One cluster of grapes ripens faster by the side of another.' " . . . " Our cyder makers have an excellent way of imitating the operation. For they take care not to bruise or squeeze the apples till they have lain together for awhile in heaps, and so ripened by mutual contact, that the too great acidity of the drink may be corrected." This fact is repeated, like most of the other facts that interest him, several times in his writings ; and he certainly was much interested in cider, as also in perry.

Yet he does not ignore mead. In the *History of Life and Death*, Part ii. 22 : " Mead, I imagine, would not be bad if strong and old ; but since all honey has some acidity in it (as may be seen by the corrosive water that the chemists extract from it, which can even dissolve metals), it would be better to make a similar drink with sugar, not lightly infused, but incorporated as firmly as honey in mead, and keep it for a year or six months, so that the water may lose its crudity, and the sugar may acquire subtlety. "

Experiment solitary touching honey and sugar, *Nat. Hist.*, 848 : " Sugar hath put down the use of honey, insomuch as we have lost those observations and preparations of honey which the ancients had, when it was more in price. First, it seemeth that there was in old time tree-honey as well as bee-honey, which was the tear or blood issuing from the tree ; insomuch as one of the ancients relateth that in Trebisond there was honey issuing from the box-trees,

which made men mad. Again, in ancient time there was
a kind of honey which, either of its own nature or by art,
would grow as hard as sugar, and was not so luscious as
ours. They had also a wine of honey which they made
thus. They crushed the honey into a great quantity of
water, and then strained the liquor : after they boiled it in
a copper to the half ; then they poured it into earthen
vessels for a small time, and after turned it into vessels of
wood, and kept it for many years. They have also at this
day, in Russia and those Northern countries, mead simple,
which, well made and seasoned, is a good wholesome drink,
and very clear. They use also in Wales a compound drink
of mead with herbs and spices. But meanwhile it were
good, in recompense of that we have lost in honey, there
were brought in use a sugar-mead ; for so we may call it,
though without any mixture at all of honey; and to brew
it, and keep it stale, as they use mead : for certainly, though
it would not be so abstersive, and opening, and solutive a
drink as mead, yet it will be more grateful to the stomach,
and more lenitive, and fit to be used in sharp diseases : for
we see that the use of sugar in beer and ale hath good
effects in such cases."

He speaks about the nourishment in odours, and suggests pouring wine on new-turned earth and inhaling it
as a thing nourishing and pleasant.   " It is certain that
odours do, in a small degree, nourish, especially the odour
of wine," and he gives the case of Democritus (*Nat. Hist.*,
934).

He advised people to inhale the odours of newly-turned
earth.   " I commend also sometimes in digging of new
earth to pour in some Malmsey or Greek wine, that the
vapour of the earth and wine together may comfort the
spirits the more " (*Nat. Hist.*, c. x. 928).

He does not forget the various steps in finishing any
drink. *Nat. Hist.*, c. iii. 308 : " The longer malt or herbs
or the like are infused in liquor, the more thick and troubled

the liquor is ; but the longer they be decocted in the liquor,
the clearer it is. The reason is plain, because in infusion
the longer it is, the greater is the part of the gross body
that goeth into the liquor; but in decoction, though more
goeth forth, yet it either purgeth at the top or settleth at
the bottom. And therefore the most exact way to clarify
is first to infuse, and then to take off the liquor and decoct
it, as they do in beer, which hath malt first infused in the
liquor, and is afterwards boiled with the hop. This is referred to separation."

In *Nat. Hist.*, c. iv. 301, he goes on to the clarification
of liquors : " Liquors are many of them at the first thick
and troubled, as must, wort, juices of fruits, or herbs expressed, and by time they settle and clarify. But to make
them clear before the time is great work; for it is a spur
to Nature, and putteth her out of her pace; and besides, it
is of good use for making drinks and sauces potable and
serviceable speedily. But to know the means of accele-
rating clarification, we must first know the causes of clarification. The first cause is by the separation of the grosser
parts of the liquid from the finer; the second, by the equal
distribution of the spirits of the liquor with the tangible
parts, for that ever representeth bodies clear and untroubled ;
the third, by the refining the spirit itself, which thereby
giveth to the liquor more splendour and more lustre."

The following paragraphs continue the subject : 302
treats of "Separation by weight; by heat; by adhesion,
as when a body more viscous is mingled with the liquor;
by percolation, &c." 303. "Of the even distribution of
spirits by heat, motion, time, or mixture of some other
body." 304. "Of heat, motion, and mixture of some other
body which hath virtue to attenuate." 305. "It is in
common practice to draw wine and beer from the lees,
which we call racking, whereby it will clarify much the
sooner; for the lees, though they keep the drink in heart
and make it lasting, yet withal they cast up some spissi-

tude, and this instance is to be referred to separation."
In 306 he gives experiments to show that "it were good
to try what the adding to the liquor more lees than
his own will work;" and also in 307, "Take new beer,
and put in some quantity of stale beer into it, and see
if it will not accelerate the clarification." In 309 he
advises experiments by putting hot embers, renewed daily,
round the bottles of new beer; and lime quenched and
unquenched, and notice the effect on even distribution or
refining of the spirit.   310. He suggests shaking: "Take
bottles and swing them, or carry them in a wheelbarrow
over rough ground twice a-day; but then you may not
fill the bottles full, but leave some air, for if the liquor
come to the stopple, it cannot play nor flower; and when
you have shaken them well either way, pour the drink into
another bottle, stopped also close after the usual manner,
for if it stay with much drink in it, the drink will pall;
neither will it settle so perfectly in all the parts.   Let it
stand some twenty-four hours; then take it, and put it
again into a bottle with air, *ut supra;* and thence into a
bottle stopped, *ut supra;* and so repeat the operations for
seven days.   Note, that in the emptying of one bottle into
another, you must do it swiftly, lest the drink pall.   This
instance is referred to the even distribution of the spirits
by motion."   Elsewhere he suggests ropes in the cask.
In 311 he treats of clarification by percolation, or separation by adhesion.   Let "milk be put into new beer, and
stirred with it, for it may be that the grosser part of the
beer will cleave to the milk; the doubt is, whether it will
sever again, which is soon tried.   It is usual in clarifying
Hippocras to put in milk, which after severeth and carrieth
with it the grosser parts of the Hippocras, as hath been
said elsewhere.   Eggs are tried by some.   Also for the
better clarification by percolation when they thin new beer,
they use to let it pass through a strainer; and it is like
the finer the strainer is the clearer it will be."

Nat. Hist., c. iv. 312, he goes on to maturation : " For the maturation of drinks, it is wrought by the congregation of the spirits together, whereby they digest more perfectly the grosser parts ; and it is effected partly by the same means that clarification is, whereof we spake before ; but then note that an extreme clarification doth spread the spirits so smooth as they become dull and the drink dead, which ought to have a little flowering. And therefore all your clear amber drink is flat." 313. "We see the degrees of maturation of drinks : in must, in wine (as it is drunk), and in vinegar. Whereas must hath not the spirits well congregated, wine hath them well united, so as they make the parts somewhat more oily ; vinegar hath them congregated, but more jejune and in smaller quantity, the greatest and finest spirit part being exhaled : for we see vinegar is made by setting the vessel of wine against the hot sun ; and therefore vinegar will not burn, for that the finer part is exhaled." 314. "The refreshing or quickening of drink palled or dead is by enforcing the motion of the spirit ; so we see that open weather relaxeth the spirit, and maketh it more lively in motion. We see also bottling of beer or ale, while it is new and full of spirit, so that it spirteth when the stopple is taken forth, maketh the drink more quick and windy. A pan of coals in the cellar doth likewise good, and maketh the drink work again. New drink, put to drink which is dead, provoketh it to work again ; nay, which is more, as some affirm, a brewing of new beer *set by* old beer maketh it work again. It were good also to enforce the spirits by some mixtures, that may excite and quicken them ; as by putting into the bottles nitre, chalk, lime, &c." 315. "It is said that the burying the bottles of drink well stopped, either in dry earth a good depth, or in the bottom of a well within water, and, best of all, the hanging of them in a deep well somewhat above the water for some fortnight's space, is an excellent means of making drink fresh and quick; for the cold doth not cause any exhaling of the spirits at all, as heat doth, though it rarefieth the rest that remain; but cold maketh the spirits vigorous and irritates them, whereby they incorporate the parts of liquor perfectly."

Novum Organum, xlvii. : "Among prerogative instances in the 23rd place is quantity, which, borrowing a term from medicine, I call also doses of Nature. . . . All particular virtues act according to the greater or less quantity of the body. Large quantities of water corrupt slowly, small ones quickly. Wine and beer ripen and become fit to drink much more quickly in bottles than in casks."

Nat. Hist., c. ix. 861 : " Time doth change fruit, as apples, pears, &c., from more sour to more sweet; but contrariwise liquors, even those that are of the juice of fruit, from more sweet to more sour; as wort, must, new verjuice, &c. The cause is the congregation of the spirits together; for in both kinds the spirit is attenuated by time; but in the first kind it is more diffused, and more mustered by the grosser parts, which the spirits do but digest. But in drinks the spirits do reign, and finding less opposition of the parts, become themselves more strong, which causeth also more strength in the liquor; such as if the spirits be of the hotter sort, the liquor becometh apt to burn; but in time it causeth likewise, when the higher spirits are evaporated, more sourness."

Novum Organum, Book ii. 50 : " Polychrest instances, or instances of general use. . . . I remember to have heard of bottles of wine being let down into a deep well to cool; but through accident or neglect being left there for many years, and then taken out, and that the wine was not only free from sourness and flatness, but much finer tasted, owing, it would seem, to a more exquisite commixture of its parts."

In *Life and Death*, Part ii. 23 : " Age in wine or liquor engenders subtlety in the parts of the liquor and acrimony in the spirits; whereof the first is beneficial, the second hurtful. To avoid, therefore, this complication, put into the cask, before the wine has settled at all, a piece of well-boiled pork or venison, that the spirits of the wine may have something to prey upon and devour, and thereby lose their pungency."

Of *Heat and Cold:* "The sunbeams do ripen all fruits, and addeth to them a sweetness or fatness; and yet some sultry, hot days, overcast, are noted to ripen more than bright days. The sunbeams are thought to mend distilled waters, the glasses being well stopped, and to make them more virtuous and fragrant. The sunbeams do turn wine into vinegar, but query whether they would not sweeten verjuice? The sunbeams do pall any wine or beer that is set in them. Bitter frosts do make all drinks to taste more dead and flat. Paracelsus reporteth, if a glass of wine be set upon a terrace in a bitter frost, it will leave some liquor unfrozen in the centre of the glass, which excelleth *spiritus vini* drawn by fire."

Nat. Hist., c. ix. 898 : "The turning of wine into vinegar is a kind of putrefaction; and in making of vinegar they use to set vessels of wine over against the noon sun, which calleth out the more oily spirits, and leaveth the liquor more sour and hard. We see also that burnt wine is more hard and astringent than wine sunburnt. It is said that cyder in navigations under the line ripeneth, when wine or beer soureth. It were good to set a rundlet of verjuice over against the sun in summer, as they do vinegar, to see whether it will ripen and sweeten."

In *History of Dense and Rare*, 3 : "I have heard that new wine just trodden out, and still fermenting, when put into a strong and thick glass (the mouth of the glass being so closed and sealed˙ that the must could neither burst it nor break through), as the spirit could find no vent, has with continued circulation and vexation, completely transformed itself into tartar, so that nothing remained in the glass except vapour and lees. But of this I am not certain."

Nat. Hist., c. viii. 781 : "It is said they have a manner to prepare the Greek wines, to keep them from fuming and inebriating, by adding some sulphur or alum, whereof the one is unctuous, the other is astringent. And certain it is that those two natures do most repress fumes. This experiment should be transferred unto other wine and strong beer by putting in some like substances, while they work, which may make them both to fume less and to inflame less."

Nat. Hist., c. iv. 339: "All moulds are inceptions of putrefaction."   341. "The 1st means of preventing putrefaction is cold ; for so we see that meat and drink will keep longer unputrefied or unsoured in winter than in summer ; . . . put in conservatories of snow, will keep fresh. This worketh by the detention of the tangible parts." 342. "The 2nd is astringents."   345. "The 3rd is excluding the air, and again exposing to the air, &c. . . ." 344. "The 4th is motion and stirring. . . ." 345. "The 6th is the strengthening of the spirits of bodies. It should be tried also whether chalk put into water or drink doth not preserve it from putrefying or speedy souring. So we see that strong beer will last longer than small, and all things that are hot and aromatical do help to preserve liquors." 347. "The 7th is the separation of cruder parts." 348. "The 8th is the drawing forth continually of the part where putrefaction beginneth."   349. "The 9th is a commixture of something that is more oily and sweet." 350. "The 10th is the commixture of something that is dry." In 378 he again mentions hanging bottles of wine, beer, and milk in wells in various stages, and the results.

He notices that "all bodies have their own dimensions and gravities ; water has more weight but less dimension than wine." In *De Augm. Scient.* he has numerous experiments to prove this scattered all over the work.

The idea of stimulants seemed to run much in his head, many of his figures of speech being taken from their technology. " Silence is the fermentation of thought " (*De Augm. Scient.*). In *Novum Organum* (xx.) he calls his first group of collected instances his " first vintage." He gives the action of yeast as an example of natural magic (li.). He explains poetically the Greek fable of Dionysus or Bacchus. " In his early youth he was the first to invent and explain the culture of the vine, and the making of wine and its use ; whereby becoming illustrious, he subdued the whole world. . . . His sacred tree was the ivy." " Founders and uniters of states were honoured but with titles of worthies or demi-gods, as Hercules ; on the other side, such as were inventors and authors of new arts, endowments, and commodities towards man's life, were ever consecrated amongst the gods themselves, as Ceres and Bacchus." In his prose poem, which contained his ideas of a perfect state—*The New Atlantis*—he said : " There were two long galleries, one in which were patterns and samples of all rare inventions, and in the other were statues of all the principal inventors, such as the Inventor of Wine, the Inventor of Bread, the Inventor of Sugar." " We had also drink of three sorts, all wholesome and good—wine of the grape ; a drink of grain, such as is with us our ale, but more clear ; and a kind of cider made of a fruit of that country, a wonderful pleasing and refreshing drink."

After describing the festivities of the " Son of the Vine," with his cluster of golden grapes, his cicerone tells him, " We have also large and various orchards and gardens, . . . where trees and berries are set, whereof we make divers kinds of drinks, besides the vineyards. . . . I will not hold you long with recounting of our brewhouses and bakehouses and kitchens, where are made divers drinks, breads, and meats, rare and of special effects. Wines we have of grapes, and drinks of other juice, of fruits, of grains, and of roots, and of mixtures with honey, sugar,

F

manna, and fruits dried and decocted. Also of the tears
or woundings of trees, and of the pulp of canes. And
these drinks are of several ages, some to the age or last
of forty years. We have these drinks also brewed with
several herbs and roots and spices; yea, with several fleshes
and white meats, whereof some of the drinks are such as
they are in effect meat and drink both. And above all,
we strive to have drinks of extreme thin parts to insinuate
into the body, and yet without all biting and sharpness or
fretting; insomuch as some of them put upon the back of
your hand will, with a little stay, pass through to the palm,
and yet taste mild to the mouth. We have also waters which
we ripen in that fashion as they become nourishing; so that
they are indeed excellent drink, and many will use no other."

The health-question was ever present to his mind, and
he is always considering the substances conducive to longevity, combining them with beer and wine, and daily using
them. As he says himself, he was always "puddering in
medicines," and he considered all medicines made more
powerful by being mixed with wine or beer. Paul's advice
to Timothy was not lost upon Bacon : "Take a little wine
for thy stomach's sake and for thy frequent infirmities."
His special combinations are worthy of a separate paper—
e.g., his "Capon-beer," "Wine for the spirits," "Wine
against adverse melancholy," "Restorative wines," "Ale of
raisins," "Methusalem water," &c. In his *History of Life
and Death* (vii. 12) he has "The preparation of drinks
suited to longevity may be comprised in one precept. Of
water-drinkers there is no need to speak, for, as has been
said elsewhere, such a diet may continue life for a certain
time, but can never prolong it to any great extent. But
in other spirituous liquors (as wine, beer, mead, and the
like), the one thing to be aimed at and observed as the sum
of all is to make the parts of the liquor as fine and the
spirit as mild as possible." And he repeats various experiments to make it so.

"I do much marvel that no Englishman, or Dutchman, or German doth set up brewing in Constantinople, considering they have such quantity of barley. For as for the general sort of men, frugality may be the cause of drinking water, for that it is no small saving to pay nothing for one's drink, but the better sort might well be at the cost. And yet I wonder the less at it, because I see France, Italy, or Spain have not taken into use beer or ale; which perhaps, if they did, would better both their healths and their complexions. It is likely it would be matter of great gain to any that should begin it in Turkey" (*Nat. Hist.*, 705).

In *Nat. Hist.*, c. viii. 727, he tells us, "The use of wine in dry or consumed bodies is hurtful; in moist and full bodies it is good;" and gives the reasons. He also brings forward a precept of Aristotle that "wine be forborne in all consumptions." "If it must be taken, let it be burnt."

He gives the quaintest causes for the effects of drunkenness in *Nat. Hist.*, c. viii. 724, 725 : "Drunken men reel, they tremble, they cannot stand, nor speak strongly. They imagine everything turneth round; they imagine also that things come upon them ; they see not well things afar off; those things that they see near at hand they see out of their place, and sometimes they see things double. The cause of the imagination that things turn round is, for that the spirit themselves turn, being compressed by the vapour of the wine, for any liquid body upon compression turneth, as we see in water, and it is all one to the sight whether the visual spirits move, or the object moveth, or the medicine moveth. And we see that long turning round breedeth the same imagination. The cause of the imagination that things come upon them is, for that the spirits visual themselves draw back, which maketh the object seem to come on ; and besides, when they see things turn round and move, fear maketh them think they come upon

them. The cause that they cannot see things afar off is
the weakness of the spirits ; for in every megrim or vertigo
there is an obtenebration joined with a semblance of turning round, which we see also in the lighter sort of swoon-
ings. The cause of seeing things out of their place is the
refraction of the spirits visual ; for the vapour is an un-
equal medium, and it is as the sight of things out of place
in water. The cause of seeing things double is the swift
and unquiet motion of the spirits, being oppressed, to and
fro ; for, as was said before, the motion of the spirits
visual and the motion of the object make the same
appearances ; and for the swift motion of the object,
we see, if you filip a lute-string, it showeth double or
treble."

726. " Men are sooner drunk with small draughts than
with great. And again, wine sugared inebriateth less than
wine pure. The cause of the former is, for that the wine
descendeth not so fast to the bottom of the stomach, but
maketh longer stay in the upper part of the stomach, and
sendeth vapours forth to the head, and therefore inebriateth
sooner. And for the same reason sops in wine, quantity
for quantity, inebriate more than wine of itself. The cause
of the latter is, for that the sugar doth inspissate the
spirits of the wine, and maketh them not so easy to resolve
into vapour. Nay, farther, it is thought to be some remedy
against inebriating if wine sugared be taken after wine
pure. And the same effect is wrought either by oil or
milk taken upon much drinking."

The works of Bacon on " Drinks " would fill a large
volume, which might be called " Wine, Beer, and Cider."
He never mentions spirits as a drink. He has very little
original matter amusing. Shakspere's wit or humour is
not suggested in his works. Some collected *quotations,*
however, may be deemed interesting ; as, for instance :—

Apophthegm 108. One was examined upon certain
scandalous words spoken against the king. He confessed

them, and said : " It is true I spake them ; and if the wine had not failed, I had said much more."

Apophthegm 53. A physician advised his patient that had sore eyes that he should abstain from wine ; but the patient said, " I think rather, sir, from wine and water, for I have often marked it in blue eyes, and I have seen water come forth, but wine never."

Apophthegm 134. Alonso of Arragon was wont to say in commendation of age, " That age appeared best in four things—old wood to burn ; old wine to drink ; old friends to trust ; and old authors to read." Let therefore the drinks in use be subtle, yet free from all acrimony and acidity, as are those wines which, as the old woman says in Plautus, " are toothless with age."

Apophthegm 29. The Lord Keeper, Sir Nicholas Bacon, was asked his opinion by Queen Elizabeth of one of these monopoly licenses ? And he answered, " Madam, will you have me speak the truth ? *Licentiæ deteriores sumus.*" We are all the worse for licenses. A good motto for Sir Wilfrid.

" It is written of Epicurus that, after his disease was judged desperate, he drowned his stomach and senses with a large draught and ingurgitation of wine ; hence he was not sober enough to taste any bitterness in Stygian waters " (*Adv. of Learning*, ii.).

In his *Promus* (1594-96), edited by Mrs. Pott, are many phrases and several proverbs in English and foreign languages, intended as suggestions for future work. Much has been made of parallelisms between the *Promus* and the plays of Shakspere ; but anything found there is certain not to be original, so nothing can be based on it. For instance, Greene says,[1] " Soft fire makes sweet malt," and

---

[1] Robert Greene's *Quippe for an Upstart Courtier*, 1592 ; also *Tib. Talk*—
"Soft Fier maketh sweete maulte, good Madge Mumblecrust."
(*Ralph Roister Doister*, 1553.)
Also—   "Softer fire makes sweeter malt."
(*Nash's Pierce Pennilesse*, 1592.)

Shakspere, in "As You Like It," says, "Good wine needs no bush."[1] We need not, however, be surprised to find that Bacon, either from them or from others, had heard the phrases and *booked them.*

470. Soft fire makes sweet malt.

512. *Lunæ radiis non maturescit botrus.* The cluster does not ripen in the rays of the moon.

517. Good wine needs no bush.

582. *Buon vin cattiva testa, dice il Griega.* Good wine makes a bad head, says the Greek.

583. *Buon vin favola lunga.* Good wine talks long.

631. As he brews, so must he drink.

777. *Ad vinum diserti.* Eloquent at wine (*Erasm.*).

878. An owl's egg. It was an old superstition that if a child ate of an owl's egg before it had tasted wine, it would be a total abstainer all its life.

910. The vinegar of sweet wine.[2]

999. *In vino veritas.*

1605. *Vin sur lait souhait ; lait sur vin, venin.*

1608. *A la trogne on cognoist l'yvrogne.*

1612. *Vin vieux, amy vieux, et or vieux, sont aimés en tous lieux.*

In the *Adv. of Learning*, Book ii. : "As Philocrates sported with Demosthenes, ' You may not marvel, Athenians, that Demosthenes and I do differ, for he drinketh water and I drink wine.' And like as we read of the ancient parable of the two gates of sleep in Virgil, if we put on sobriety and attention, we shall find it a sure maxim in knowledge, that the more pleasant liquor of wine is the more vaporous, and the braver gate of ivory sendeth forth the falser dreams."

---

[1] John Davies of Hereford says—

> "Good wine doth need no bush, Lord, who can tell !
> How oft this old said saw hath praised new books."
>
> (1603.)

[2] Also, "The sweetest wine turneth to the sharpest vinegar."
(Euphues' Anatomy of Wit, 1579.)

In the *Interpretation of Nature* (cxxii.), "I may say then of myself that which one said in jest (since it marks the distinction so truly), 'It cannot be that we should think alike, when one drinks water and the other drinks wine.' Now, other men, as well in ancient as in modern times, have in the matter of sciences drunk a crude liquor like water, whereas I pledge mankind in a liquor strained from countless grapes, from grapes ripe and fully seasoned, collected in clusters, and gathered and then squeezed in the press, and finally purified and clarified in the vat. And, therefore, it is no wonder if they and I do not think alike."

The authors of Shakspere's and of Bacon's works drank different liquors, and therefore they did not think alike. The first drank nectar; the second, wine and beer. The first could not have yoked the horses of Apollo to the car of commonplace experiment; the second would have fallen like Icarus, with melted wings from his high flight, had he essayed it.

CHAPTER IV.

WHETHER WERE THE POEMS AND PLAYS CLAIMED BY SHAKSPERE OR BACON?

SHAKSPERE wrote his Sonnets and *gave* them to his friends, which Meres proves. He wrote his poems, printed them, signed and *dedicated* them to Southampton, which was never considered less than proof he composed them. He wrote his plays and *sold* them to his company, which credited him with them by giving him place and power, and publishing them with his name after his death. He *acted* his own plays and others, so that he knew just what would tell on an audience, and thence he won his fame; and he must have spoken to many of *his plots* and *his alterations.*

A claim of three hundred years ago can only be *proved* by inference. But if the premises are good, the inference can be sound. If all of the works named as Shakspere's were not definitely claimed by him in his lifetime, some were, and that is quite sufficient for the purpose in hand.

The earliest signed work was his *Venus and Adonis,* 1593.

In 1592 the Plague had been in London, and the players were not allowed to play often, lest the concourse of people should spread infection.

Doubtless Shakspere found thereby more leisure to write a poem unconnected with the stage, or at least to correct, beautify, and expand one he had in hand.

We have already pointed out that Shakspere only wrote two dedications, both simple, manly, and like modern forms; nevertheless, the first, the dedication to *Venus and Adonis*, is written as to a patron:—

1593. To the Right Honourable Henry Wriothesly, Earl of Southampton, &c. :—

Right Honourable,
I know not how I shall offend in dedicating my unpolished lines to your Lordship, nor how the world will censure me for choosing so strong a prop to support so weak a burden; only if your Honour seem but pleased, I account myself highly praised, and vow to take advantage of all idle hours, till I have honoured you with some graver labour. But if the first heir of my invention prove deformed, I shall be sorry it had so noble a godfather, and never after ear so barren a land, for fear it yield me still so bad a harvest. I leave it to your honourable survey, and your Honour to your heart's content; which I wish may always answer your own wish, and the world's hopeful expectation.
Your Honour's in all duty,
WILLIAM SHAKSPERE.[1]

Consider the meaning of the phrases "unpolished lines," "take advantage of all idle hours," "first heir of my invention," "some graver labour"—these cannot fit into the Baconian story in any way.

In one year, however, the admiration of his poetic power had caused Southampton to receive him and honour him as a friend, by which degree of intimacy Shakspere opened his heart like a flower to the sun. Shakspere did take advantage of all idle hours, and soon produced a witness of his

[1] The second editions I have not seen; the third edition of 1596 retains the dedication.
"18 April 1593, Richard Field entered for his copie under the handes of the Archbishop of Canterbury and Master Warden Stirrup, a book entituled Venus and Adonis."
That publishers had a right in the editions is evident. On 25th June 1594 is an entry in the Stationers' Register. "Master Harrison, senior, assigned over unto him from Richard Field in open court holden this day a Book called Venus and Adonis, the which was before entered to Richard Field, 18 April 1593."

"graver labour." The dedication of *The Rape of Lucrece* in the following year reads very differently, but still less like Bacon. The address is to a friend—a friend superior in rank, but one who could feel Burns's idea, even then common to the heart of man :—

> " The rank is but the guinea stamp,
> The man's the gowd for a' that."

1594.[1] To the Right Honourable Henry Wriothesly, Earl of Southampton, &c. : —

The love I dedicate to your Lordship is without end ; whereof this pamphlet without beginning is but a superfluous moiety. The warrant I have of your honourable disposition, not the worth of my untutored lines, makes it assured of acceptance. What I have done is yours ; what I have to do is *yours;* being part in all I have devoted yours. Were my worth greater, my duty would show greater ; meantime, as it is, it is bound to your Lordship, to whom I wish long life, still lengthened with all happiness.—Your Lordship's in all duty,

WILLIAM SHAKSPERE.

He acknowledges his love, his duty, and the warrant given him of Southampton's honourable disposition. He confesses his lines to be *untutored*, which Bacon would not have done, and devotes all past and future work to Southampton, which Bacon could not have done, as he shared his dedications amongst many, reserving his best for queens and kings.

I do not think Baconians gather the full import of these *simple* prose lines because they are so natural. The fawning

---

[1] In the Stationers' Registers for this year appears :—

6th Feb. 1594. To John Danter. "A Noble Roman History of Titus Andronicus."

12th March. To Thomas Myllynton, "The Firste Parte of the Contention," &c.

14th May. To Master Harrison, senior. "The Ravishment of Lucrece."

14th May. "The Most Famous Chronicle History of Leire, King of England and his three Daughters," to Edward White.

19th June. To Thomas Creede. "The Tragedy of Richard the Third."

servility and ambitious expediencies in Bacon's dedications, though harmonious enough to the ideas of his time, are not so to ours. They remind us of one of the Apophthegms he preserved. " Of the like nature was the answer which Aristippus made, when, having a petition to Dionysius and no ear given to him, he fell down at his feet, whereupon Dionysius staid, and gave him the hearing and granted it; and afterwards some person, tender on behalf of philosophy, reproved Aristippus that he would offer the profession of philosophy such an indignity, as for a private suit to fall at a tyrant's feet; but he answered that it was not his fault, but the fault of Dionysius, that had ears in his feet."

In 1599 the first edition of *The Passionate Pilgrim* was published; a second edition published has not been preserved.

In 1612 the third edition was republished as Shakspere's by William Jaggard. Two of Thomas Heywood's sonnets were included; and in an *Apology for Actors*, 1612, Heywood said that his Epistle of *Helen to Paris* and *Paris to Helen* had been printed in his *Troja Britannica*, 1609, which might make the world think he had stolen them from Shakspere, and that Shakspere, to do himself right, had reprinted them; " but as I must acknowledge my lines not worth Shakspere's patronage, under whom Jaggard hath published them, so the *author* I know to be much offended with M. Jaggard, that altogether unknown to him, presumed to make so free with his name." And Jaggard was forced to publish his next edition without Shakspere's name on the title-page.

That " friendly Shakspere," as Scoloker calls him, should have thus sided with Heywood and others in regard to their claims, may be taken as an inverse assumption of the property of the remainder of the verses, unclaimed by others. The world then knew very much of private matters, and made these as public as possible, as we may see in the Nashe-Harvey scurrilous series of pamphlets, rising out of

Greene's, but not a word is said against Shakspere. The plays printed under his name would have been contested by some rival, made a shelter for attacks by some enemy, had they not been really his. Pirated as they doubtless often were, he gives a negative assent by silence.

Now, it is perfectly certain that the two poems at least were signed by Shakspere, and that even though the plays were pirated, they must have been claimed by him before the printers would have thought of putting his name to them. That any one who invented an author would have certainly chosen one " excellent in the art he professed," is self-evident ; and the very ascription to him is a sign of his known capability to write them. Therefore, while we cannot be absolutely sure that he either printed or signed the following works, we may be sure he claimed them. That neither in title-page or Stationers' Registers there should ever have been any variation in the ascription to him (if any name is mentioned), and that there never should have been in contemporary literature the slightest hint of the rights of other people in them, must be remembered now to enforce this claim, though we treat it fully in the next chapter.

Probably the high praise of Meres made booksellers aware of the value of his name, and henceforth we see it appear on title-pages, and sometimes even in Stationers' Registers.

Love's Labour's Lost . . . . . . 1598.

> A pleasant conceited Comedie called, Loues labors lost. As it was presented before her Highnes this last Christmas. Newly corrected and augmented by W. Shakespere. Imprinted at London by W. W. for Cuthbert Busby. 1598. 4to.

Copies in Bodleian, &c.

Richard the Second . . . . . . 1598.

The Tragedie of King Richard the Second. As it hath beene publikely acted by the right Honourable the Lord Chamberlaine his Seruants. By William Shake-speare. Lond. Printed by Valentine Simmes for Andrew Wise, and are to be sold at his shop in Paules church yard at the signe of the Angel. 1598. 4to.

An edition published in 1597, but without author's name.

Copies in British Museum, &c.

Richard the Third . . . . . . 1598.

The Tragedie of King Richard the Third. Containing his treacherous Plots against his brother Clarence; the pitiful murther of his innocent Nephewes; his tyrannicall vsurpation, with the whole course of his detested life and most deserued death. As it hath beene lately Acted by the Right Honourable the Lord Chamberlaine his seruants. By William Shake-speare. Lond. Printed by Thomas Creede for Andrew Wise, dwelling in Paules Church-yard, at the signe of the Angell. 1598. 4to.

A previous edition without author's name.

Copies in B. Museum, &c.

Henry IV., Part I. . . . . . . 1599.

The History of Henrie the Fourth. With the battell at Shrewsburie, betweene the King and Lord Henry Percy, surnamed Henry Hotspur of the North. With the humorous conceits of Sir John Falstalffe. Newly corrected by W. Shake-speare. At London. Printed by S. S. for Andrew Wise, dwelling in Paules Church-yard, at the signe of the Angell. 1599. 4to.

Several copies known.   One in British Museum.

There was an earlier copy of this play printed but without author's name.

The Passionate Pilgrime   .   .   .   .   .   1599.

By W. Shakespeare. At London. Printed for W. Jaggard, and are to be sold by W. Leake, at the Greyhound in Paules Churchyard. 1599. 16mo. First edition, 30 leaves, on the 18th of which is a title, " Sonnets to Sundry Notes of Musicke."

———

A copy in Capell's Collection, and is the only one known.

Henry IV., Part II. .   .   .   .   .   1600.

The second part of Henrie the Fourth, continuing to his death, and coronation of Henrie the Fift. With the humours of Sir John Falstaffe, and swaggering Pistoll. As it hath been sundrie times publikely acted by the Right Honourable, the Lord Chamberlaine his seruants. Written by William Shakespeare. Lond. Printed by V. S. for Andrew Wise and William Aspley. 1600. 4to.

———

Several copies exist.   Three in British Museum.

Merchant of Venice[1]   .   .   .   .   .   1600.

The excellent History of the Merchant of Venice. With the extreme cruelty of Shylocke the Jew towards the saide Merchant, In cutting a iust pound of his flesh. And the obtayning of Portia by the choyse of three

---

[1] On the 22nd July 1598 an entry was made in the Stationers' books. " James Robertes, a booke of the Marchaunte of Venyse, or otherwise called the Jewe of Venyse, provided that it be not prynted by the said James Robertes or any other whatsoever without licence first had of the Right Honourable the Lord Chamberlain."

Caskets. Written by W. Shakespeare. Printed by
J. Roberts. 1600. 4to.

Copies in British Museum, &c.

The Most Excellent Historie of the Merchant of Venice,
    with the extreame crueltie of Shylock the Jewe towards
    the sayd Merchant in cutting a just pound of his flesh;
    and the obtayning of Portia by the choyse of three
    chests. As it hath beene divers times acted by the
    Lord Chamberlaine his Servants. Written by William
    Shakespeare. At London. Printed by J. R. for Thomas
    Hayes, and are to be sold in Paules Churchyard at the
    signe of the Greene Dragon. 1600.

Entered by Thomas Haies on October 28, 1600.

A Midsummer Night's Dreame   1600
    As it hath beene sundry times publikely acted by the
    Right Honourable the Lord Chamberlaine his Servants.
    Written by William Shakespeare. Printed by James
    Roberts. 1600. 4to.

Copies in British Museum, &c.
Stationers' entries. A Booke called a Mydsomer Night
Dreame is entered by Fisher. Oct. 8, 1600.

Much Adoe About Nothing   1600
    As it hath beene sundrie times publikely acted by the
    Right Honourable the Lord Chamberlaine his Servants.
    Written by William Shakespeare. Lond. Printed by
    V. S. for Andrew Wise and William Aspley. 1600. 4to.

Copies in British Museum, &c.
Stationers' Registers. Andrewe Wise entered for their
copies under William Apsley thandes of the Wardens, two
bookes, the one called "Much Adoe About Nothing," the

other the 2nd part of the " History of King Henry the 4th with the humours of Sir John Folstaff." Written by Master Shakespeare,—xijd.

———

This is the first time the *name* appears in the Register. Though just before this Eleazar Edgar entered for his copie under the handes of the Wardens, a booke called "Amours " by J. D. with certyene other sonnets by W. S. vjd. January 3, 1600.

Robert Chester, in 1601, printed *Love's Martyr, or Rosalin's Complaint*, allegorically shadowing the Truth of Love in the constant fate of the Phœnix and Turtle. "To these are added some new compositions . . . done by the *best* and *chiefest* of our moderne writers, with their names subscribed to their particular workes, never before extant ; and now first consecrated by them all generally, to the love and merit of the true noble knight, Sir John Salisburie," among whom Shakspere writes and *signs* his only philoso-phic poem, in which he makes a notice of the obsequies of the Phœnix and the Turtle-dove figure forth mystically the idea of spiritual union. What makes it all the more certain that this was really from the pen of Shakspere is, that, unlike other poems invited from friends in that period to accompany any author's work, there is no flattery in it either to Chester or Salisbury.

Merry Wives of Windsor [1] .   .   .   .   . 1602.

A most pleasaunt and excellent conceited Comedie of Syr John Falstaffe and the Merrie Wiues of Windsor. Entermixed with sundrie variable and pleasing humors of Sir Hugh the Welch Knight, Justice Shallow, and

———

[1] Said to have owed its origin to the Queen's express desire to see Falstaff on the stage in love. The play is remarkable and unique, as containing the sole attempt by Shakspere in the direction of a panegyric on royalty.

his wise cousin M. Slender ; with the swaggering vaine
of Auncient Pistoll and Corporal Nym. By Wm.
Shakespeare. As it hath beene divers times acted
by the Right Honourable my Lord Chamberlaine's
servants. Both before Her Maiestie, and else-where.
Lond. Printed by T. C. for Arthur Johnson, and are
to be sold at his shop in Powles Churchyard, at the
signe of the Flower de Leuse and the Crowne. 1602.
4to.

Copies in the Bodleian, &c.

Hamlet . . . . 1603.
The Tragicall Historie of Hamlet, Prince of Den-
marke. By William Shake-speare. As it hath beene
diverse times acted by his Highnesse servants in the
Cittie of London : as also in the two Vniversities of
Cambridge and Oxford, and else-where. At London,
printed for N. L. and John Trundell. 1603. 4to.

First edition, only two copies known. One copy (imperfect) in Library of the Duke of Devonshire, and one
copy in British Museum.

"Lowndes' Bibliographer's Manual" (H. G. Bohn's
edition, 1863), Part viii. p. 2276.

The Tragicall Historie of Hamlet, Prince of Denmark.
By William Shakspere. Newly imprinted and enlarged to almost as much againe as it was, according
to the true and perfect coppie. At London. Printed
by J. R. for N. L., and are to be sold at his shoppe
under St. Dunstan's Church in Fleet Street. 1604.

James Roberts had entered at Stationers' Hall the
Revenge of Hamlet in. July 1602 ; this was doubtless the
tragedy as published in 1604.

G

Lear[1]   .   .   .   .   1608.

M. William Shak-speare : His True Chronicle Historie
of the life and death of King Lear and his three
Daughters.   With the vnfortunate life of Edgar, sonne
and heire to the Earle of Gloster, and his sullen and
assumed humur of Tom of Bedlam.   As it was played
before the Kings Maiestie at Whitehall vpon S.
Stephens night in Christmas Hollidayes.   By his
Maiesties servants playing vsually at the Gloabe on
the Bancke-side.   Lond.   Printed for Nathaniel
Butter, and are to be sold at his shop in Paul's
Churchyard, at the signe of the Pide Bull, neere St.
Austin's gate.   1608.   4to.

————

Two other editions published in same year.
Many copies exist, but with differences in the text.
Copy in British Museum.

Pericles   .   .   .   .   1609.

The late and much admired Play called Pericles, Prince
of Tyre, with the true Relation of the whole Historie,
aduentures, and fortunes of the said Prince : As also,
the no lesse strange and worthy accidents in the Birth
and Life of his Daughter Mariana.   As it hath been
diuers and sundry times acted by his Maiesties Seruants
at the Globe on the Banck-side.   By William Shake-

[1] 26th Novr. 1607. Stationers' Registers. "Nathaniel Butter and
John Busby entred for their copie under the handes of Sir George
Back, Knt., and the Wardens, a book called Master William Shakespeare his historie of King Lear, as yt was played before the King's
Majestie at Whitehall upon St. Stephen's night (26th Dec.) at Christmas last by his Majesties servants, playinge usually at the Globe on
the Bank-side vjd."
  2nd May 1608. "Master Payer entered for his copy under the
handes of Master Wilson and Master Warden Seton a book called a
Yorkshire Tragedy written by William Shakespeare vjd."

speare. Imprinted at Lond. for Henry Gosson, and
are to be sold at the signe of the Sunne in Pater-
noster row, &c.   1609.   4to.

Copies in the British Museum, &c.

Troilus and Cressida[1]   .   .   .   .   .   1609.

> The Famous Historie of Troylus and Cresseid.   Ex-
> cellently expressing the beginning of their loues, with
> the conceited wooing of Pandarus, Prince of Licia.
> Written by William Shakespeare. Lond. Imprinted by
> G. Eld for R. Boniau and H. Walley, and are to be
> sold at the spread Eagle in Paules Church yard near
> against the great North doore.   1609.   4to.

Copies in British Museum, &c.

Lucrece   1616

> By Mr. William Shakespeare.   Newly reuised.   Lon-
> don.   Printed by T. S. for Roger Jackson, and are to
> be solde at his shop neere the Conduit in Fleet-street.
> 1616.   8vo.

This edition is supposed to have appeared before his
death, on 23rd April 1616.

Copies in British Museum, &c.

Several earlier editions without author's name on title-
page.

Though I only notice those works printed during his life,
it is not to be considered that he did not claim, while alive,
those works printed after his death, or his "fellows" would
not have credited them to him.   There is no reason to

---

[1] February 7, 1603.   Stationers' Registers.   "Master Robertes
entered for his copy in full court holden this day to print when he hath
got sufficient authority for yt, the booke of Troilus and Cressida, as
yt is acted by my Lord Chamberlain's men."

doubt the verbal word he must have given to many of his
authorship of these works. Every notice we have of him
shows that he was not only honourable, honest, but *exact* in
his dealings; and there is no ground on his side to believe
that he would have fathered such a huge literary dishonesty.

Though some of these had not been printed before the
1623 folio, many of them had been alluded to before.

The plays which were for the first time printed in the
folio of 1623 are—

*The Tempest, The Two Gentlemen of Verona, Measure for
Measure, The Comedy of Errors, The Taming of the Shrew,
All's Well that Ends Well, Twelfth Night, The Winter's Tale,
Henry VI., Part I., Henry VIII., Coriolanus, Timon of
Athens, Julius Cæsar, Macbeth, Antony and Cleopatra, Cym-
beline.*

Of those mentioned before 1623 are—

Henry VI., Part I., alluded to by Greene and by Nash in
    Pierce Pennilesse, 1592.
All's Well that Ends Well, held to be *Love's Labours
    Wonne* of Meres, 1598.
The Two Gentlemen of Verona. Meres, 1598.
Comedy of Errors, Played at Gray's Inne Revels, 1594.
    Meres, 1598.
Twelfth Night, Manningham. Played at Middle Temple,
    February 1601–2.
Othello. Acted at Harefield, 1602. Wurmser saw it at
    the Globe, 1610.
Measure for Measure, by Shaxberd. Acted by his Ma[ies]
    Plaiers, St. Stephen's Night, at Whitehall, February
    1604.
The Tempest, acted at Whitehall, 1611.
The Winter's Tale, acted at Whitehall, 1611. Mentioned
    by Dr. Forman at Globe, May 15, 1611.

Henry VIII., being acted as a new play when the Globe was burnt, 1613.

Macbeth. Dr. Forman mentions and summarises it as acted at the Globe, April 20, 1610.

Timon of Athens, alluded to in Marston's *Scourge of Villany*, 1598.

Taming of the Shrew, acted at Henslow's Theatre, 1593. Entered at Stationers' Hall 1607.

So that there are really only

Cymbeline, Julius Cæsar, Antony and Cleopatra, Coriolanus introduced to us as entirely new plays.

King John we find in Meres. Published anon, 1591. By W. Sh. 1611. By William Shakespeare, 1622.

Knight gives a chronological order of Shakspere's plays, showing the facts that determine the dates previous to which they must have been written :—

Henry VI. Part II. Printed as First Part of the *Contention*, 1594.

Henry VI. Part III. Printed as the *True Tragedy of Richard Duke of York*, 1595.

Richard II. Noticed by Meres. Printed 1597.

Richard III. Noticed by Meres. Printed 1597.

Romeo and Juliet. Noticed by Meres. Printed 1597.

Love's Labour Lost. Noticed by Meres. Printed 1598.

Henry IV. Part I. Noticed by Meres. Printed 1598.

Henry IV. Part II. Printed 1600.

Henry V. Printed 1600.

Merchant of Venice, Noticed by Meres. Printed 1600.

Midsummer Night's Dream. Noticed by Meres. Printed 1600.

Much Ado About Nothing. Printed 1600.

As You Like It. Entered at Stationers' Hall, 1600.

Titus Andronicus. Printed 1600.

Merry Wives of Windsor. Printed 1602.

Hamlet. Printed 1603.

Lear. Acted at Whitehall, 1604. Printed 1608.
Troilus and Cressida. 1609.
Pericles. 1609.

"*The Tragedie of Othello the Moore of Venice.* As it hath beene diverse times acted at the Globe, and at the Black-Friars, by his Majesties' Servants. Written by William Shakespeare," was entered at Stationers' Hall, 6th October 1621, by Thomas Walkley, and published in 1622. It has an unusual introduction.

"THE STATIONER TO THE READER.

"To set forth a book without an Epistle were like to the old English proverb, 'a blue coat without a badge;' and the *author being dead*, I thought good to take that piece of work upon me: to commend it I will not: for that which is good, I hope every man will commend, without entreaty; and I am the bolder, because the author's name is sufficient to vent this work. Thus leaving every one to the liberty of judgment, I have ventured to print this play, and leave it to the general censure. Yours,

THOMAS WALKLEY."

I imagine he thought himself imitating Shakspere's prose style of dedication in this.

Bacon *never* at any time claimed any of Shakspere's works, nor did he ever claim to be a poet. But he did claim to be a great prose writer, and was most careful of his property. Bacon's habit was first to plan a work, then by slow steps of experiment and verification to execute it; he wrote, re-wrote, altered, improved, translated. He preserved every scrap he ever wrote, he kept even copies of his private letters, notes of his speeches, memoranda of his smart sayings, even of things he only meant to have said, and quotations from his reading, and he signed his name to all his own compositions. He had no faith in the perpetuity or universality of the English language, and had

most of his works translated into Latin, that all might
read. "These modern languages will play the bankrupt
with books," he said. Further, as he copies his works,
some of them even twelve times, and "alters ever as he
adds, writes, or translates," "nothing is finished until all
is finished." Each of his copies, to himself and his executors, is a separate entity, however separated by language or
time. In his last will he said : " For my *name* and *memory*,
I leave it to man's charitable speeches, and to foreign nations,
and the next ages. But as to that durable part of my
memory which consisteth in my works and writings, I
desire my executors to take care that of all my writings,
both of English and of Latin, there may be books fair bound
and placed in the King's Library, and in the library of the
University of Cambridge, and in the library of Divinity
College, and in the library of Benet College, and in the
library of the Archbishop of Canterbury, and in the library
of Eton. Also, whereas I have made up two register-books,
the one of my orations or speeches, the other of my epistles
or letters, whereof there may be use ; I do devise and be-
queath them to the right honourable my very good Lord
Bishop of Lincoln."

Is it likely that a man so careful of every scrap, of every
duplicate, so desirous of fame, after all possible danger was
over of losing his mother's affections or his Queen's advancement, as the Baconians dream, because of his passion
for writing plays, would have voluntarily ignored at death
a mass of writings that, even in bulk, bore no mean proportion to those he had printed, and that in quality bore
a nobler impress of genius and thought than any he had
acknowledged ? For at the end of the *Resuscitatio*, published in 1657, Dr. Rawley gives what he entitles "a perfect list of his Lordship's works, both in English and
Latin," which he concludes by these words : " As for other
pamphlets, whereof there are several put forth under his
Lordship's name, *they are not to be owned for his.*" So that

even in the most private and confidential relations, it was unsuggested even by a verbal claim.

Is it possible that executors or dependents so devoted as Rawley and Matthew could have examined his papers without finding some rough draft, some memorandum, some private copy, some *cipher* that would have revealed that these poems and plays had also a right to be bound in the "fair volumes" and sent to all the learned universities? The *Promus* was the only scrap unprinted by them, because they knew it contained nothing original even in arrangement; and the *Conference of Pleasure* in its *complete form*, which was found in the box of papers in Northumberland House, but which Bacon had not though worthy of being remembered as but "a toy." The speeches are, however, in a separate form incorporated in his works.

The only ghost of authority for a claim that has been brought forward is connected with this Northumberland MS. But it is a ghost that was never alive. There Bacon's *Conference of Pleasure* is copied by a clerk, probably for some of his patrons, who were to act in it, or dress and speak in it. The paper volume formerly contained other works now lost. A list appears on the outer page, among which are "*Richard II., Richard III., Asmund and Cornelia, Isle of Dogs*, by Nashe and inferior plaiers." Over the page is scribbled "Shakspeare," "Bacon," "Neville," "Ne vile velis," &c.—probably by some fine thread of association or classification. The old "Percy" may have played in these other pieces too. But there is no claiming the authorship of any of them for anybody. The prosy and flattering speeches of the Squire, the Hermit, the Soldier, the Statesman, and the reply of the Squire, are just as like Bacon as they are unlike anything of Shakspere's. Certainly *The Isle of Dogs* was by Nash.[1] The *Asmund and Cornelia* might have been his also; but though the Baconians give it to

---

[1] He was imprisoned for it. "As Actæon was worried of his own hounds, so is Tom Nash of his *Isle of Dogs.*"—*Harvey.* See Appendix 13.

Bacon, no one in the British Museum knows anything about it. Whether the *Richard II. and III.* were Shakspere's rendering of these histories, we have no means to prove. Other men wrote of these histories after William Baudwin in his *Mirror for Magistrates.*[1] Yet this chance scribble of a copying-clerk is one of the strongest pillars of the Baconian edifice ! Another is like to it.

Bacon writes a letter to the poet Sir John Davies,[2] asking him to help his advancement under King James, and be good to "concealed poets ;" but one has only to turn to his remarks on poesy to understand what he means by that. We can see that he separates the matter from the form, that he sets parabolical poetry above dramatic, and calls it an artifice for *concealment*, independent of the conditions of verse or prose.

"The measure of words has produced a vast body of art —namely, Poesy, considered with reference not to the matter of it, but to the style and form of it, that is to say, metre and verse. But for Poesy, whether we speak of *Inventions* or metre, it is like a luxuriant plant that comes out of the lust of the earth, without any formal seed. Wherefore, it spreads everywhere and is scattered far and wide, so that it would be vain to take thought about the defects of it. With this, therefore, we need not trouble ourselves." —*De Augm. Sci.* lib. vi.

(Poesy—feigned History or Fables.) *De Augmentis*, Book ii. : "It is concerned with individuals ; . . . it commonly exceeds the measure of nature, joining at pleasure things which in nature would never have come together, and introducing things which in nature would never have come together, and introducing things which in nature would never have come to pass. . . . This is the work of Imagination."

Chap. xiii. : "Under the name of Poesy, I treat *only* of feigned History. . . . Narrative poetry is a mere imita-

---

[1] See Appendix, Note 17.   [2] See Appendix, Note 15.

tion of History. . . . Dramatic poetry is History made
visible; for it represents actions as if they were present,
whereas History represents them as past." " A sound
argument may be drawn from Poesy to show that there is
agreeable to the spirit of man a more ample greatness, a
more perfect order, and a more beautiful variety than it
can anywhere find in nature. . . . Dramatic poetry, which
has the Theatre for its world, would be of excellent use if
well directed. For the stage is capable of no small influence both of discipline and corruption. Now of corrup-
tions of this kind we have enough; but the discipline has
in our times been plainly neglected. And though in
modern states play-acting is esteemed but as a toy, except
when it is too satirical and biting; yet among the ancients
it was used as a means of educating men's minds to virtue.
Nay, it has been regarded by learned men and great
philosophers as a kind of musician's bow by which men's
minds may be played upon. And certainly, it is most true,
and one of the great secrets of nature, that the minds of
men are more open to impressions and affections when
many are gathered together than when they are alone.
. . . . True history may be written in verse, and feigned
history in prose. . . . It˙ is of double use, and serves
for contrary purposes, for it serves for an enfoldment;
and it likewise serves for illustration. In the latter case
the object is a certain method of teaching; in the former,
an artifice for *concealment.* . . . The numbers of Pythagoras, the enigmas of the Sphinx, the fables of Æsop, the
apophthegms of ancient sages were parabolical poesy . . .
a mystery involved in many of them." . . .

The *New Atlantis* and the *Masques* would quite fit these
definitions. His being " wholly exercised in inventions "
is also evidently explained by the *experiments* and inventions
he made. " I have taken all knowledge to be my province;
and if I could purge it of two sorts of rovers, whereof the
one with disputations, confutations, and verbosities, the

other with blind experiments and auricular traditions and impostures, hath committed so many spoils; I hope I should bring in industrious observations, grounded conclusions, and profitable *inventions* and discoveries; the best state of that province. This, whether it be curiosity, or vainglory, or nature, or, if one take it favourably, philanthropia, is so fixed in my mind that it cannot be removed." —*Letter to Burghley*, 1592. He often uses the word in this sense, as well as his previous one—a poetic conception of a fictitious tale, such as would suggest our modern novel. On the other hand, he distinctly states to the Earl of Essex: "I profess not to be a poet; but I prepared a sonnet directly tending to draw on Her Majesty's reconcilement to my Lord, which I remember I also showed to a great person, one of my Lord's nearest friends, who commended it. This, though it be, as I said, but a toy, yet it showed plainly in what spirit I proceeded." We may rest assured that, if Bacon did not profess to be a poet, he was not one. The "Lines to a Retired Courtier" are not claimed by Bacon, but given to him by Baconians. I should much rather think them by Raleigh.

The few lines in the "Masque of an Indian Prince," and the few lines published in Sir Walter Raleigh's poems as by Bacon, are very probably his.

" The man of life upright, whose guiltless heart is free
From all dishonest deeds and thoughts of vanity.
That man whose silent days in harmless joys are spent,
Whom hopes cannot delude nor fortune discontent,
That man needs neither tower nor armour for defence."

There are few prose writers who have not occasionally tried verse.

Of the translations of certain Psalms into English verse by Bacon, 1624, Spedding says: "These were the only verses certainly of Bacon's making that have come to us, and probably, with one or two slight exceptions, the only verses he ever wrote."

That a man capable in 1623 of altering and editing the blank verse Plays, should have become so disorganised as to be able to *print, even* if he had written, the commonplace rhymed versifications of the Psalms in 1624, could be accounted for only by some unknown disease.

We may therefore rest assured that William Shakspere claimed his works during his life, though he had so bestowed the copyrights as not to have them to *leave* in his will.

We may exonerate Bacon not only from claiming the *Plays* in life or in death, but from suggesting in his works that he might have written them.

But not only were the Poems and Plays printed as Shakspere's at the outset, both in the early editions and the standard editions of 1623 and 1632, but they continued to be so by the old stationers and by the modern editors without exception or scepticism. We must not forget the old proverb, " Possession is nine points of the law." Our arguments, then, do not require to be one quarter as strong as those of the other side to overwhelm them. But we have an opinion, shared by many, that they are stronger.

CHAPTER V.

EXTERNAL EVIDENCE.

THE external evidence of other people's writings, however, is the most convincing proof.

1592. The earliest printed notice which alludes to Shakspere is in Greene's *Groat's-worth of Wit*, where he, in an oft-quoted passage, evidently aims at Shakspere's growing fame as an actor, and his entrance on a dramatic career as the critic and adapter of other men's dramas, and calls him "an absolute *Johannes Factotum*" and "the only Shakescene in a country." Besides quoting from one of Shakspere's plays, Greene suggests that he also assisted in stage-management, and points to the fact that he was *dominant* by that time, and that other witty writers were *subject* to his pleasures.

Greene's scorn of the actors, the "puppits," the "buckram gentlemen," seems embittered by the fact that one of them should be "able to bumbast out a blanke verse as well as the best of you." As a rival of Shakspere it is wonderful he had so little else to say against him; and yet it came very badly from him, who only just before, in Greene's *Quip for an Upstart Courtier*, had translated wholesale, from verse into his prose, *The Debate between Pride and Lowliness*, by T. F., probably Francis Thynne, printed by Charlewood several years before Greene's pamphlet.

"Young Juvenal, that biting satyrist,[1] and thou no less

---

[1] Nash.

deserving than the other two. . . . Base-minded men all three of you, if by my miserie ye be not warned; for unto none of you (like me) sought those burres to cleave : those Puppits (I meane) that speak from our mouths, those anticks garnished in our colours. Is it strange that I, to whom they all have been beholding; is it not like that you, to whom they all have been beholding, shall (were ye in that case that I am now) be both at once of them forsaken ? Yes, trust them not: for there is an upstart crow, beautified with our feathers, that with his *Tiger's Heart Wrapt in a Player's Hide* [1] supposes he is as well able to bumbast out a blanke verse as the best of you; and being an absolute Johannes factotum, is in his own conceit the only Shake-scene in a countrie. Oh, that I might intreate your rare wits to be employed in more profitable courses; and let these Apes imitate your past excellence, and never more acquaint them with your admired inventions. . . . Whilst you may, seeke you better maisters, for it is pittie men of such rare wits [2] should be subject to the pleasures of such rude groomes. In this I might insert two more that both have writ against these buckram gentlemen. For other new comers I leave them to the mercy of those painted monsters, who, I doubt not, will drive the best-minded to despise them."—*Greene's Groat's-worth of Wit.*

This and Greene's *Quippe for an Upstart Courtier* really led to the Nash-Harvey dispute, as Nash was by some supposed to have aided Greene; by others, Chettle, the editor, was blamed. The one point, however, in which all concerned *agreed* was the praise of Shakspere, and the clearing his name from *any blame.*

"Greene, the coney-catcher of this dreame, the autour—

---

[1] "Oh, Tyger's heart wrapt in a woman's hide."—3rd Part, *King Henry VI.* Probably Marlowe and Greene were part authors of the two Parts of *The Contention* and *The True Tragedie,* upon which Parts II. and III. of *King Henry VI.* are based.

[2] Marlow, Lodge, and Nash.

for his dainty device deserveth the Hauter. . . . I would
not wish a sworn enemie to be more basely valued, or more
vilely reputed than the common voice of the citie esteemeth
him that sought fame by diffamation of other, but hath
utterly discredited himself, and is notoriously grown a pro-
verbe of infamy and contempt. . . . Honour is precious,
worship of value, fame invaluable. They perillously threaten
the Commonwealth that go about to violate the inviolable
partes thereof ; many will sooner lose their lives than the
least jott of their reputation." [1]

1592. In *Pierce Pennilesse*, by Thomas Nash, we find :
" Other newes I am advertised of, that a scald triviall lying
pamphlet called Green's *Groat's-worth of Wit* is given out
to be of my doing. God never have care of my soule, but
utterly renounce me, if the least word or syllable in it
proceeded from my pen." Farther on he alludes to Shakspere's *Henry V.* " How would it have joyed brave Talbot
(the terror of the French) to thinke that after he had lyen
two hundred yeares in his toombe, he should triumph again
on the stage, and have his bones new embalmed with the
teares of 10,000 spectators at least (at several times), who,
in the tragedian that represents his person, imagine they
see him fresh-bleeding." And again, " If you tell them
what a glorious thing it is to have *Henry V.* represented
on the stage, leading the French king prisoner and forcing
both him and the Dolphin to swear fealtie. Aye, but (will
they say) what doo we get by it ? respecting neither the
right of fame that is due to the nobility deceased, nor what
hopes of eternity are to be proposed to adventurous minds,
to encourage them forward." Nash further praises plays
in general.

1592. In *Foure Letters and Certain Sonnets*, especially
touching Robert Greene and other parties by him abused,
Gabriel Harvey seems to praise Shakspere : " Vile Greene,
would thou wearest halfe so honest as the worst of the

_____
[1] Very suggestive of Cassio's regard for " reputation."

foure whom thou upraidest, or halfe so learned as the un-
learnedst of the three ! Thanke others for thy borrowed
and filched plumes of some little Italianated bravery, and
what remaineth but flat impudence and grosse detraction ;
the proper ornaments of thy sweet utterance." . . .

He adds : " If any distresse be miserable, diffamation is
intolerable, especially to mindes that would rather deserve
just commendation than unjust slander. That is done, cannot *de facto* be undone ; but I appeale to wisedome how dis-
creetly, and to justice, how deservedly it is done ; and request the one to do us reason in shame of impudency, and
beseech the other to do us right in reproach of calumny.
It was my intention so to demeane myself in the whole, and
so to temper my stile in every part, that I might neither
seeme blinded with affection, nor enraged with passion ;
nor partiall to friend, nor prejudiciall to enemie, nor injurious to the worst, nor offensive to any, but mildly and
calmly show how discredite reboundeth upon the autors, as
dust flyeth back into the wag's eyes, that will need be puff-
ing it out." And in the next year, in Pierce's *Supererero-
gation* he adds, " He is very simple who would fear a rayling
Greene."

1592. Greene's friend Chettle, who had edited his *Groatsworth of Wit*, publishes *Kind Hart's Dream*, in which he
says of Shakspere : " About three months since died Mr.
Robert Greene, leaving many papers in sundry bookseller's
hands, among others, his *Groatsworth of Wit*, in which a
letter written to divers playmakers is offensively by one
or two of them taken. With neither of them that take
offence was I acquainted, and with one of them, I care not
if I never be ; the other, whom at that time I did not so
much spare as since I wish I had, for that as I have
moderated the heat of living writers, I mighte have used
my own discretion (especially in such a case), the author
being dead. That I did not, I am as sorry as if the ori-
ginall fault had beene my fault, because myselfe have seene

his demeanour no less civille than he, exelent in the qualitie he professes. Besides, divers of worship have reported his uprightness of dealing, which argues his honesty, and his facetious grace in writing, which aprooves his art." This proves him no "rude groome," but of civil demeanour, excellent in the "qualitie he professes"—*i.e.*, acting and improving on plays, with a facetious grace in writing, with art, and with good friends.

1593. A letter written to Lord de Clifford styles Shakspere "our English tragedian." In this year *Venus and Adonis* was printed.

1594. Henry Willobie, in his *Avisa*, says :—

> " Yet Tarquyne plucked his glistering grape,
> And Shakspere paints poor Lucrece' rape."

In his introductory verses on his love-troubles, Willobie "bewrayeth the secresy of his disease unto his familiar friend Will Shakespeare, who not long before had tried the courtesy of a like passion, and was but newly recovered of the like infection." The verses alternate between the complaint of the lover and the answer and advice of W. S. This was entered in the Stationers' Registers on 3rd Sept. 1594, as "Willobie his Avisa, or the true picture of a modest maid and of a chaste and constante wyfe."

1594. " You that to shew your wits have taken toyle
In registering the deeds of noble men,
And sought for matter on a forraine soyle
As worthier subjects of your silver pen,
Whom you have raised from dark oblivion's den ;
You that have writ of chaste Lucretia,
Whose death was witness of her spotless life ;
Or penned the praise of sad Cornelia,
Whose blameless name hath made her name to rise
As noble Pompey's most renowned wife.
Hither unto your home direct youre eies
Whereas unthought on, much more matter lies."
(Sir William Herbert : *Epicedium of Lady Helen Branch.*)

H

1594.   " Lucrece, of whom proud Rome hath boasted long,
      Lately revived to live another age."
                      (Drayton's *Matilda.*)

1594.   " Christ's thorn is sharp, no head his garland weares. . . .
      Still finest wits are 'stilling Venus' rose."
             (*Peter's Complaint*, Robert Southwell.)

Though these allusions are nameless, the context shows that Shakspere is meant.

1595. Clark's *Polimanteia.* Thomas Watson, a Londoner bred in Oxford, the writer of a book of passionate sonnets written in and after 1582, is strangely connected with Shakspere in a literary sense in W. Clark's *Polimanteia*, published at Cambridge, 1595 :—

Let other countries (sweet
Cambridge) envie (yet admire)
My Virgil, thy Petrarch, divine
Spenser. And unlesse I erre (a thing
All praise-
worthy Lu-
crecia, sweet
Shake-
speare,
eloquent
Gaveston.
Easie in such simplicitie), deluded
By dearly beloved Delia, and fortunately
Fortunate Cleopatra ; Oxford thou maist
Extoll thy courte-deare verse-happie
Daniell, whose sweete refined Muse, in
Wanton
Adonis,
Watson's
Heyre.
Contracted shape, were sufficient amongst
Men to gaine pardon of the sinne to Rosamond,
Pittie to distressed Cleopatra, and ever-loving
Praise to his loving Delia.

It is difficult to catch the connection of the ideas associated in Clark's mind.

Perhaps Watson wrote poems on Adonis, and Shakspere seemed to have inherited the inspiration.[1]

---

[1] Thomas Watson's poems, published posthumously in 1593, were " The passionate centurie of love, divided into two parts ; whereof the first expresseth the author's sufferance in Love, the latter his long farewell to Love and all his tyranny." He also wrote *Meliboeus* and sixty Sonnets, very much in the same style as Shakspere's. He was much admired by his contemporaries, and it is strange he was so soon forgotten.

1595.
> " And there, though last, not least is Aëtion,
> A gentler shepherd may nowhere be found,
> Whose Muse, full of high thought's invention,
> Doth like himself heroically sound." [1]
> > (Spenser's *Colin Clout's Come Home Again.*)

1595. In George Markham's tragedy of *Sir Richard Grenville,* he addresses Southampton thus :—

> "Thou, the laurel of the Muses' hill,
> Whose eyes doth crown the most victorious pen."

—meaning Shakspere.

1595. In L'Envoy to *Cephalus and Procris,* Thomas Edwardes names the poets by the best-known of their works.

> "Adon deafly making thro'
> Stately troupes, rich conceited.
> Shewed he well deserved to
> > Love's delight on him to gaze,
> And had not Love herself intreated
> > Other nymphes had sent him hayes.'

1596. The Prologue to Ben Jonson's *Every Man in His Humour* alludes to Shakspere's *Henry V.* and *Henry VI.* He said that the world had had enough of Shakspere's style, and that he was going to show it how plays *should be written.*[2]

> " Though need make many poets, and some such
> As art and nature have not bettered much ;

---

[1] This surely could not be *Bacon.* Aëtion means eagle-flight, suggesting his poetry. Shakspere was the only *heroic name* of the period. All poets then were *poetically* called shepherds.

[2] John Cleveland writes to the memory of Ben Jonson :—

> " Who first reformed our stage with justest laws,
> And was the first best judge in his own cause,
> Who, when his actors trembled for applause,
> Could with a noble confidence prefer
> His own, by right to a whole theatre ;
> From principles which he knew could not err."

Yet ours for want hath not so loved the stage,
As he dare serve the ill customs of the age,
Or purchase your delight at such a rate
As, for it, he himself must justly hate :
To make a child now swaddled, to proceed
Man, and then shoot up, in one beard and weed,
Past threescore years ; or, with three rusty swords,
And help of some few foot and half-foot words,
Fight over York and Lancaster's long jars,
And in the tyring-house bring wounds to scars ;
He rather prays you will be pleased to see,
One such to-day, as other plays *should be,*
Where neither chorus wafts you o'er the seas,
Nor creaking throne comes down the boys to please ;
Nor nimble squib is seen to make afeared
The gentlewomen ; nor roll'd bullet heard
To say it thunders ; nor tempestuous drum
Rumbles, to tell you when the storm doth come ;
But deeds and language, such as men do use,
And persons such as Comedy would choose,
When she would show an image of the times
And sport with human follies, not with crimes.
Except we make them such, by loving still
Our popular errors, where we know they're ill ;
I mean such errors as you'll all confess,
By laughing at them, they deserve no less :
Which, when you heartily do, there's hope left then
You, that have so graced monsters, may like men."

This seems to prove that Shakspere had been " graced,"
even though abnormal in his developments of art.

1596. "Will you reade Catullus ? Take Shakspere and
Marlowe's fragment," says Richard Carew, in his essay on
The Excellency of the English Tongue, attached to his *Survey
of Cornwall, Remains concerning Britain,* by W. Camden,
2nd edition. Shakspere was therefore able to write in
good style.

1596. The *De Witt Papers.*

1597. An interesting series of three university plays
commence.

I. The *Pilgrimage to Pernassus* shows the difficulties of

scholars. II. The *Return from Pernassus*, Part i., their impecuniosity. III. The *Return from Pernassus*, Part ii., or *The Scourge of Simony.* But the interest to us lies not in the first, but in the second and third, in which are allusions to Shakspere's *Returne from Pernassus* (Act iii. sc. 1) : —

Gull. Pardon, faire ladie, thoughe sicke-thoughted Gullio maks amaine unto thee, and like a bould-faced sutore 'gins to woo thee.[1]

Ingenioso. (We shall have nothinge but pure Shakspeare and shreds of poetrie he hath gathered at the theators.)

Gull. Pardon mee, moy mittressa, ast am a gentleman, the moone in comparison of thy bright hue a meere slutt, Anthonie's Cleopatra a black browde milkmaid, Hellen a dowdy.

Ingen. (Marke, Romeo and Juliet! Oh monstrous theft,[2] I thinke he will runn through a whole book of Samuel Daniell's.)

Gull. Thrise fairer then myselfe (thus I began)
  The gods faire riches, sweet above compare,
  Staine to all nymphes, more lovely then a man,
  Nature that made thee with herself at strife
  Saith that the worlde hath ending with thy life.[3]

Ingen. Sweet Mr. Shakspeare!

Gull. Make mee verses in two or three different vayns, in Chaucer's, Gower's, and Spenser's, and Mr. Shakspeare's. Marry, I thinke I shall entertaine those verses which run like these : —

  Even as the sunne, with purple-coloured face,
  Had tane his laste leave on the weeping morne, &c.[3]

O, sweet Mr. Shakspeare! I'll have his picture in my study at the courte. . . .

Gull. Let mee heare Mr. Shakspeare's veine.

Ingen. Faire Venus, queene of beutie and of love,[3]
  Thy red doth stayne the blushing of the morne,
  Thy snowie necke shameth the milkwhite dove,
  Thy presence doth this naked world adorne ;
  Gazing on thee all other nymphes I scorne.
  When ere thou dyest slowe shine that Satterday
  Beutie and grace muste sleepe with thee for aye.

---

[1] Sick-thoughted Venus makes amain unto him,
   And like a bold-faced suitor 'gins to woo him.

[2] *Romeo and Juliet*, ii. 4.   [3] *Venus and Adonis.*

Gull. Noe more ! I am one that can judge accordinge to the pro-
verbe, *bovem ex unguibus.* Ey, marry, these have some life in them !
Let this duncified worlde esteeme of Spenser and Chaucer, I'le wor-
shipp sweet Mr. Shakspeare, and to honoure him will lay his *Venus
and Adonis* under my pillow, as we reade of one (I doe not well
remember his name, but I am sure he was a Kinge) slept with Homer
under his bed's heade.

It closes with the strange lines :—

    Ingenioso. Whatever schollers—
    Studiosus.   Discontented be—
    Philomusus. Let none but them—
    All.   Give us a plauditie.

Though the preference of the "Gull" for Shakspere's
poems was a dubious compliment, it is now a historical
reference of no mean value. The contemporary type of
character here satirised is illustrated in Decker's *Gull's
Hornbook,* yet it is possible that some special individual was
aimed at. John Weever writes an epitaph : "Here lies fat
Gullio," &c.

These two plays were first edited by the Rev. W. D.
Macray. The third play is also edited by him, but was
previously brought out in the "Arber" series. It will be
treated under its own date.

1598. The familiar passage in the *Palladis Tamia* of
Francis Meres, Master of Arts of both Universities, which
places Shakspere in this year above all ancient or modern
writers, was republished in the edition of 1634.

This history of literature (written probably in 1596)
shows that in about ten years Shakspere had taken the
first rank in literature as well as on the stage, and no one
so much as Francis Meres, Professor of Rhetoric in Oxford,
would have naturally studied the subject so carefully and
critically in his period. "As the Greek tongue is made
famous and eloquent by Homer, Hesiod, &c., and the Latine
tongue by Virgil, Ovid, Horace, &c., so the English tongue
is gorgeously invested in rare ornaments and resplendent
habiliments by Sydney, Spenser, Daniell, Drayton, Warner,

Shakespeare, Marlowe, Chapman." . . . "As the soule of Euphorbus was thought to live in Pythagoras, so the sweet wittie soule of Ovid lives in mellifluous and hony-tongued Shakespeare. Witness his *Venus and Adonis*, his *Lucrece*, his sugred *Sonnets* among his private friends, &c. . . . As Plautus and Seneca are accounted the best for Comedy and Tragedy among the Latins, so Shakespeare among ye Englishe is the most excellent in both kinds for the stage; for comedy, witness his *Gentlemen of Verona*, his *Errors*, his *Love's Labour Lost*, his *Love's Labour Wonne*, his *Midsummer Night's Dream*, and his *Merchante of Venice;* for tragedy, his *Richard II.*, *Richard III.*, *Henry IV.*, *King John*, *Titus Andronicus*, and his *Romeo and Juliet*. As Epius Stolo said that the Muses would speak with Plautus' tongue, if they would speak Latine, so I say, that the Muses would speak with Shakespeare's fine-filed phrase if they would speak English. As Ovid said . . . and as Horace saith of his works . . . so say I severally of Sir Philip Sydney's, Spenser's, Drayton's, Daniell's, Shakespeare's, and Warner's works. . . . As Pindarus, Anacreon and Callimachus among the Greeks, and Horace and Catullus among the Latines, are the best lyricke poets, so in this faculty the best among our poets are Spenser (who excelleth in all kinds), Daniell, Drayton, Shakespeare, Bretton. . . . For tragedie, our best are . . . Lord Buckhurst, Shakespeare, &c.; for comedie, our best are . . . Lyly, Lodge, Gascoigne, Greene, Shakespeare, &c. The most passionate among us to bewail the perplexities of love are Surrey, Wyatt, Brian, Sydney, Rawley, Dyer, Spenser, Daniell, Drayton, Shakespeare, Whetstone, Gascoyne, Page, Churchyard, Bretton, &c."—Meres' *Wit's Treasury*, second part of *Wit's Commonwealth*.

One interesting fact may be noted, that Meres, at the time of this publication, was living near the Globe Theatre, and must have heard Shakspere, and most probably knew him personally.

1598. Richard Barnfield, in his *Remembrance of some English Poets*, praises Shakspere for his *Lucrece* :—

> " And Shakspere, thou whose honey-flowing vaine
> (Pleasing the world) thy praises doth obtaine ;
> Whose Venus and whose Lucrece (sweet and chaste)
> Thy name in Fame's immortell Booke have placed.
>   Live ever you—at least, in fame live ever—
>   Well may the body dye, but Fame dies never."
>   (*A Remembrance of some English Poets.*)

1598. John Marston, in his *Scourge of Villainy*, says :—

>   "A hall ! a hall !
> Room for the Spheres, the Orbes celestial
> Will dance Kemp's jigge. . . .
> I set thy lips abroach, from whence doth flow
> Nought but pure Juliet and Romeo.[1]
> Say, who acts best ? Drusus or Roscio ?
> Now I have him, that nere of oughte did speake
> But when of playes or plaiers he did treate,
> Hath made a common-place book out of plaies,
> And speaks in print ; at least whate'er he sayes
> Is warranted by curtaine plaudeties.
> If ere you heard him courting Lesbia's eyes,
> Say (courteous sir) speaks he not movingly
> From out some new pathetic tragedy.
> He writes, he rails, he jests, he courts, what not
> And all from out his huge long-scraped stock
> Of well-penned playes." (*Humours*, Satyr 10.)

"Drusus" was a name applied to Shakspere for his noble bearing, and "Roscius" to Burbage.

In Satyr 7, Marston also says, 1598 :—

> " A man, a man ; a kingdom for a man.[1]
> Why, how now, currish mad Athenian ?"

1598. Gabriel Harvey's note on Speght's *Chaucer*, now lost :—

"The younger sort take much delight in Shakspere's *Venus and Adonis;* but his *Lucrece,* and his tragedy of *Hamlet, Prince of Denmark,* have it in them to please the wiser sort."

---

[1] Suggesting *Romeo and Juliet, Richard III.,* and *Timon.*

1599. John Weever, *Ad Gulielmum Shakspere:*—

> "Honie-tongued Shakspere, when I saw thine issue,
> I swore Apollo got them and none other,
> Their rosie-tinted features clothed in tissue
> Some heaven-born godesse said to be their mother.
> Rose-cheeked Adonis with his amber tresses,
> Faire fier-hot Venus charming him to love her—
> Chaste Lucretia, vergine like her dresses,
> Prowd lust-stung Tarquine seeking still to prove her,
> Romeo, Richard ; more whose names I know not.
> Their sugred tongues and power attractive beauty,
> Say they are saints although that saints they shew not,
> For thousand vowes to them subjective dutie,
> They burne in love thy childre Shakspere bet the
> Go, woo thy muse, more nymphish brood beget the."
>
> (*Epigrams in Oldest Cut and Newest Fashion.*)

1600. Samuel Nicholson compliments Shakspere by cribbing largely from him without acknowledgment in *Acolastus his After-Witte ;*" which, however, only proves the existence of the plays, and Nicholson's knowledge and appreciation of them.

1600. Shakspere is mentioned seventy-nine times in *England's Parnassus*, compiled by Robert Allot, himself a poet.[1] He had two sonnets prefixed to Markham's *Devereux*, 1597, and is complimented in conjunction with Middleton in the *Epigrammes* of John Weever, 1599. His quotations are not literal according to any modern text ; nor are any of the plays specified. The quotations selected from Shakspere are ranged under the subjects : "Angels, Affection, Avarice, Beautie, Care, Danger, Death, Delay (two), Feare, Gentlenesse, Gluttonie, Good name, Griefe (two), Paine, Haste, Hope, Jealousie, Justice, Kings (three),

---

[1] Robert Allot in 1599 had brought out *The Wit's Theatre of the Little World*, dedicated to John Bodenham, printed by James Robertes for Nicholas Ling, gathered out of divers *learned* authors. He does not call it his own writing, but brings lives before the world that may set a good example. Observe the distinction in " *Wit.*" Shakspere is not mentioned in it.

Lechery, Love (eleven), Miserie, Nature, Opportunitie,
Pleasure, Pollicie, Princes, Senses, Sorrow (two), Teares,
Thoughts (three), Time (two), Virtue, Use, Woe, Words
(five), Women (two); the Division of the Day, Naturall
(three), August, Description of Beautie in Persons (two),
Comparisons (eight)."

To the Reader.

> "I hang no ivie out to sell my wine :
>   The nectar of good witts will sell itselfe : . . .
> Go fearless forth, my book ! Hate cannot harm thee ;
> Apollo bred thee, and the Muses arm thee." R. A.

Imprinted at London for N. L. C. B. and J. H. 1600.

1600. In *England's Helicon*, edited by Bodenham, among
other pieces appear the lines from *Love's Labour's Lost*
beginning, "On a day, alack the day," with the name of
Shakspere attached to it.

1600. J. M. *The newe Metamorphosis : a Feast of Fancie.*

> " It seems 'tis true that W(illiam) S(hakspere) said,
>   When once he heard one courting of a mayde, ·
>   ' Beleeve not thou men's feigned flatteries,
>   Lovers will tell a bushelful of lies.' "

1601. Among the poems prefixed to Robert Chester's
Love's Martyr is one written and signed by William Shakspere, showing that [he had been invited to honour the
poet's publication, as was then usual, by accompanying
verses from distinguished friends.

1602. The *Returne from Pernassus*, Part ii., *or The Scourge
of Simony*, publicly acted by the students of St. John's
College in Cambridge in January 1602, was printed in 1606.[1]
In the reprint edited by E. Arber, the Introduction tells us
that it was :—

---

[1] On 16th October 1605, John Wright entered for his copy under
the handes of Master Owen Gwyn and the Wardens, an interlude
called *The Retourne from Pernassus, or The Scourge of Simony*, pub-
liquely acted by the students in Sanct John's College in Cambridge
vjd.—*Stationers' Records.*

A comedy written by a University pen in 1601, and addressing
itself to one of the most cultivated audiences possible at that time in
the country ; which thus publicly testifies on the stage, in the character
of Richard Burbage and William Kempe (Shakspere's fellow-actors)
to his confessed supremacy at that date, not only over all University
dramatists, but also over all the London professional playwrights,
Ben Jonson included. . . . We must point out important testimony
first, to the disreputability, and then to the profitableness, of the new
vocation of the professional play-actor ; not of the poet-actor, like
Shakspere and Jonson. It was probably owing to the fact that they
had written no plays that Burbage and Kempe were singled out for
their posts in the play.

" *The Pilgrimage to Pernassus and the Returne from Pernassus* have stood the honest stage-keepers in many a
crown's expense." [1]

The characters of Part i. reappear in this Part ii., and
seem to teach that there is no opening for scholars but on
the stage.

In judging the various poets, Ingenioso asks Judicio [2]
what he thinks of William Shakspere, referring to the
Sonnets, &c. :—

> " Who loves Adonis love or Lucre's rape,
>   His sweeter verse containes Hart-robbing life ;
>   Could but a graver subject him content,
>   Without love's foolish languishment ? "

Act iv. sc. 5, Burbage, Kempe. [3]
Kempe makes criticism on Cambridge acting :—

Burbage. A little teaching will mend these faults, and it may be
besides they will be able to pen a part.
Kempe. Few of the University pen plaies well, they smell too much
of that writer Ovid, and that writer Metamorphoses, and talke too

---

[1] See p. 117. This was the third play by the same writer.
[2] The criticism by Ingenioso and Judicio is of Francis Meres' *List
of Poets,* among whom is William Shakspere. " These being modern
and extant poets, that have lived together, from *many* of their *extante
workes and some kept in private.*"
[3] The Kempe of the *Jigge* and the *Nine Days' Wonder.*

much of Proserpina and Juppiter.   Why, here's our fellow Shakspere
puts them all downe, aye, and Ben Jonson, too.   O, that Ben Jonson
is a pestilent fellow, he brought up Horace,[1] giving the poets a pill,
but our fellow Shakspere hath given him a purge that made him
bewray his credit.

Burbage. It's a shrewd fellow indeed. . . .

Kempe. Be merry, my lads ; you have happened upon the most excellent vocation in the world for money ; they come north and south to
bring it to our playhouse ; and for *honours,* who of more report than
Dick Burbage and Will Kempe ?

Kempe to Philomusus. Thou wilt do well in time, if thou wilt be
ruled by thy betters—that is, by myself and such grave aldermen of
the playhouse.

Burbage. I like your face and the proportion of your body for
Richard III.   I pray, M. Philomusus, let me see you act a little of it.

Phil. Now is the winter of our discontent,
        Made glorious summer by the sonne of York.

It concludes thus :—

" This last is the last part of *The Returne from Pernassus,* that is the
last time that the authour's wit wil turne upon the toe in this veine."

It seems evident, then, that Shakspere's fame by this time
had reached the University less likely to know of him than
Oxford.

The French phrases in the play bear a strong resemblance to those of Shakspere.

Allusion is made also to the " Isle of Dogs."

Deckar advises Jonson " not to hang himself if he thought
any one could write plays as well as himself; not to bumbast out a new play with the old linings of jests from the
Temple's Revels, and not to venture on the stage when
your play is ended, and exchange courtesies and compliments with the gallants to make all the house rise and cry,
' That's Horace ! That's he that pens and purges humours.' "[1]   (Deckar on Jonson.)

---

[1] Jonson's *Poetaster,* Act v. sc. 3, 1602.

" It would seem that Shakespeare had espoused the cause of Deckar
in his quarrel with Jonson, though we search in vain for the ' purge '
he gave the latter."—*Old British Drama.*   See Appendix, Note 14.

1603. *A Mournful Dittie, entituled Elizabeth's Losse :—*

> " You poets all, brave Shakspere, Jonson, Greene,
>   Bestow your time to write for England's Queene,
>   Lament, lament, lament you English peeres,
>   Lament your losse, possest so many years,
>   Return your songs and sonnets and your layes,
>   To set forth sweet Elizabetha's praise.
> > Lament, lament, &c."

1603. Chettle's *England's Mourning Garment :—*

> " Nor doth the silver-tongued Melicert,
>   Drop from his honied muse one sable teare
>   To mourne her death, who gracèd his desert,
>   And to his laies opened her Royall eare.
>   Shepherd, remember our Elizabeth,
>   And sing her rape, done by that Tarquin, Death."

1603.[1] Davies of Hereford's *Microcosmos*, "The Discovery of the Little World, with the Government thereof," reprinted in 1605. To W. S. and R. B. :—

> " Players, I love you and your qualitie,
>   As you are men that pass time not abused :
>   And some I love for painting poesie,

Simonides saith poetry is a speaking painting.

> And say fell Fortune cannot be excused,[2]
>   That hath for better uses you refused :
>   Wit, courage, good shape, good parts and all good,
>   As long as all these goods are no worse used,
>   And though the stage doth stain pure gentle blood,
>   Yet generous ye are in minde and mood. . . .

Stage-plaiers.

> Some followed her by acting all men's parts,
>   These on a stage she raised in scorne to fall,
>   And made them mirrors by their acting arts,

W. S. & R. B.

> Wherein men saw their faults though ne'er so small.
>   Yet some she guerdoned not to their deserts,
>   But other some were but ill-action all,
>   Who while they acted ill, ill stayed behinde
>   (By custom of their manners) in their minde."
> > (*The Civil Warres of Death or Fortune.*)

---

[1] See Appendix, Note 15.

[2] "Roscius was said for his excellency in his quality to be only worthy to come on the stage ; and for his honesty to be more worthy than to come thereon."—*Author's Note.*

1504. Scoloker, in the Introduction to *Diaphantus*, refers to " friendly Shakspere's tragedies."

" It should come home to the vulgar's element, like friendly Shak-spere's Tragedies, where the comedian rides, where the tragedian stands on tip-toe. Faith, it should please all, like Prince Hamlet. But in sadnesse, then it were to be feared he would run mad ; in sooth, I will not be moonsick to please ; nor out of my wits though I displease all."—Anthony Scoloker, *Diaphantus, or the Passions of Love*, 1604.

1604. John Cook's *Epigrams*.[1] In the twelfth we find :—

> " Some dare do this, some other humbly craves,
> For helpe of spirits in their sleeping graves,
> As he that calde to Shakspere, Johnson, *Greene*,
> To write of their dead noble Queene."

Cook's evidence is unusually weighty, as he also was an actor, and *knew* the truth behind the scenes. Cook was the author of the play *Green's Tu Quoque*, 1614.

1605. There may be mentioned here, on Mr. Cunning-ham's authority, which I have not been able to verify :—

The Revel's Book, accompte of the year 1605.

By the King's Maties Plaiers.

1st Nov.—*The Moore of Venis*, a play in the Banketing House at Whitehall.

Sunday following, a play of *Merry Wives of Windsor*.

On St. Steven's Night in the Hall, a play called *Measure for Measure*.   Shaxberd.

On Inosents Night *The Plaie of Errors*.   Shaxberd.

Between New Years Day and Twelfe Day, a play of *Love's Labour's Loste*.

On 7th January the play of *Henry the Fifth*.

On Shrove Sunday a play of *The Merchante of Venis*.

Shaxberd.

---

[1] Cook's authorship of the volume cited is ascertained from the Stationers' Register.

On Shrove Tuesday a play cauled *The Merchante of Venis*
againe.   Shaxberd.

Commaunded by the King's Matie.

1605. Camden, in his *Remaines concerning Britain*, brackets
Shakspere with Sydney and other foremost wits of that
time.

"These may suffice for some poetical descriptions of our ancient
poets. If I would come to our time, what a world could I present to
you out of Sir Philip Sydney, Ed. Spenser, Samuel Daniell, Hugh
Holland, Ben Jonson, Th. Campion, Mich. Drayton, George Chapman,
John Marston, William Shakspere and other most pregnant wits of
these our times, whom succeeding ages may justly admire."

(*Remaines Concerning Britaine*, William Camden, ed. 1605.)

1606. *Ratsey's Ghost* [1] appears in this year, a pamphlet
in which we can see the way a spendthrift rival sees other
people's economy and self-denial. As this was only an ima-
ginary memoir of a great burglar who had been hanged
on 27th March 1605, we have the views of the writer probably superimposed upon some known opinions of Ratsey
himself. A company of actors in the provinces had played
before Ratsey for forty shillings, of which money the high-
wayman robbed them, and he advised the chief man to go
to London to a manager supposed to be Burbage.

"Get thee to London, for if one man were dead, they will have much
nede of such a one as thou art. There would be none, in my opinion,
fitter than thyselfe to play his parts : my conceipt of thee is such that
I durst wager all the money in my purse on thy head to play Hamlet
with him for a wager."

"There shalt thou learn to be frugal (for players were never so
thrifty as they are now about London), and to feed upon all men ; to
let none feede upon thee ; to make thy hand a stranger to thy pocket,
thy heart slow to perform thy promise, and when thou feelest thy purse
well lined, buy thee some place of lordship in the country, that, growing
weary of playing, thy money may bring thee to dignity and reputation ;
then thou needest care for no man."

---

[1] In the Stationers' Registers we find first part entered 2nd May 1605 ;
second part, 31st May 1605.

The player answers :—

"Sir, I thanke you for this good counsell, I promise you I will make use of it. I have heard, indeed, of some that have gone to London very meanly, and have come in time to be exceeding wealthy."

Shakspere had not entirely retired at this time, but was still working to support his family and widowed mother, though he had already bought New Place. Ratsey's satire may not altogether be meant for him; others were also rich —as Alleyn. We take the tract as at least of much contemporaneous interest.

1607. Barkstead's *Mirrha, the mother of Adonis.*

> "But stay, my muse! in thine own confines keep,
>   And wage not warre with so deare loved a neighbour.
> But having sung thy day-song, rest and sleepe.
>   Preserve thy small fame, and his greater favour.
> His song was worthy merit (Shakspere hee),
>   Sung the faire blossom, thou the withered tree,
> Laurell is due to him, his art and wit
> Hath purchased it, Cypress thy brow will fit."

John Barkstead, like Kempe and Cook above cited, was a player.

1609.[1] *Troilus and Cressida* is published with a preface headed *Newes*, praising Shakspere.[2]

"A never writer to an ever reader. Newes. Eternal reader, you have here a new play never staled with the stage,[3] never clapper-clawed with the palmes of the vulgar, and yet passing full of the palme comicall; for it is a birth of the brain that never undertooke anything comicall vainly; and were but the vaine names of commedies changed for the titles of commodities, or of playes for pleas, you should

---

[1] On 7th February 1603, Master Robertes entred for his copy in full court holden this day to print when he hath gotten sufficient authority for yt. The booke of Troilus and Cressida, as yt is acted by my Lord Chamberlain's men.—Stationers' Records."

It was a time when an enigmatic vein must have been in favour, for in a tract of 1607, a translation from the Dutch, the editor heads a sort of preface in this same fashion. "Newes to the Reader, or to whom the Buyer desires to send newes."

[3] This phrase was a mistake, and afterwards withdrawn.

see all those grand censors, that now stile them such vanities, flock to them for the maine grace of their gravities; especially this author's commedies, that are so framed to the life that they serve for the most common commentaries of all the actions of our lives; showing such a dexteritie and power of witte, that the most displeased with plays are pleased with his commedies. And all such dull and heavy-witted worldlings as were never capable of the witte of a commedie, coming by report of them to his representations, have found that witte there that they never found in themselves, and have parted better-wittied than they came; feeling an edge of wit set upon them, more than ever they dreamed they had brain to grind it on. . . . Amongst all there is none more wittie than this. . . . It deserves such a labour as well as the best commedie in Terence or Plautus, and believe this, that when hee is gone, and his commedies out of sale, you will scramble for them, and set up a new English Inquisition."

1609. Dedication by Thorpe[1] to Mr. W. H. of *Shak-spere's Sonnets,* as they are explicitly termed on the laconic title, which reminds us of *Venus and Adonis* and *Lucrece.*

To the onlie begetter of
These ensuing sonnets
Mr. W. H.[2] All happinesse
And that eternitie
promised
by
Our ever-living poet
wisheth
The well-wishing
Adventurer in
setting
forth.
                    T. T., May 20, 1609.
Never before imprinted." [3]

---

[1] Thomas Thorpe was a Warwickshire man. *Vide* unpublished MSS. of Rev. J. Hunter, British Museum.

[2] Was this the same W. Hammond to whom, in an early MS. copy of Middleton's *Witch,* that drama is inscribed? Hammond is there mentioned as a patron of literature.

[3] Edward Alleyn notes that he bought a copy for fivepence, which price is mentioned on the copy preserved in Earl Spenser's library at Althorpe.

This could not have been addressed to William Herbert, afterwards Earl of Pembroke, as it is not reverent enough. Poems by a Mr. W. H. appear in *England's Helicon*, 1600. Whether this was William Hughes, W. Hammond, W. Herbert, or whoever it was, it refers only to the person who got them or collected them for Thorpe, not to the inspirer or composer.[1]

1610. From Haslewood's Essays upon English Poets, 1815.

Edmund Bolton. "The choice of English. As, for example, language and style (the apparell of matter), hee who would penn our affaires in English, and compose unto us an entire body of them, ought to have a singular care ther of. For albeit our tongue hath not received dialects, or accentuall notes as the Greeke, nor any certaine or established rule either of gramer or true writing, is notwithstanding very copious, and few there be who have the most proper graces thereof, in which the rule cannot be variable : for as much as the people's judgments are uncertaine, the books also out of which wee gather the most warrantable English are not many to my remembrance, of which, in regard they require a particular and curious tract, I forbeare to speake at present. But among the chiefe, or rather the chiefe are in my opinion these: Sir Thomas More's Works . . . Sidney's Queen Elizabeths, Francis Bacon in his Henry VII., George Chapman's first seaven bookes of Iliades, Samuel Danyell, Michael Drayton in his Heroicall Epistles of England, Marlowe his excellent fragment of Hero and Leander.

"Shakespeare, Mr. Francis Beaumont and innumerable other writers for the stage and presse tenderly to be used in this argument, Southwell, Parsons, and some fewe others of that sort, Constable, Dorset." *Hypercritica*, or a

---

[1] 19th May 1609, Thomas Thorpe entred for his copie under the handes of Master Wilson and Master Lownes Warden, a Booke called Shakespeare's Sonnettes, vjd.—Entries in Stationers' Registers.

Rule of Judgment for Writing or Reading our Histories.
Note to Address the 4th concerning historicall language
and style. An enumeration of the best authors for written
English. Rawlinson MSS., Oxford, Bodleian.

1610. Dr. Simon Forman notes in his *Diary* that he had
witnessed the performance of *Macbeth, Winter's Tale,* &c.,
and criticises them without alluding to the author.

1610–1611. Davies [1] of Hereford mentions Shakspere in
the most complimentary manner, as a man fit to be a companion to a king.

> " Some say (good Will), which I, in sport do sing,
>   Hadst thou not played some kingly parts in sport,
>   Thou hadst been a companion for a king—
>   And beene a king among the meaner sorte.
>   Some others rail, but rail as they think fitt,
>   Thou hast no rayling but a raygning witt.
>   And honesty thou sow'st which they do reape,
>   So to increase their stock which they do keepe."
>   —*The Scourge of Folly.*

1611. In the Hawthornden MSS. we find William Drummond writing—

> *The Table of my English Books.* 1611.
> Venus and Adonis by Schaksp. (6th and 7th ed. 1602).
> The Rap of Lucrece. idem (two eds. in 1607).
> The Tragedie of Romeo and Juliet.
> A Midsomer's Night's Dreame. 4d.

1612. Preface to Webster's *White Devil* couples Shakspere with Dekker and Heywood, and praises their "right
happy and copious industry."

" Detraction is the sworn friend to ignorance; for my
own part, I have ever truly cherished my good opinion of
other men's worthy labours; especially of that full and
heightened style of Master Chapman, the laboured and
understanding works of Master Jonson, the no less worthy
composures of the both worthily excellent Master Beaumont

[1] See Appendix, Note 15.

and Master Fletcher; and lastly (without wrong last to be named) the right happy and copious industry of Master Shakspere, Master Dekker, and Master Heywood; wishing what I write may be read by their light; protesting that, in the strength of mine own judgment, I know them so worthy, that though I rest silent in my own work, yet to most of theirs I dare (without flattery) fix that of Martial, ' Non norunt hæc monumenta mori.' "   Preface to *The White Devil, or Vittoria Corrombona.*   John Webster.

We should prize this attestation particularly, as it brings Shakspere before us as a diligent student and painstaking writer, as we know otherwise he must have been.

1612. Thomas Heywood's *Apology for Actors* speaks of the injury done to him by Jaggard's carelessly inserting two of his epistles in the third edition of Shakspere's *Passionate Pilgrim.*   " But as I acknowledge my lines not worthy his patronage under whom he hath published them, so the author I know much offended with M. Jaggard, that altogether unknown to him presumed to make so bold with his name."

1613.[1] Globe Theatre burned down during performance of Henry VIII., and probably much of Shakspere's MS.

1614. Sir William Drummond says :—

" The last we have are Sir William Alexander and Shakspere, who have lately published their works," showing that Shakspere had at least published some of the plays.

In 1614. Thomas Freeman to Master William Shakspere.   After being very satirical upon players in general, he writes his only really amiable and complimentary

---

[1] On the Stationers' Registers we find Symon Stafford entered for his copy under the Warden's handes a ballad called The Sodayne Burninge of the Globe on the Bankside (in Southwark) in the Playtime, on St. Peters Day (29 June) last 1613 vjd., 30th June 1613.   Edward White entered for his copie under Master Warden Wargson's hand a doleful ballad of the generall overthrow of the famous theater on the Banksyde called "The Globe," &c., by William Parrat vjd., 30th June 1613.

epigram to this great player, for after eulogies to his sovereign he says :—

> " Not like your player, who prophanes his lips
> With scurril jeasts of some lewd ribald play,
> And after all upon the scaffold skips,
> And for his soveraigne then begins to pray
> More manerly, whilst pure, this pen of mine
> Presents her praiers (great King) for thee and thine."

Epigram 92, Part II.

> " Shakspere, that nimble mercury, thy brain,
> Lulls many hundred Argus-eyes asleepe ;
> So fit, for so thou fashioneth thy vaine,
> At the horse-foot fountain thou hast drunke full deepe.
> Vertues or vice, the theme to thee all one is.
> Who loves chaste life, there's Lucrece for a teacher ;
> Who list read lust, there's Venus and Adonis,
> True model of the most lascivious leatcher.
> Besides in plays thy wit winds like Meander,
> Whence needy new composers borrow more
> Than Terence doth from Plautus and Menander.
> But to praise thee aright I want thy store ;
> Then let thine own works thine own worthe upraise
> And help to adorne thee with deserved baies."
> (Freeman's *Epigrams, Runne and a Great Cast,*[1] Dedicated to
> Thomas Lord Windsor.)

1614. An edition of *England's Helicon, or the Muses Harmony,* published by Richard More in this year, has " The Passionate Shepherd's Song, by William Shakespeare," in the table of " All the Songs and Pastoralls," with the authors' names, contained in this book.

1614. Christopher Brooke, *Ghost of Richard III.,* celebrates the author of the antecedent drama, but does not name him.

---

[1] The carelessness of Elizabethan printers is illustrated in the title of this little book. On the title-page it is spelt, " Rubbe and a great caste," on the sub-title page, " Rub and a great cast," and on the titles of Part ii. " Runne and a great caste." As Shakspere's Epigram is in Part ii., I have retained this, evidently the correct spelling.

> " To him that imped my Fame with Clio's quill,
>   Whose magick raised her from Oblivion's den,
> That writ my storie on the Muses' Hill,
>   And with my actions dignified his pen ;
> He that from Helicon sends many a rill,
>   Whose nectared veines are drunke by thirstie men ;
>   Crowned be his stile with fame, his head with bays ;
>   And none detract, but gratulate his praise."
>   (*The Ghost of Richard III.* expressing himself.)

1615. John Stow's *Chronicles*, augmented by Edmund Howes, mention Shakspere: " Our modern and present excellent poets, which worthily flourish in their owne workes, and all of them in my own knowledge, lived together in this Queene's raigne ; according to their priorities as neere as I could, I have orderly set downe" . . . the 13th is " M. Willie Shakspeare, gentleman."

1615. From certain extracts in it, we judge that not later than this year, and probably earlier, is the manuscript note-book of Edward Pudsey ; edited and printed this year,[1] by Mr. Richard Savage, Librarian of Shakspere's birthplace, Stratford-on-Avon.   These are selections from the plays of Shakspere, Jonson, and others ; and give slightly varied renderings and contractions ; but with act and scene entered. For instance, *M͠chant of Ve. Shakspear—*

> " The'll not shew their teeth in way of smile
>   tho' nestoʳ swear y jest bee laughable."   (Act. i. sc. 1.)

Titus Andronicus, Romeo & Juliet, King Richard 2nd, King Richard 3rd, Much Adoe ab: no: Hamlet. Several quotations from each occur.

1616. Inscription on Shakspere's Tomb :—

> "Judicio Pylium, Genio Socratem, Arte Maronem,
>   Terra Tegit, Populus Maeret, Olympus Habet."

---

[1] Shakespearean Extracts from Edward Pudsey's Book. Simpkin & Marshall, 1888.   The original is now in possession of Mr. Halliwell-Phillips.

"Stay, passenger, why goest thou by so fast ;
  Read, if thou canst, whom envious death hath placed
  Within this monument—Shakspere, with whome
  Quick Nature dide ; whose name doth deck ys tombe
  Far more than cost ; see all yt he hath writt
  Leaves living art, but page to serve his witt."
      Obiit. Ano. Doi. 1616, Ætatis 53, Die 23 Ap.

"Good frend, for Jesu's sake forbeare
  To digg the dust encloased heare ;
  Blest be ye man yt spares these stones
  And curst be he yt moves my bones."

1618. Elegies on the death of Richard Burbage.

1618. Ben Jonson to Drummond : "Shakspere wanted art and sometimes sense; for, in one of his plays, he brought in a number of men saying they had been ship-wrecked in Bohemia, where is no sea by near a hundred miles."

1620–1636. On the Time-Poets.

"One night the great Apollo, pleased with Ben,
  Made the odd number of the Muses ten,
  The fluent Fletcher, Beaumont rich in sense,
  In compliment and courtship's quintessence,
  Ingenious Shakespeare : Massinger that knows
  The strength of plot to write in verse or prose."
(*Choice Drollery, Songs and Sonnets.* Anonymous. Printed 1656.
  Dr. Ingleby's *Centurie of Prayse.*)

1621. Robert Burton,[1] in his *Anatomy of Melancholy,* published at Oxford, says, " When Venus ranne to meet her rose-cheeked Adonis, as an elegant Poet [Shakspere][2] of ours sets her out " (Part III. sec. ii., numb. 2, subs. 2).

[1] The first edition, 1621, has at the end " A conclusion to thereader," which is signed Robert Burton, and dated " From my studie in Christ Church Oxon., Decemb. 5, 1620." Omitted in subsequent editions, and not signed again until the 1652 edition.
[2] Author's side-note.

Robert Burton is careful in giving his author, saying, " I have wronged no man ; I have given every man his own."

1622. *The Tragedy of Othello, the Moore of Venice,* as it hath beene diverse times acted at the Globe and at the Black-Friars by His Majesties' Servants. Written by William Shakspere, London. Printed by N. O. for Thomas Walkley, and are to be sold at his shop at the Eagle and Child in Brittans Burse, 1622.

TRANSCRIPT OF STATIONERS' REGISTERS.

8° Novembris, 1623.

Master Blounte and Isaak Jaggard entered for their copie under the hands of Master Doctor Worrall and Master Cole, warden, Master William Shakspeer's Comedyes, Histories, and Tragedyes, soe manie of the said copies as are not formerly entered to other men, vizt.

Comedyes.—*The Tempest, The Two Gentlemen of Verona, Measure for Measure, The Comedy of Errors, As You Like It, All's Well that Ends Well, Twelfe Night, The Winter's Tale.*

Histories.—*The Thirde Parte of Henry ye Sixt, Henry the Eight, Coriolanus, Timon of Athens.*

Tragedies.—*Julius Cæsar, Mackbeth, Anthonie and Cleopatra, Cymbeline.*   vijs.

1623. We now come to the credentials presented in the introduction to the first folio.

To THE READER.

This figure that thou here seest put,
  It was for gentle Shakspere cut,
Wherein the graver had a strife
  With Nature to outdo the life.

Ah, could he but have drawne his wit
As well in brasse as he hath hit
His face ; the print would then surpass
All that was ever writ in brasse ;
But since he cannot, reader, looke
Not on his picture but his book.

B. J.

(Prefixed to Droeshouts's portrait of Shakspere.)

Dedication, To the most noble and Incomparable paire of Brethren, William Earl of Pembroke, &c., and Philip Earl of Montgomery, &c. "Right Honourable—Whilst we studie to be thankful in one particular for the many favours we have received from your lordships, we are falne upon the ill fortune, to mingle two the most diverse things that can be, feare and rashnesse ; rashnesse in the enterprize and feare of the successe. For, when we valew the places your Highnesses sustaine, we cannot but know their dignity greater than to descend to the reading of these trifles ; and, while we name them trifles, we have deprived ourselves of the defence of our Dedication. But, since your lordships have been pleased to consider these trifles something heretofore, and have prosecuted both them and their author living with so much favour, we hope that (they outliving him and he not having the same fate, common with some, to be executor to his owne writings) you will use the like indulgence towards them, you have done unto their parent. There is a great difference whether any booke choose his patrones or find them. This hath done both. For so much were your Lordship's likings of the severall parts when they were acted, as before they were published, the volume asked to be yours. . . . We have collected them and done an office to the dead to procure his orphanes guardians ; without ambition either of self-profit or fame, only to keep the memory of so *worthy* a friend and fellowe alive, as was *our* Shakspere, by humble offer of his playes, to your most noble patronage. . . . We most humbly consecrate to your Highnesses these remaines of your

servant Shakspere; that what delight is in them may be
ever your lordships', the reputation his, and the faults ours,
if any be committed by a payre so careful to show their
gratitude both to the living and the dead as is your lordships most bounden.   JOHN HEMINGE.
                                HENRY CONDELL.

TO THE GREAT VARIETY OF READER.

From the most able to him that can but spell.   There
you are numbered.   We had rather you were weighed.
Especially when the fate of all bookes depends upon your
capacities, and not of your heads alone but of your purses.
Well! it is now publique, and you will stand for your privi-
leges wee know, to read and censure.   Do so, but buy it
first.   That doth best commend a book the stationer sayes.
Then, how odde soever your braines be, or your wisedomes,
make your license the same, and spare not. . . . Whatever
you do, buy.   Censure will not drive a trade or make the
Jacke go.   And though you be a magistrate of wit, and sit
on the stage at Black Friars, or the Cock Pit, to arraigne
plays daily, know these playes have had their trial already,
and stood out all appeales and do now come forth quitted
rather by a decree of Court than any purchased letters of
recommendation.

It had been a thing, we confesse, worthy to have been
wished that the author himself had lived to have set forth
and overseen his owne writings, but since it hath been
ordained otherwise, and he by death departed from that
right, we pray you do not envie his friends the office of
their care and paine, to have collected and published them,
and so to have published them, as where (before) you were
abused with diverse stolen and surreptitious copies, maimed
and deformed by the frauds and stealths of injurious im-
postors, that exposed them; even those are now offered
to your view cured, and perfect of their limbes; and all the

rest as he conceived them. Who, as he was a happy imitator of nature, he was a most gentle expresser of it. His mind and hand went together, and what he thought he uttered with that easiness that we have scarce received from him a blot in his papers. But it is not our province, who onely gather his works and give them you, to praise him.

It is yours that reade him. And there we hope, to your divers capacities, you will find enough, both to draw and hold you; for his wit can no more lie hid than it could be lost. Read him therefore again and again; and then, if you do not like him, you are in some manifest danger, not to understand him.　　　　　JOHN HEMINGE.

HENRY CONDELL.[1]

　　　To the memorie of Mr. W. Shakspere.
　　　Wee wondred (Shakspere) that thou wentst so soone,
　　　From the world's stage to the grave's tyring-roome.
　　　Wee thought thee dead, but this thy printed worth
　　　Tels thy spectators that thou went'st but forth,
　　　To enter with applause. An actor's art
　　　Can dye and live, to acte a second part
　　　That's but an exit of mortalitie,
　　　This, a re-entrance to a Plaudite.　　　J. M.

1623. The verses before the book by W. Basse, "On Mr. William Shakspere :—

　　　" Renowned Spenser, lie a thought more nigh
　　　To learned Beaumont, and rare Beaumont ly
　　　A little nearer Chaucer to make roome
　　　For Shakspere, in your threefold, fourfold tomb.
　　　To lodge all four in one bed make a shift
　　　Until Domesday, for hardly will a fifte
　　　Betwixt this day and that by fate be slaine
　　　For whom the curtains shall be drawn again.

---

[1] Prefixed to the plays comes the list of the chief actors who acted in them, in which Shakspere's name stands first. See Appendix, Note 16.

But if Precedency in death doe barre,
A fourth place in your sacred sepulcher
In this uncarved marble of thy own,
Sleep, brave Tragedian, Shakspere sleep alone.
Thy unmolested rest, unshared cave
Possesse as Lord, not tenant to thy grave,
   That unto others it may counted be
   Honour hereafter to be laid by thee."

1623. Hugh Holland upon the lines and life of the famous scenic poet Master William Shakspere.

"Those hands, which you so clapt, go now and wring
You Britaine's brave ; for done are Shakspere's days.
His days are done that made the dainty playes,
Which made the globe of Heaven and Earth to ring.
Dried is that vein, dried is the Thespian Spring,
Turned all to teares, and Phoebus clouds his rays.
That corps, that coffin now bestick with bays,
Which crowned him Poet first, then Poet's King.
If Tragedies might any Prologue have
All those he made, would scare make one to this,
Where fame, now that he gone is to the grave,
(Death's public tyring-house) the Nuncius is.
For though his line of life went soone about
The life yet of his lines shall never out."

1623. The magnificent eulogy of Jonson is almost a household word, so to speak, in our literature.

"Ben Jonson, To the memory of my beloved ; the Author, Mr. William Shakspere :—

" To draw no envy (Shakspere) on thy name,
Am I thus ample to thy Booke and Fame ;
While I confess thy writings to be such
As neither man nor muse can praise too much.
'Tis true, and all men's suffrage. . . .
I therefore will begin. Soule of the Age !
The Applause ! delight ! the wonder of our stage ;
My Shakspere, rise ! I will not lodge thee by
Chaucer, or Spenser, or bid Beaumont lye
A little further to make thee a roome ;
Thou art a monument, without a tombe,

And art alive still, while thy Booke doth live,
And we have wits to read, and praise to give.
And though thou hadst small Latin and less Greeke
From thence to honour thee, I would not seeke
For names ; but call for thundering Æschylus,
Euripides, and Sophocles to us ;
Paccuvius, Accius, him of Cordova dead
To life again, to hear thy buskin tread,
And shake a stage ; or, when thy socks were on,
Leave thee alone for the comparison
Of all that insolent Greece, or haughty Rome
Sent forth, or since did from their ashes come.
Triumph, my Britaine, thou hast one to shewe
To whom all scenes of Europe homage owe.
He was not for an age, but for all time.
Nature herselfe was proud of his designes,
And joyed to wear the dressing of his lines
Which were so richly spun, and woven to fit
As, since, she will vouchsafe no other wit.
Yet must I not give nature all ; thy art,
My gentle Shakspere, must enjoy a part ;
For, though the poet's matter nature be,
His art doth give the fashion, and that he
Who casts to write a living line must sweat,
(Such as thine are) and strike the seconde heat
Upon the muse's anvil, turn the same
(And himself with it) that he thinks to frame,
Or for the laurel he may gain a scorne,
For a good poet's made, as well as born ;
And such wert thou.
                    Look how the Father's face
Lives in his issue, even so the race
Of Shakspere's mind and manners brightly shines
In his well-turned and true-filed lines.
Sweet Swan of Avon ! what a sight it were
To see thee in our waters yet appeare,
And make those flights upon the banks of Thames
That so did take Eliza and our James !
But stay, I see thee in the hemisphere
Advanced, and made a constellation there !
Shine forth thou star of poets, and with rage
Or influence chide or cheere the drooping stage,

> Which, since thy flight fro hence hath mourned like night,
> And despairs day, but for thy volumes light." [1]
>
> *(Ben Jonson.)*

Drummond said of Jonson, "He is a great lover and praiser of himself, a contemner and scorner of others." [2] For that very reason his praise is stronger than that of others.

1623. Leonard Digges writes a poem to the memory of the deceased author, Maister William Shakspere :—

> Shakspere, at length thy pious fellows give
> The world thy works ; thy workes by which outlive
> Thy tomb, thy name must, when that stone is rent
> And time dissolves thy Stratford monument,
> Here we alive shall view thee still.   This booke,
> When brasse and marble fade, shall make thee looke,
> Fresh to all ages ; when posteritie
> Shall loathe what's new, think all is prodegie
> That is not Shakspere's ; every line, each verse
> Here shall revive, redeeme thee from thy herse.
> Nor fire, nor cankering age, as Naso said
> Of his, thy wit-fraught book shall once invade
> Nor shall I e'er believe, or think thee dead
> (Though mist) untill our bankrout stage be sped
> (Impossible) with some new strain to out-do
> Passions of Juliet and her Romeo ;
> Or till I heare a scene more nobly take
> Than when thy half-sword parleying Romans spake.
> Till these, till any of thy volumes rest,
> Shall with more fire, more feeling be exprest,
> Be sure, our Shakspere, thou canst never dye,
> But crowned with laurel live eternally.   *(L. Digges.)*

---

[1] Dryden concurred with Rowe in thinking these verses sparing and invidious, while Boswell thought them sincere because so appropriate. Supported by the passage in *Timber*, I think there is no doubt he felt and meant all he said.

[2] John Davies, of Hereford, says to Ben Jonson, in his *Scourge of Folly*, 1611 :—

> "Thou art sounde in body ; but some say, thy soule
> Envy doth ulcer ; yet corrupted hearts
> Such censurers must have."

This portion of the Anti-Baconian evidence is a singularly valuable and representative series of affidavits, so to speak, from men who knew Shakspere in many relations. Condell was probably, like Burbage, a native of Stratford or the immediate vicinity, where a family of this not very common name remains.

1623. The office-book of Sir Henry Herbert, Master of the Revels to James I., Charles I., and Charles II., *Variorum*, vol. iii. 1623–36. To the Duchess of Richmond, in the King's absence, was given the *Winter's Tale*, by the King's company, the 18th January 1623. At Whitehall.

Upon New Year's night, the Prince only being there, the first part of *Sir John Falstaff*, by the King's company. At Whitehall, 1624.

For the King's players. An olde play, called *Winter's Tale*, formerly allowed of Sir George Bucke, and likewise by mee, on Mr. Hemmings his worde that there was nothing profane added or reformed, though the allowed booke was missinge ; and therefore I returned it without a fee this 19th August 1623.

Received from Mr. Hemmings in their company's name, to forbid the playing of Shakspere's plays to the Red Bull Company, this 11th of April 1627, £5, os. od.

On Saturday, the 17th of November (mistake for 16th), being the Queen's Birthday, *Richarde the Thirde* was acted by the K. players at St. James, when the King and Queene were present, it being the first play the Queene sawe since her M^{ty's} delivery of the Duke of York, 1633.

On Tuesday night, at Saint James, the 26th of November, 1633, was acted before the King and Queene, the *Taminge of the Shrew*. Likt.

On Wednesday night, the 1st of January 1633, *Cymbelyne* was acted at Court by the King's players. Well likt of the King.

The *Winter's Tale* was acted on Thursday night at Court, the 16th January 1633, by the K. players and likt.

Julius Cæsar at St. James, the 31st January 1636.
This, of course, only proves that Shakspere wrote plays.
Those mentioned we know, from other sources, to be
his.

1625. Richard James to Sir Henry Bourchier :—

"A young gentle Lady of your acquaintance, having
read ye works of Shakspere, made me this question.   How
Sir John Falstaffe or Fastolf, as he is written in ye Statute
Book of Maudlin College in Oxford, where every day that
society were bound to make memorie of his soule, could be
dead in ye time of Harrie ye fifte, and again live in ye
time of Harrie ye Sixt, to be banished for cowardice.
Whereunto I make answer that it was one of those humours and mistakes for which Plato banished all poets out
of his commonwealth. . . . In Shakspere's first show of
Harry the Fift, the person with which he undertook to
playe a buffoon was not Falstaff, but Sir John Oldcastle."
—D. Ingleby's *Centurie of Prayse.*

1623. William Davenant : [1]—

ODE

IN REMEMBRANCE OF MR. WILLIAM SHAKSPERE.

I.

Beware (delighted poets) when you sing
To welcome nature in the early spring :
    Your numerous feet not tread
The banks of Avon ; for each flower
(As it ne'er knew a sun or shower)
    Hangs there the pensive head.

II.

Each tree whose thick and spreading growth hath made
Rather a night beneath the boughs than shade
    (Unwilling now to grow)

---

[1] Born 1605-6.   One of his early poems.   Appeared among his
poems published in 1638.

Looks like the plume a captain wears,
Whose rifled falls are steept i' th' tears,
Which from his last rage flow.

III.

The piteous river wept itself away
Long since (alas) to such a swift decay,
That reach the map and look
If you a river there can spy,
And for a river your mock'd eye
Will find a shallow brook.

1625. Ben Jonson's *Timber*, or *Discoveries.*

Jonson, speaking of poets in general, says—" Poetry in this latter age hath proved but a mean mistress to such as have wholly addicted themselves to her, or given their names up to her family. They who have but saluted her on the by, and now and then tendered their visits, she hath done much for, and advanced in the way of their own professions (both the law and the gospel), beyond all they could have hoped or done for themselves without her favour." Immediately after this, as if he had taken Shakspere as the illustrative poet, he says—

De Shakspeare Nostrat.—Augustus in Hat.

" I remember the players have often mentioned it as an honour to Shakspere, that in his writing (whatsoever he penned), he never blotted out a line. My answer hath been, would he had blotted a thousand—which they thought a malevolent speech. I had not told posterity this, but for their ignorance, who chose that circumstance to commend their friend by, wherein he most faulted; I to justify mine own candour : for I loved the man, and do honour his memory, on this side idolatry, as much as any. He was (indeed) honest, and of an open and free nature; had an excellent phantasy, brave notions, and gentle expressions; wherein he flowed with that facility, that sometimes it was necessary he should be stopped. '*Sufflaminandus erat,*' as Augustus said of Haterius. His wit was in his own power,

K

would the rule of it had been so too. Many times he fell
into those things, could not escape laughter; as when he
said in the person of Cæsar, one speaking to him, ' Cæsar,
thou dost me wrong,' he replied, ' Cæsar did never wrong
but with just cause,' and such like, which were ridiculous.
But he redeemed his vices with his virtues. There was
ever more in him to be praised than pardoned." This
conclusively proves that Jonson loved "the man," and not
the works only, and that the man had extraordinary con-
versational powers. It is but a step to the writing of
thoughts, which here is also proved; so that, even had
Bacon written the plays, Shakspere is shown *capable* of
having done so himself.

LVI. Jonson's Epigram. Poet-Ape.

> Poor Poet Ape, that would be thought our chief,
>   Whose works are e'en the frippery of wit
> From bondage is become so bold a thief,
>   As we the robbed, leave rage, and pity it.
> At first he made low-shifts, would pick and glean,
>   Buy the reversion of old plays; now grown
> To a little wealth, and credit in the scene,
>   He takes up all, makes each man's wit his own.
> And, told of this, he slights it. Tut, such crimes
>   The sluggish gaping auditor devours;
> He marks not whose 'twas first: and after times
>   May judge it to be his, as well as ours.
> Fool! as if half eyes will not know a fleece
> From locks of wool, or shreds from the whole piece?

Ben Jonson is supposed to have expressed in this his feelings of
jealousy towards Shakspere's successes in his early days, before he
knew and "loved the man."

1625. William Camden completely finished his *Britannia*
in 1617, commenced in 1597, and was printed in 1625. He
says of Stratford—"In the Chancel lies William Shakespeare, a native of this place, who has given ample proof of
his genius and great abilities in the forty-eight plays he
has left behind him."

1627. Drayton's *Epistle to Henry Reynolds.* This is one Warwickshire man writing to another, both personal acquaintances of Shakspere :—

> " Shakspere, thou had'st as smooth a comicke vaine,
> Fitting the socks, and in thy natural braine,
> As strong conception and as clear a rage
> As any one that trafficked with the stage."
>   —*Third edition*, 1628.

1628. In Burton's 3rd edition of this year of *Anatomy of Melancholy* he adds the illustration of " Benedict and Beatrice " to his former words. " And many times those which at the first sight cannot fancy or affect each other, but are harsh and ready to disagree, offended with each other's carriage (like Benedict and Beatrice in the comedy) [Shakespeare's],[1] in whom they finde many faults ; by the living together in a house, by conference, kissing, colling, and such like allurements, begin at last to dote insensibly upon one another " (Part III. sec. ii., numb. 2, subs. 4.)[2] Other allusions also appear to the plays.

1630. Abraham Cowley's *Poetical Revenge*, a minor poem in " Silva " :—

> " May hee,
> Bee by his father in his study tooke,
> At Shakespeare's plays instead of the Lord Cooke."

1630. John Taylor (the Water-Poet), in his *Travels in Bohemia*, alludes to Shakspere's seaports there, and in *The Praise of Hemp Seed* he says :—

> " Spenser and Shakspere did in art excel
> Sir Edward Dyer, Greene, Nash, Daniel."
>   *(John Taylor, the Water-Poet,* vol. iii.)

1630. Archy's *Banquet of Jests* (first printed in 1630) has a story of one travelling through Stratford, " a town

---

[1] Author's side-note.
[2] In the 1652 edition a printer's error makes this stand Part iii. sect. 2, numb. 3, instead of 2, subs. 4.

most remarkable for the birth of famous William Shakspere."

1630. John Milton's splendid Epitaph, though printed later in the editions of 1632 and 1640, was said to have been written in this year. Coming from a Puritan, printed in the time of Puritan ascendency, it is very powerful in this argument.

"An Epitaph on the admirable dramatic poet, William Shakspere :—

> " What needs my Shakspere, for his honoured bones,
>   The labour of an age in piled stones ?
>   Or that his hallowed reliques should be hid
>   Under a star y-pointing pyramid ?
>   Dear son of memory, great heir of fame,
>   What need'st thou such weak witness of thy name.
>   Thou, in our wonder and astonishment,
>   Hast built thyself a live-long monument.
>   For whilst, to the shame of slow-endeavouring art,
>   Thy easy numbers flow ; and that each heart
>   Hath, from the leaves of thy unvalued book,
>   Those Delphic lines with deep impression took.
>   Then thou, our fancy of itself bereaving,
>   Dost make us marble with too much conceiving.
>   And so sepulchred, in such pomp dost lie,
>   That kings for such a tomb would wish to die."
>
>   (*John Milton.*)

1632. Milton also alludes to Shakspere in *L'Allegro*—

> " Then to the well-trod stage anon,
>   If Jonson's learned socks be on ;
>   Or sweetest Shakspere, Fancy's child,
>   Warble his native wood-notes wild."

1632. The second folio edition repeats the portraits and lines by Jonson. It is printed by Thomas Cotes for Robert Allot ; but the address to Lords Pembroke and Montgomery remain.

Then comes the lines " Upon the effigies of my worthy friend, the author, Master William Shakspere :—

"Spectator, this life's shadow is to see,
The truer image of a livelier he.
Turn reader ; but observe his comic vaine,
Laugh and proceed next to a tragic strain.
Then weep, so when thou find'st two contraries,
Two different passions from thy rapt soul rise.
Say (who alone effect such wonders could)
Rare Shakspere to the life thou dost beholde."

1632. On worthy Master Shakspere and his poems :—

" A mind reflecting ages past, whose cleere
And equal surface can make things appeare
Distant a thousand years, and represent
Them in their lively colours just extent. . .
In that deepe duskie dungeon to discerne
A Royal Ghost from Churls ; by art to learne
The physiognomie of shades and give
Them suddaine birth, wondering how oft they live.
What story coldly tells, what poets faine
At secondhand, and picture without braine,
Senseless and soullesse showes.   To give a stage
(Ample and true with life) voyce, action, age ;
To raise our ancient sovereigns from their hearse ;
Make kings his subjects by exchanging verse. . .
This and much more, which cannot be exprest
But by himselfe, his tongue, and his owne brest,
Was Shakespeare's freehold, which his cuning braine
Improved by favour of the nine-fold traine.
The buskined Muse, the Comick Queen, the grand
And louder tone of Clio : nimble hand,
And nimbler foote of the melodious paire,
The silver-voiced lady, the most faire
Calliope, whose speaking silence daunts,
And she whose prayse the heavenly body chants.
These joyntly woo'd him, envying one another
(Obeyed by all as spouse but loved as brother),
And wrought a curious robe of sable grave,
Fresh greene, and pleasant yellow, red most brave,
And constant blew, rich purple, guiltless white,
The lowly russet, and the scarlet bright,
Brancht and embroidered like the painted spring ;
Each leaf matched with a flower, and each string

Of golden wire, each line of silke : there run
Italian workes, whose thread the sisters spun ;
And there did sing, or seem to sing, the choyse
Birdes of a forrayn note and curious voyce. . .
Now when they could no longer him enjoy
In mortall garments pent, death may destroy,
They say, his body, but his verse shall live.
And more than nature takes our hands shall give.
In a lesse volume but more strongly bound,
Shakspere shall breathe and speake, in laurel crowned
Which never fades.   Fed with Ambrosian meate,
In a well-lined vesture rich and neate,
So with this robe they clothe him, bid him weare it,
For time shall never staine nor envy teare it."
—*J. M. S.*

The copy of 1632 in the Memorial Library at Stratford
has another portrait bound up with it from a later folio
than this.   The lines under it are also different, being—

   " This Shadowe is renowned Shakespeare's Soule of the Age,
   The applause, delight, the wonder of the stage.
   Nature herself was proud of his designes,
   And joyed to weare the dressing of his lines,
   Which were so richly spun and woven to fit,
   As, since, she will vouchsafe no other wit,
   For ever live the same, the world to tell
   Thy like no age shall ever parallel."

   1632. Thomas Randolph alludes to Shakspere and to
some of his plays :—

   " Did not Will Summers break his wind for thee?
   And Shakespeare therefore write his Comedy?
   All things acknowledge thy vast power divine
   (Great God of Money), whose most powerful shine
   Gives motion, life.   Day rises from thy sight,
   Thy setting, though at noon, makes night
   Sole Catholic cause of what we feel or see,
   All in this All are but effects of thee."
        (*Hey for Honesty, Down with Knavery.*   Play by Thomas
               Randolph.   After Aristophanes, his *Plutus*.)

He mentions in this play Pericles, Sir John Oldcastle, Sir

John Falstaff, and the ghost of Hamlet's father. These poems were not published till later, but Randolph died in 1634.

1632. " Read Jonson, Shakspere, Beaumont, Fletcher, or
Thy neat limned pieces, skilful *Massinger.*"
(Sir Aston Cokaine, lines prefixed to *Massinger*.)

1633. John Hales of Eton, " In a conversation between Sir John Suckling, Sir William Davenant, Endymion Porter, Mr. Hales of Eaton, and Ben Jonson, Sir John Suckling, who was a professed admirer of Shakspere, had undertaken his defence against Ben Jonson with some warmth; Mr. Hales, who had sat still some time hearing Ben frequently reproaching him with the want of learning and Ignorance of the Antients, told him at last 'that, if Mr. Shakspere had not read the Antients, he had likewise not stolen anything from them (a fault that the other made no conscience of), and that if he would produce any one Topick finely treated by any of them, he would undertake to show something upon the same subject, at least as well written, by Shakspere.' "—*Rowe's Life.*

1633. A marginal note to William Prynne's *Histrio-mastix* refers to Shakspere's plays as printed on finer paper and more in demand than the Bible.

"Another Barrister of Lincoln's Inn to the Fellows of Lincoln's Inn. In spite of the statutes of our Kingdom branding all professed stage-plaiers for infamous rogues; and stage-plaiers for unlawful pastimes, yet other Innes of Court permit them, though we do not, having excluded long before these amusements, for feare they should corrupt the young students. . . I say the number of Players, Play-books; Play-haunters, and Play-houses still increasing; there being 40,000 play-bookes printed within these 2 years (as the Stationers inform me), they being now more vendible than the choicest sermons. The multitude of our London Play-haunters being so augmented now, that all the ancient Divvels Chapels, for so the Fathers call the Play-houses, are not sufficient, two old Play-houses being also

lately re-edified,[1] enlarged, and one [2] new theater erected.
Some play-bookes since I first undertook this subject are
grown from quarto into folio; which yet bear so good a
price and sale, that I cannot but with grief relate it, they
are now new printed in far better paper than most octavo
or quarto Bibles " (Ben Jonson's, Shakspere's, and others).
—To the *Christian Reader.*

. . . " Note, Shakspere's plays are printed in the best
crown paper, far better than most Bibles. Above 40,000
play-books have been printed and vented within these last
two years."

1634. William Habington glances at this in his *Castara ;*
To a friend inviting him to a meeting upon promise :—

> May you drinke beare, or that adulterate wine,
> Which makes the zeale of Amsterdam divine,
> If you make breache of promise. I have now
> So rich a sacke, that even yourselfe will bow
> T' adore my *Genius.*   Of this wine should Prynne
> Drinke but a plenteous glasse, he would beginne
> A health to Shakspere's ghost.   —*Castara.*

1635. T. Heywood's *Hierarchy of the Blessed Angels,*
alluding to the writers and actors being called by their
Christian names, specifies " the enchanting quill of mellifluous Shakspere :—

> Our moderne poets to that passe are driven,
> Those names are curtailed that they first had given . . .
> Mellifluous Shakspere, whose enchanting quill
> Commanded mirth and passion, was but *Will.*

In 1636 Sir John Suckling's *Fragmenta Aurea* were
written, but were printed by a friend to perpetuate his
memory in 1646. They contain—

> The sweat of learned Jonson's brain
> And gentle Shakspere's easier strain.

---

[1] The Fortune and the Red Bull.
[2] The White Friars Theatre.—*Author's notes.*

In his *Prologue to the Goblins*, same year, he says :—

> When Shakspere, Beaumont, Fletcher ruled the stage,
> There scarce were ten good pallats in the age.
> More curious cooks than guests ; for men would eat
> Most heartily of any kind of meat.

1636. Sir John Suckling's *Letters :* "We are at length arrived at that river, about the uneven running of which my friend Mr. William Shakspere makes Henry Hotspur quarrel so highly with his fellow-rebels."

Also : "I must confesse it is a just subject for our sorrow, to hear of any that does quit his station, without his leave that placed him there ; and yet as ill a mine as this act has 'twas *à la Romantic ;* as you may see by a line of Mr. Shakespeare's, who, bringing in Titinius after a lost battel, speaking to his sword, and bidding it find out his heart, adds :—

> 'By your leave, gods, this is a Roman's part.'"

He also writes *A Supplement of an Imperfect Copy of Verses of Mr. Wil. Shakespeare.* On Lucrece.

1637. To the memory of Immortal Ben :—

> "So, in our halcyon days we have had now
> Wits, to which all that after come must bow ;
> And should the stage compose herself a crown,
> Of all those wits which hitherto she has known ;
> Though there be many that about her brow
> Like sparkling stones, might a quick lustre throw ;
> Yet Shakspere, Beaumont, Jonson, these three shall
> Make up the Gem in the point verticall."
> > (Owen Feltham, *Jonsonius Virbius.*)

1637. "Shakspere may make grief merry ; Beaumont's stile
> Ravish, and melt anger into a smile.
> In winter nights or after meals they be,
> I must confess, very good company ;
> But thou exact'st our best hour's industry,
> We may read them, we ought to study thee."
> > (Richard West, *Jonsonius Virbius.*)

1637.   " What are his faults (O Envy) that you speake
      English at court, the learned stage acts Greek ;
      That Latine hee reduced and could command
      That which your Shakspere scarce could understand."
                  (H. Ramsay, *Jonsonius Virbius.*)

1637. To the memory of Jonson, by Jasper Mayne :—

    " Though the priest had translated for that time
    The Liturgy, and buried thee in rime,
    So that in meter we had heard it said,
    Poetique dust is to poetique laid ;
    And though that dust being Shakspere's thou mightst have
    Not his roome, but the Poet for thy grave. . . .
    So that, as thou didst Prince of numbers die
    And live, so now thou mightst in numbers lie
    'Twere frail solemnity. . . .
    Who without Latine helps hadst been as rare
    As Beaumont, Fletcher, or as Shakspere were ;
    And, like them, from thy native stock couldst say,
    Poets and kings are not born every day."
                  (*Jonsonius Virbius.*)

1637. J. Terrent, *Jonsonius Virbius*—

    " Nec geminos vates ; nec te Shakspeare silebo
    Aut quicquid sacri nostros conjecit in annos
    Conselium Fati."

1637. Samuel Holland's *Don Zara del Fogo* (not printed till 1656) mentions that "Shakspere and others were willing to water their bays with their blood rather than part with their proper right."

1637. Manuscript commonplace book of Abraham Wright, vicar of Okeham in Rutlandshire, speaks of " Othello " by Shakspere.

1638. James Mervyn prefixed to Shirley's *Royal Master :—*

    " That limbus I could have believed thy brain
    Where Beaumont, Fletcher, Shakspere, and a traine
    Of glorious poets in their active heate
    Move in that orbe as in their former seate. . . .
    Each casting in his dose, Beaumont his weight,
    Shakspere his mirth, and Fletcher his conceit."

1638. Richard Brome, in *Antipodes*, acted in this year, but printed in 1640—

> " These lads can act the Emperors' lives all over,
> And Shakespeare's chronicled histories to boot,
> And were that Cæsar, or that English Earle
> That lov'd a play and player so well, now living,
> I would not be outvied in my delights."

1638. Davenant's *Ode*, published along with *Madagascar* and other poems, see page 144.

1639. " Robert Chamberlain. One asked another what Shakespeare's works were worth all being bound together. He answered, not a farthing. Not worth a farthing, said he, why so ? He answered that his playes were worth a great deale of money, but he never heard that his works were worth anything at all."—*Conceits, Clinches, Flashes, and Whimsies.*

1640. Thomas Bancroft to Shakspere :—

> " Thy muse's sugared dainties seem to us
> Like the famed apples of old Tantalus ;
> For we (admiring) see and hear thy straines,
> But none I see or heare those sweets attaines. . . .
> Thou hast so used thy pen or (shooke thy speare),
> That poets startle, nor thy wit come neere."
> 				(*Two bookes of Epigrammes and Epitaphs.*)

1640. The 12mo edition of the poems of Shakspere gives new testimonials :—

To the Reader,—I here presume under favour to present to your view some excellent and sweetely composed poems of Master William Shakspere, which in themselves appeare of the same purity, the Authour himselfe then living avouched ; they had not the fortune by reason of their Infancie in his death, to have the due acomodation of proportionable glory with the rest of his ever living works, yet the lines of themselves will afford you a more authentick approbation than my assurance any way can, to invite your allowance, in your perusall you shall finde them seren,

cleere and elegantly plaine, such gentle straines as shall
recreate and not perplexe your braine, no intricate or
cloudy stuff to puzzell your intellect, but perfect-eloquence,
such as will raise your admiration to his praise: this
assurance I know will not differ from your acknowledgment. And certain I am my opinion will be seconded by
the sufficiency of these ensuing lines. I have been somewhat solicitous to bring this forth to the perfect view of
all men, and in so doing, glad to be serviceable for the
continuance of glory to the deserved Author in these his
poems.   JOHN BENSON.

Of Mr. William Shakspere.

What, lofty Shakspere, art again revived?
And virbius-like now show'st thyself twice-lived
'Tis love that thus to thee is showne
The labours his, the glory still thine owne.
These learned poems amongst thine after-birth
That makes thy name immortall on the earth

Will make the learned still admire to see
The muses' gifts so full, infused on thee.
Let carping Momus barke, and bite his fill,
And ignorant Davus slight thy learned skill.[1]
Yet those who know the worth of thy desert,
And with true judgment can discern thy art,
Will be admirers of thy high-tuned straine,
Amongst whose number let me still remain.
                                        JOHN WARREN.

Upon Master William Shakspere.

Poets are borne not made, when I would prove
This truth, the glad remembrance I must love
Of never dying Shakspere who alone
Is argument enough to prove that one.
First that he was a poet none could doubt,
That heard the applause of what he sees set out
Imprimed ; where thou hast (I will not say)
Reader, his workes for to contrive a play ;

----

[1] There were some carpers even in those days.

(To him 'twas none) the patterne of all wit
Art without art unparalleled as yet.
Next Nature onely helpt him, for looke thorow
This whole booke thou shalt finde he doth not borowe.
One phrase from Greekes nor Latines imitate,
Nor once from vulgar languages translate,
Nor plagiari-like from others gleane,
Nor begges he from each witty friend a scene
To piece his Acts with ; all that he doth write
Is pure his owne, plot, language, exquisite.
Then vanish upstart Writers to each stage,
You needy Poetasters of this age. . . .
I doe not wonder when you offer at
Black-Friers, that you suffer, 'tis the fate
Of richer veines, prime judgments that have fared
The worse with this deceased man compared.
So have I seene, when Cæsar would appeare
And on the stage at half-sword parley were
Brutus and Cassius ; oh, how the audience
Were ravished, with what wonder they went thence,
When some new day they would not brook a line
Of tedius, though well-laboured Catiline.
Sejanus, too, was irksome, they prized more
Honest Iago or the jealous Moore.
And though the Fox and subtle Alchemist
Long intermitted, could not quite be mist,
Though these have shamed all Ancients, and might raise
Their authours' merit with a crown of Bayes.
Yet these sometimes, even at a friend's desire,
Acted, have scarce defrayed the sea-cole fire,
And doore-keepers ; when let but Falstaffe come,
Hal, Poines, the rest, you scarce shall have a roome.
All is so pestered ; let but Beatrice
And Benedicke be seene ; loe, in a trice
The cockpit, galleries, boxes, all are full
To heare Malvoglio, that cross-gartered gull,
Briefe, there is nothing in his wit-fraught booke,
Whose sound we would not heare, or whose worth looke
Like old coynd gold, whose lines in every page
Shall passe true currant to succeeding age.

LEONARD DIGGES.

1640. After the elegies by J. M. and W. B., reprinted

from the 1632 edition, comes "An Elegie on the Death
of that famous Writer and Actor, Mr. William Shakspere : "—

> . . . Let learned Johnson sing a dirge for thee,
> And fill our Orbe with mournful harmony.
> But we neede no remembrancer, thy fame
> Shall still accompany thy honoured name
> To all posterity, and make us be
> Sensible of what we lost in losing thee.
> Being the Age's wonder, whose smooth rhymes
> Did more reforme than lash the looser times.
> Nature herselfe did her own selfe admire,
> As oft as thou wert pleased to attire
> Her in her native lusture and confesse
> Thy dressing was her chiefest comlinesse.
> How can we then forget thee, when the age,
> Her chiefest tutor, and the widdow'd stage.
> Her onely favourite in thee hath lost ;
> And Nature's selfe, what she did bragge of most.
> Sleep then, rich Soule of numbers, whilst poor we,
> Enjoy the profits of thy legacie.
> And think it happinesse enough we have
> So much of thee redeemed from the grave
> As may suffice to enlighten future times,
> With the bright lustre of thy matchless rhimes.   ANON.

1640. To Mr. William Shakspere :—

> " Shakespeare, we must be silent in thy praise,
> 'Cause our encomiums will but blast thy bays,
> Which envy could not, that thou didst so well.
> Let thine own histories prove a chronicle."   ANON.
>   (*Witt's Recreations, selected from Finest Fancies of
>   Modern Muses.*)

1640. Poems.

TO HIS MISTRIS SHADE.

> Then soft Catullus, sharpe fanged Martiall
> And towering Lucan, Horace, Juvenall,
> And snakie Perseus ; these and those whose rage
> (Dropt from the jarre of heaven) filled to enrage
> All times unto their phrensies, thou shalt there
> Behold them in an Amphitheatre,

Amongst which Synod crowned with sacred bayes,
And flattering joy weele have to recite their playes—
Shakespeare and Beaumond, Swannes to whom the spheres
Listen, while they call backe the former yeares.
To teach the truth of Scenes, and more for thee
There yet remaines, brave soule than thou canst see
By glimmering of a fancie : doe but come
And there Ile shew thee that illustrious roome
In which thy father Johnson shall be placed
As in a globe of radiant fire, and graced
So he of that high Hyrarchy, where none
But brave soules take illumination
Immediately from heaven.

" An addition of some excellent Poems to those precedent of re-nowned Shakespeare, by other Gentlemen."

Bound at the end of the 1640 edition. See British Museum.

1642. Charles Butler, Vicar of Wotton, in this year produced his 2nd edition, in Latin, of his Rhetorica, Libri Duo. Quorem Prior de Tropis et Figuris, Postirior de Voce et Gestu præcepit : in usuum scholarum postremo recognita, Quibus recens acesserunt de oratoria Libri duo. Lib. I. cap. 13. The 1st edition, London 1629, has not this Shakesperean passage :—"The kinds of rhythm may be distinguished partly by the number of their syllables, partly by the different arrangement of the echoing sounds ; but observation of the best poets teaches these things best.

" Such among us, fit to be compared to Homer, Virgil, Ovid, and others of the better ancient fame, are Sir Philip Sydney, Edmund Spenser, Samuel Daniel, Michael Drayton, Joshuah Sylvester, the naturally serious Francis Quarles, and he whom I name with honour, that divine poet, George Wither, and others now eminent in genius and in skill, of whom this age is most fruitful. To whom is added of the dramatic poets, in no whit inferior to Seneca, Plautus, Terence— the tragi-comic-historic William Shakespeare ; and not a few professing that special art."—LUCY TOULMIN SMITH, trans. edit. Dr. Ingleby's *Centurie of Prayse.*

1641. John Johnson speaks of Shakspere as being read

secretly at night by young people, "The Academy of Love."

1641. Martin Parker in this year writes :

> " All poets, as addition to their fames,
> Have by their works eternized their names,
> As Chaucer, Spenser, and that noble Earl
> Of Surrie thought it the most precious pearle
> That decked his honour to subscribe to what
> His high ingenue ever aimed at.
> Sydney and Shakespeare, Drayton, Withers, and
> Renowned Jonson, glory of our land."

1641. There appears this year a complaint of poor players out of occupation because of the plague—and doubtless, also, Puritan ascendency. This factor in public opinion cannot be ignored in any critical review of the period.

1642. James Shirley, Prologue to *The Sisters.*

> " You see
> What audience we have, what company
> To Shakspere comes, whose mirth did once beguile,
> Dull hours, and buskined, made even sorrow smile,
> So lovely were the wounds that men could say,
> They could endure the bleeding the whole day,
> He has but few friends lately, think of that ! "

1643. Sir Richard Baker's *Chronicle* says :—

"For writers of Plays, and such as had been Players themselves, William Shakspere and Benjamin Jonson have specially left their names recommended to posteritie."

1644. Dugdale in his *Warwickshire :*—" One thing more in relation to this ancient town of Stratford is observable, that it gave birth and sepulture to our late famous poet, Will Shakespeare, whose monument I have inserted in my discourse of the church."

1644. *Mercurius Britannicus,* No. 20, gives an account of the misfortunes befalling a man who edited a Sunday news-

paper :—" Aulicus " is " a wofull spectacle and object of dul-
nesse and tribulation, not to be recovered by the Protestant
or Catholique liquor, either ale or strong beer, or sack or
claret, or hippocras, or muscadine, or rosalpis, which has
been reputed formerly by his grandfather, Ben Jonson, and
his uncle, Shakspere, and his cowzen Germains, Beaumont
and Fletcher, the onely blossoms for the brain, the restora-
tives for the wit, the bathing for the nine muses ; but
none of these are now able either to warm him into a
quibble, or to inflame him into a sparkle of invention, and
all this because he hath prophaned the Sabbath by his
pen."

1644. *Vindex Anglicanus :*—" There is no sort of verse,
either ancient or modern, which we are not able to equal
by imitation.   We have our English Virgil, Seneca, Lucan,
Juvenal, Martial, and Catullus ; in the Earl of Surrey,
Daniel, Jonson, Spenser, Don, Shakespeare, and the glory
of the rest, Sandys and Sydney."—Dr. Furnival's *Collection.*

1644–5. *The great Assises holden in Parnassus by Apollo
and his Assessours*, at which sessions are arraigned the news
papers of the time.

In this one point I must specially notice the peculiar
manner the Baconians have of disobeying their great
master, to seek after " negative instances " of any opinion
one may hold.   They *bring forward* the *title-page* to prove
that Bacon was set high above Shakspere, and only next
Apollo, and therefore the author of the plays, and they
withhold the contents.

Lord Verulam is Chancellor, as fitted his office, and
placed among the learned men, who have also benefited by
the printer's art.   Shakspere is placed among the jurors,
as a *poet* among poets.   Joseph Scaliger, the Censor, tells
Apollo, considering typography :—

> " This instrument of Art is now possest
> By some who have in Art no interest."

L

Apollo sends for Torquato Tasso with troops to bring in all that had defiled the Press with scurrilous pamphlets, to

> " Where Phœbus on his high tribunall sate,
> With his assessours in triumphant state,
> Sage Verulam, *sublimed for science great*,
> As Chancellor, next him had the first seat."

The others were arranged in order of consideration of their learning, and the amount of detraction they had suffered at the hands of the various newspapers of the time. Jonson was made the keeper or jailor. He first brought forth " Mercurius Britannicus." Then the jury was impanelled, twelve good men :—

> " Hee who was called first in all the list,
> George Withers hight, entitled satyrist ;
> Then Cary, May, and Davenant were called forth,
> Renowned poets all and men of worth,
> If wit may passe for worth.   Then Sylvester,
> Sands, Drayton, Beaumont, Fletcher, Massinger,
> Shakespeare and Heywood, poets good and free ;
> Dramatic writers all but the first three.
> These were empanelled all, and, being sworne,
> A just and perfect verdict to returne.   .   .   .
> Then Edmund Spenser, Clerke of the Assize,
> Read the endictment loud, which did comprise
> Matters of scandall and contempt extreme,
> Done 'gainst the Dignity and Diademe
> Of great Apollo, and that legal course
> Which throughout all Parnassus was in force."

The prisoner, Mercurius Britannicus, pleads not guilty, and requests the jurors' names to be read over again, excepting to George Withers on the plea that he himself was " a cruel satyrist." He next tried to set aside two other able jurors, on the plea they were translators :—

> " Deserving Sands and gentle Sylvester."

But Apollo judges that translators can be poets. The next culprit, Mercurius Aulicus, is blamed for bringing in the

exploded doctrine of the Florentine Machiavelli. He objects
to the juror May, because, though a poet, he " cannot trust
his truth." Another prisoner objects to other jurors, but
Apollo quenches him :—

> " He should be tried
> By twelve who were sufficient men and fit,
> Both for integrity and pregnant wit."

Bribery is attempted, but Apollo scorns it, and puts the
briber in prison under " Honest Ben." Another prisoner
objects to Cary for a " luxurious pen " " with foule conceits." The last prisoner objected :—

> " By Histrionicke Poëts to be tryed,
> 'Gainst whom he thus maliciously enveighed.
> Shakspere's a mimicke, Massinger a sot,
> Heywood for Aganippe takes a plot,
> Beaumont and Fletcher make one poët ; they
> Single dare not adventure on a play. . . .
> Thus spake the prisoner, then among the crowd
> Plautus and Terence 'gan to mutter loud,
> And old Menander was but ill-apayd,
> While Aristophanes his wrath bewrayed
> With words opprobrius, for it galled him shrewdly
> To see dramatic poets taxed so lewdly."

Another prisoner, Spye, objects to Drayton. Apollo is
indignant :—

> " How boldly hath this proud traducing Spye
> And his comrades our honest poets checkt,
> Who from the *best* have ever found respect."

There is nothing for Bacon—all for Shakspere here.

1645. Paul Aylward to his deere friend Mr. Henry
Burkhead upon his Tragedy of Cola's Fury or Lirenda's
Miserie :—

> "The fame declines
> Of ne're enough-praised Shakespeare if thy lines
> Come to be published."

1645. Daniel Breedy to the same :—

" Deere frend, since then this peece so well limned
As most would thinke 'twas by Ben Jonson trimmed,
That Shakespeare, Fletcher, and all did combine
To make Lirenda through the Clouds to shine."

1646. S. Shepherd, in *The Times displayed in Six Sestiads*, says :—

" See him whose tragic scean Euripides
Doth equal, and with Sophocles we may
Compare great Shakspere."

1647. George Daniel of Beswick :—

"Though Shakespeare, Story, and Fox legend write " . . .

Again :

"To the Sceane and Act
Read Comicke Shakespeare ; or, if you would give
Praise to a just desert, crowning the stage,
See Beaumont, once the honour of his age "—
(*Poems, Vindication of Poetry*, Dr. Grosart's Collection.)

1647. "'Twixt Jonson's grave and Shakespeare's lighter sound
His muse so steered, that something still was found . . .
Shakespeare to thee was dull, whose best wit lies
I' the Lady's question and the Fool's replies,
Old fashioned wit, which walked from town to town."
(William Cartwright on Fletcher.)

1647. "The flowing compositions of the then-expired Sweet Swan of
Avon—Shakspere."
(James Shirley, *Dedicatory Epistle of Ten Players*,
Beaumont and Fletcher's Works.)

1647. " When Jonson, Shakspere, and thyself did sit
And swayed in the triumvirate of wit,
Yet what from Jonson's oyle and sweat did flow,
Or what more easy nature did bestow
On Shakspere's gentler muse, in thee full-growne,
Their graces doth appeare."
(Sir John Denham on Fletcher.)

Others also connect these names.

1647. James Howell :—

> " Had now grim Ben bin breathing, with what rage,
>   And high swoln fury had Hee lashed this age,
>   Shakespeare with Chapman had grown madd, and torn
>   Their gentle Sock, and lofty Buskins worne —
>   To make their muse welter up to the chin
>   In blood."
>
> (Commendatory verses on Fletcher's Dramas.)

1647. Sir George Buck :—

> " Let Shakespeare, Chapman, and applauded Ben
>   Weare the eternal merit of their pen.
>   Here I am sicke : and were I to choose
>   A mistris co-rival, 'tis Fletcher's muse.
>
> (1st edition Fletcher's Works.)

1648. Wednesday, 27th December. Parliamentary notices : —" The King is pretty merry, and spends much time in reading of sermon-books, and sometimes Shakespeare's and Ben Jonson's plays."

1649. Milton in *Eikonoklastes* also says that " Shakspere was the closet companion of Charles."

1649. As also said J. Cooke, *Appeal to all Rational Men*, on King Charles's trial, " Had King Charles but studied Scripture half so much as Ben Jonson or Shakespeare, he would have learned that Hezekiah," &c.

1649. The epitaph upon his daughter, Mrs. Susanna Hall, shows the estimation of his character by his surviving relatives :—

" Here lyeth ye body of Susanna, wife to John Hall, Gent., ye daughter of William Shakspere, Gent. She deceased ye 11th of July, A.D. 1649, aged 66.

> " Witty above her sexe, but that's not all—
>   Wise to salvation was good Mistress Hall.
>   Something of Shakspere was in that, but this
>   Wholy of Him with whom she's now in blisse.
>   Then, passenger, hast ne'ere a teare
>   To weepe with her, that wept with all?

> That wept, yet set herself to chere
> Them up with comfort's cordiall.
> Her love shall live, her mercy spread
> When thou hast ne'er a tear to shed."

1650.   "Then Petrarch, Sydney, none can move
> Shakespeare out of Adonis' grove ;
> There sullenly he sits ; but these
> Admire thy novel rhapsodies."

Samuel Sheppard to Anthony Davenport.

1650. Also Samuel Sheppard on Davenport's play of *The Pirate :—*

> "Thou rival'st Shakespeare, though thy glory's less."

1651. Again he says, "Shakespeare trod on English earth," &c., and in another dedicatory poem :—

> "Fletcher and Beaumont, who so wrot
> Johnson's fame, was soon forgot,
> Shakespeare no glory was allowed,
> His sun still shrank beneath a cloud."

1651. Samuel Sheppard, in his *Epigrams,* includes one on Shakspere :—

> "1. Sacred Spirit, while thy lyre
>   Echoed o'er the Arcadian plains
> Even Apollo did admire,
>   Orpheus wondered at thy strains.
>
> 3. Who wrote his lines with a sunbeame,
>   More durable than Time or Fate ;
> Others boldly do blaspheme,
>   Like those who seem to preach, but prate.
>
> 4. Thou wert truly priest-elect,
>   Chosen darling to the nine,
> Such a trophy to erect
>   By thy wit and skill divine.
>
> 5. That were all their other glories
>   (Thine excepted) torn away,
> By thine admirable stories
>   Their garments ever shall be gay.

6. Where thy honoured bones do lie,
   As Statius once to Maro's urn,
   Thither every year will I
   Slowly tread and sadly turn."

1651. Jasper Mayne. Prefixed to William Cartwright's
Plays :—

" For thou to nature hadst joined Art and Skill,
  In thee Ben Jonson still held Shakespeare's Quill,
  A quill ruled by sharp judgment, and such laws
  As a well-studied mind and reason draws."

1651. " Shakespeare's Othello, Johnson's Catiline,
         Would lose their lustre, were thy Albovine
         Placed betwixt them."—*From the same.*

1651. William Bell speaks of—

" Heywood's old iron, Shakespeare's Alchemy."

1651. J. S. :—" The true and primary intent of the Trage-
dians and Commedians of old, was to magnify Virtue, and
to depress Vice : And you may observe throughout the
works of incomparable Johnson, excellent Shakespeare, and
elegant Fletcher, &c.—they, (however vituperated by some
streight-laced brethren not capable of their sublimity) aim
at no other end." (An excellent Comedy called *The Prince
of Priggs Revels*, Address to the Reader.)

1652. Jo. Tatham, commendatory verses prefixed to
Richard Brome's *The Merry Beggars :*—

" But Shakespeare, the Plebean Driller, was
  Founder'd in 's Pericles, and must not pass."

1652. *A Hermeticall Banquet, drest by a Spagiricall
Cooke :*—

"Poeta is her minion, to whom she (Eloquentia) resigns the whole
government of her family. Ovid she makes Major Domo ; Homer,
because a merry Greek, Master of the Wine-cellars ; Shakspere,
Butler ; Ben Jonson, Clerk of the Kitchen ; Fenner, his Turnspit ;
and Taylor, his scullion."

1653. Sir Richard Baker's *Chronicles,* another edition :—

> "Richard Burbage and Edward Alleyne—two such actors as no age must ever look to see the like. . . . For writers of plays, and such as had been players themselves, William Shakspere and Benjaman Jonson, have specially left their names recommended to posterity."

1653. Sir Aston Cokaine, Prelude to *Brown's Plays :*—

> "Shakspere (more rich in humours) entertaine
> The crowded Theatres with his happy vaine."

1654. Henry Vaughan's sacred poems say that George Herbert's poems gave the first check to Shakspere, "a most flourishing and advanced wit" of his time. It was the Puritan period.

Henry Vaughan, Silurist, born 1621 ; he wrote poems in 1646 ; published them with preface, September 1654, in which "The First that with any effectual success attempted a diversion of this foul and overflowing stream, was the blessed man Mr. George Herbert, whose holy life and verse gained many pious converts, of whom I am the least, and gave the first check to a most flourishing and admired wit of his times."

George Herbert was born 1593 ; was made public orator, Cambridge, 1619; published poems, previously written, 1633.

1654. Edmund Gayton's pleasant Notes upon Don Quixote alludes to Shakspere and his plays several times ; but clearly says, "Let Englishmen write of their owne wits, their fancies, subjects, disputes, sermons, histories, romances, are as good, vigorous, lasting, and as well worthy reading as any in the world. Our Faery Queene, the Arcadia, Drayton, Beaumont and Fletcher, Shakespeare, Johnson, Randolph, and lastly Gondibert, are of eternal fame."

1655. *The Hectors, or The False Challenge,* a comedy. "*Mrs. Love-wit :* Sometimes to your wife you may read a piece of Shakespeare, Suckling, and Ben Jonson too, if you can understand him."—*Dr. Ingleby (Anonymous).*

1656. Samuel Holland, *Wit and Fancy in a Maze :—*

"Behold Shakspere and Fletcher appeared (bringing with them a strong party) as if they meant to water the bays with bloud, rather than part with their proper right, which indeed Apollo and the Muses had (with much justice) conferred upon them, so that now there is likely to be a trouble in Triplex. . . . Shakspere and Fletcher, surrounded with their life-guard—viz., Gosse, Massinger, Decker, Webster, Suckling, Cartwright, Carew."

1656. Abraham Cowley, in the author's preface to his poems, says, "That many writers have had their works stuffed out by the publishers, as has been done with Shakespeare, Jonson, and many others."

1658. Sir Aston Cokaine to Mr. John Honeyman :— "Lessen the loss of Shakespeare's death by thy successful pen and fortunate phantasie."

1658. In verses to Mr. Clement Fisher of Wincot, accompanying his *Small Poems*, Sir Aston Cokaine says :—

"Shakspere, your Wincot Ale hath much renowned,
That fox'd a beggar so (by chance was founde
Sleeping), that there needed not many a word
To make him to believe he was a Lord ;
But you affirm (and in it seem most eager)
'Twill make a Lord as drunk as any beggar.
Bid Norton brew such Ale as Shakspere fancies
Did put Kit Sly into such Lordly trances,
And let us meet there (for a fit of Gladnesse),
And drink ourselves merry in sober sadness."

Also,

"Now, Stratford-upon-Avon, we would choose
Thy gentle and ingenuous Shakspere Muse. . . .
Our Warwickshire the heart of England is,
As you most evidently have proved by this ;
Having it with more spirit dignified
Than all our English counties are beside."
        To my worthy and learned friend Mr. Dugdale
        upon his *Warwickshire Illustrated.*

1658. Anonymous. To the Readers. Prefixed to five new Playes by Richard Brome :—

"There are a sort who think they lessen this Author's worth when they speak the relation he had to Ben Jonson. We very thankfully embrace the objection, and desire they would name any other Maister that could better teach a man to write a good play. . . . We have here prefixed Ben Jonson's own testimony to his servant our Author; we grant it is (according to Ben's own nature and custome) magisterial enough; and who looks for other, since he said to Shakespeare—'I shall draw envy on thy name' (by writing in his praise), and threw in his face small Latine and less Greek ! "

1658. "To thee compared, our English poets all stop
    An' vail their bonnets, even Shakespeare's Falstop," *i.e.*
    Falstaff.

           (Samuel Anstie's *Naps upon Parnassus*).

1660. Elegie on R. Lovelace :—

   "Where each man's Love and Fancy shall be try'd
    As when great Johnson or brave Shakespeare dyed."

1660. Restoration.

1660. (*Circa.*)   Richard Flecknoe writes :—

"In this time Poets and Actors were in their greatest flourish, Jonson, Shakespear, with Beaumont and Fletcher, their Poets; and Field and Burbidge their actors.

"For playes, Shakspere was one of the first who inverted the Dramatic Stile, from dull History to quick Comedy, . . . upon whom Jonson refined.

"Another said of Shakespeare's writings 'that it was a fine garden but wanted weeding."

"Shakespeare excelled in a natural vein, Fletcher in wit, and Johnson in gravity and ponderousness of style, . . . Comparing him with Shakespeare, you shall see the difference betwixt Nature and Art."

           (*Essays on the English Stage.*)

1660. Sir Richard Baker's *Chronicle of England,* "Whereunto is now added in this 3rd edition, the reign of King Charles I." :—

"Poetry was never more resplendent, nor more graced; wherein Jonson, Silvester, Shakspere, &c., not only excelled their own countrymen, but the whole world beside."

1662. Fuller's *Worthies*, under Warwickshire, has :—

" William Shakspere was born at Stratford-on-Avon in this county ; in whom three eminent poets may seem to be confounded. 1. Martial, in the warlike sound of his surname (whence some conjecture him of a military extraction). Hastivibrans or Shakspere. 2. Ovid, the most natural and witty of all poets. 3. Plautus, who was an exact comedian, yet never any scholar, as our Shakspere (if alive) would confess himself. Add to all these, that though his genius generally was jocular, and inclining him to festivity, yet he could, when so disposed, be solemn and serious, as appears by his tragedies ; so that Heraclitus himself (I mean if secret and unseen) might afford to smile at his comedies, they were so merry ; and Democritus scarce forbear to sigh at his tragedies, they were so mournful. He was an eminent instance of the truth of that rule, *Poeta non fit sed nascitur.* [One is not made, but born a poet.] Indeed, his learning was very little. . . . Nature itself was all the art which was used upon him. Many were the wit combats betwixt him and Ben Jonson, which two I beheld like a Spanish great galleon and an English man-of-war. Master Jonson, like the former, was built far higher in learning, solid but slow in his performances ; Shakspere, like the English man-of-war, lesser in bulk, but lighter in sailing, could turn with all tides, tack about, and take advantage of all winds, by the quickness of his wit and invention." [1]

1648–1679. Diary of Rev. J. Ward, Vicar of Stratford :—" I have heard that Mr. Shakespeare was a natural wit, without any art at all. . . . Shakespeare frequented the plays all his younger time, but in his elder days lived at Stratford, and supplied the stage with two plays every year, and for it had an allowance so large that he spent at the rate of £1000 a year, as I have heard.

" Remember to peruse Shakespeare's Plays and bee versed in them, yt that I may not be ignorant in the matter. . . . Shakespeare, Drayton, and Ben Jonson had a merrie meeting, and itt *seems* drank too hard, for Shakespeare died of a feavour there contracted. . . . Whether Dr. Heylin does

[1]   " What things we have seen
Done at the Mermaid. Heard words that have been
So nimble and so full of subtle flame,
As if that every one from whom they came
Had meant to put his whole soul in a jest."
(Beaumont's " Lines on the Mermaid Tavern.")

well in reckoning up the dramatic poets which have been famous in England, to omit Shakespeare? . . . A letter to my brother to see Mrs. Quiney," *i.e.* Judith Shakespeare.

1661–1663. Pepys' Diary speaks of the revival of Shakspere's Plays.

1663. "Not unlike Falstaffe in Shakespeare."—*Hudibras*, 2nd part, Anonymous.

1664.[1] Another folio edition of Shakspere's works have the same verses attached in different order, and the same portrait as the 1632 one. But it has seven other plays added, said to have been written by Shakspere, namely, *Pericles, The London Prodigall, The History of Thomas Lord Cromwell, Sir John Oldcastle, The Puritan Widow, A Yorkshire Tragedy, Locrine*, all now believed to be spurious. The copy in the British Museum has some early manuscript notes added, which ascribe still other poems to Shakspere, but makes many errors. It also speaks of a quarto edition of the Plays in 1639. It may be interesting to some to have these notes, apparently from the Poetical Register, Historical Account :—

"Mr. William Shakespeare was son of Mr. John Shakespeare, and born on Stratford-on-Avon in 1564. His family, as it appears by the registers and publick writings relating to the town, were of good figure and fashion there, and are mentioned as gentlemen.

"The latter part of his life was spent, as all men of good sense will wish theirs may be, in ease, retirement, and the conversation of his friends. He had the good fortune to gather an estate equal to this occasion, and in that to his wish; and is said to have spent some years before his death at his native place in Stratford. His pleasurable wit, good nature, and most agreeable conversation, engaged him here in the acquaintance and intituled him to the

---

[1] Some copies of the 1664 edition are dated 1663, and do not contain these extra plays, and in some a space is left in the title-page for the portrait.

friendship of the gentlemen of the neighbourhood, who had a true taste of wit and merit, as it had done at London, whilst he attended on the stage. He died Anno Dom. 1616, in the fifty-third year of his age, and was buried on the north side of the Chancel in the great Church of Stratford, where a monument is placed in the wall, representing his statue leaning on a cushion with these inscriptions. . . .

" Besides the plays collected in this volume, I find mentioned *The Two Noble Kinsmen*, by John Fletcher and William Shakespear, imprinted 1634. Mr. Shakspere also wrote the following poems, which, though inferior to his dramatic performances, yet have they numerous beauties. They are :—I. *Venus and Adonis*, dedicated to his great patron the Earl of Southampton, and printed 1602. This poem has been very much admired, and there are a great many very good and incomparable lines in it. II. *Tarquin and Lucrece*, printed 1594. This piece is not so well done as the former one, but it has some admirable lines, such as the following. . . . III. *Mars and Venus*. In this poem is described Vulcan's net, and his securing *Mars and Venus*. . . . IV. *The Amorous Epistle of Paris to Helen.*[1] V. *Helen to Paris*. VI. *The Tale of Cephalus and Procris*.[2] VII. *Achilles' Concealment of his Sex in the Court of Lycomedes*. VIII. *A Lover's Complaint*. IX. *The Passionate Shepherd*. X. *Cupid's Treachery*, and several other miscellaneous poems, particularly on the subject of love."

1664. In General Prologue to her Playes, Lady Margaret Cavendish, Duchess of Newcastle, says :—

" As for Ben Jonson's brain, it was so strong
He could conceive or judge what's right, what's wrong;
His language plain, significant and free,
And in the English tongue the Masterie ;
Yet gentle Shakespeare had a fluent wit,
Although less learning, yet full well he writ ;

[1] Heywood's.   [2] Edwarde's.

For all his Playes were writ by Nature's light,
Which gives his Readers and Spectators sight.
But noble readers, do not think my Playes
Are such as have been writ in former daies,
As Jonson, Shakespeare, Beaumont, Fletcher writ,
Mine want their Learning, Reading, Language, Wit."

1664. Sociable letter by the same, ccxi. cxxiii. clxix.:—
" I wonder how that person you mention in your letter
could either have the conscience or confidence to dispraise
Shakespear's playes as to saye they were made up only
with clownes, fools, watchmen and the like; but to
answer that person, though Shakespear's wit will answer
for himself, I say that it seemes by his judging or censuring, he understands not playes or wit; for to express pro-
perly, rightly, usually and naturally a clown's or fool's
humour, expressions, phrases, garbs, manners, actions,
words and course of life, is as witty, wise, judicious, ingenious and observing, as to write and express the expressions,
phrases, garbs, manners, actions, words, and course of life,
of kings and princes. . . . Shakespear did not want wit to
express to the life all sorts of persons, of what quality, profession, degree, breeding or birth soever; nor did he want
wit to express the divers and different humours or natures
or several passions in mankind; and so well he hath expressed in his playes all sorts of persons as one would think
he had been transformed into every one of those persons
he hath described; and as sometimes one would think he
was really himself the clown or jester he feigns, so one
would think he was also the king and privy counsellor,"
&c., and much more." This letter is interesting as leading
up to Dryden.

With the new folio edition, and with this dawn of inci-
pient criticism, the centenary of the birth of the great dramatist was reached.

While we survey such an extraordinary assemblage of
certificates, which speak of William Shakspere's clear and

incontestable title to the works which have always been
taken by the world to be his, we feel that the authenticity
of *no other poet* could be supported by so many or so powerful public allusions within a period through which he
might have lived. It is a singular *consensus* of opinion on
the part of intelligent and educated persons, many of whom
were contemporaries, and to some of whom the poet was as
perfectly well known as Tennyson or Browning is to the
present age. The attestations are clear and definite. They
all tell one story.

The critical period began with Dryden.

There is one psychological fact deserving notice here.
The love of novelty inherent in human nature makes us
charmed by the new and the contemporary. Things that
grow old as we grow old fade in charm and interest; but
there is a time when the commonplace and stale passes
away from the old, and it becomes invested with a new
charm of romance and historical interest. Because it is
farther away from us, it becomes more purely objective.
Hence the warm contemporary admiration of Shakspere
partially ceased, and he suffered, with other meaner things,
from the changes of fashion and of thought. But at the
time of his centenary he appears in a new aspect, adjusted
by the powers of perspective into his true proportion
among his fellows in the distance. It is judgment rather
than feeling that is now exercised upon his works; more
centuries must elapse before feeling comes once more
justly into play.

Essay on Dramatic Poesie.

John Dryden, 1688. "To begin then with Shakespeare :
he was the man who, of all modern, and perhaps ancient
poets, had the largest and most comprehensive soul. All
the images of Nature were still present to him, and he drew
them not laboriously, but luckily. When he describes anything, you more than see it, you feel it too. Those who

accuse him to have wanted learning give him the greater commendation; he was naturally learned; he needed not the spectacles of books to read Nature; he looked inwards and found her there. I cannot say he is everywhere alike; were he so, I should do him injury to compare him with the greatest of mankind. He is many times flat, insipid; his comick wit degenerating into clenches, his serious swelling into bombast. But he is always great when some great occasion is presented to him: no man can say he ever had a fit subject for his wit, and did not then raise himself as high above the rest of the poets. 'Quantum lenta solent, inter viberna cupressi.'" Yet one may criticise without understanding a poet, without even being able to understand him. Davenant had introduced a new style of heroic plays; Dryden established them, and among their efforts were corrections and alterations of Shakspere's plays.

Dryden says in his Prologue to *Secret Love, or The Maiden Queen* :—

I.

He who writ this, not without pains and thought,
From French and English theatres has brought
The exactest rules by which a play is wrought.

II.

The unities of action, place, and time,
The scenes unbroken, and a mingled chime
Of Johnson's humour with Corneille's rhyme.

Villiers satirises Dryden, and this in his *Rehearsal*, "to ridicule these rhyming mouthing plays" (1672), meaning Dryden in Bayes, who "transverses and transproses," *i.e.* if he finds a good book in prose, turns it into verse, if in verse, turns it into prose, and calls it his own. He also has a table-book. Bayes: "I come into a coffee-house, or some other place where wittie men resort. I make, as if I minded nothing (do you mark?), but as soon as any one speaks, pop I slap it down, and make it my own." Bayes: "Why, sir, when I have anything to invent, I never trouble my head about it, but presently turn o'er this book, and there I have at one view all that Perseus, Montaigne, Seneca's tragedies, Horace, Juvenal, Claudian, Pliny, Plutarch's lives, and the rest, have ever thought upon this subject, and so in a trice, by leaving out a few words, or putting in others of my own, the business is done."

The traditional period begun with Aubrey, in 1680, after criticism had shown that he was worthy of having had traditions.[1] But he was easily imposed upon, and his demands often caused a manufactured supply. Even Aubrey's "traditions," however, support the chief facts to be proved. "This William, being inclined naturally to poetry and acting, came to London, I guess about eighteen years of age ; and was an actor at one of the playhouses, and did act exceedingly well. Now Ben Jonson was never a good actor, but an excellent instructor. He began early to make essaies at dramatique poetry, which

---

[1] Most of the "traditions" arise from him, though a few had arisen earlier through personal idiosyncrasies, as the Davenant scandal—see Halliwell's *Life of Shakespeare*. Though John Aubrey had a good education and intellectual tastes, he was credulous and inexact to an extraordinary degree. Malone said he was a dupe to every gossip. Perhaps a list of his other works best give the qualities of his mind :—

Vol. I. Miscellanies ; Day-Fatality ; Local-Fatality ; Ostenta ; Omens ; Dreams ; Apparitions ; Voices ; Impulses ; Knockings ; Blows Invisible ; Prophecies ; Marvels ; Magic ; Transportation in the Air ; Visions in a Beril or Glass ; Converse with Angels and Spirits ; Corps-Candles in Wales ; Oracles ; Exstacy ; Glances of Love ; Envy ; Second-sighted Persons.

II. A Perambulation of the County of Surrey.

III. 1. The Natural History of Wiltshire.

    2. Architectonica Sacra.

    3. An Apparatus for the Lives of our English and other Mathematical Writers.

    4. An Interpretation of Villare Anglicanum.

    5. The Life of Thomas Hobbes of Malmesbury (his friend).

    6. An Idea of Education of Young Gentlemen.

    7. Designatio de Easton Piers in Com. Wilts. per me (eheu) infortunatum Johannem Aubrey, R. S. Socium.

M

at that time was very lowe, and his playes took well. He
was a handsome, well-shaped man, and very good company,
and of a very ready and pleasant smooth witt."

Several other "traditions" came into existence in 1748;
and another fresh supply arose in connection with the
Ireland forgeries in 1796.

We may then say that the observational period lasted
for a century from the date of his birth; the critical period
began in 1668 with Dryden; the traditional period with
Aubrey in 1680; the elaborative period in our own century; the sceptical outburst in our own decade, *i.e.*, since
1850. We have only here dealt with facts and contemporary witnesses.

We find that Warwickshire and Stratford were considered
honoured for being the birthplace of Shakspere; that he
had come to town to seek his fortune, and laboured faith-
fully and patiently in doing so; was handsome and gifted,
welcomed and loved by the actors; adored by the people,
received by the nobles, and honoured by both sovereigns;[1]
jealously spoken of only by Greene, whose opinion was
worth nothing, by Ben Jonson in his first acquaintance,
who nobly made up for it, and *perhaps* by the jealous author
of *Ratsey's Ghost;* and the sum total of their blame was,
that he had acted the works of others, altered them, improved on them, rivalled them, eclipsed them; economised
in a reckless age, and retired rich. At that time of savage
attacks and gross raillery, no other word was ever said
against Shakspere, whose life *must* have been open to the
Argus-eyed scrutiny of many rivals. Beyond rancour and
above reply, he was called "gentle," "honey-tongued,"
"friendly," "silver-tongued," "noble," "rare," "having no
rayling, but a rayning wit." There would be nothing

---

[1] It is said (1709 edition of his plays) that a letter was written in
his own hand by James I. to Shakspere, and was in the possession of
Sir William Davenant till his death, "as many credible persons now
living can testify."

peculiar in considering so dominant a personality capable of writing poems, had he not been proved to have done so. His wit and conversation made him *reign* in his own circles; his acting powers were great; his literary powers unparalleled. Had this *great cheat* been perpetrated, Ben Jonson *must* have known. Upon what principle could we explain his panegyric to the beloved "departed sweet Swan of Avon," if applied to the "living Lord Keeper of York House, Strand"? Had the Baconians demanded the honour for *Anthony* Bacon, it would not have been so utterly incongruous; for he was dead, yet at the same time obviously a man whose life had not shown the fruits of wit possible to it. Had they demanded it for Raleigh, with any show of authority, it might have been believed, for he was a *poet*. Had they claimed it for Beaumont or Fletcher, or any one of the other drama writers, there might have seemed *some* probability in it; for an actor must have written the plays.

We have to consider further the *psychological improbability that so many men must* have been in the secret, if secret there was; and that *all* should have been able to keep it, not only to keep it even in silence, but to go out of their way to falsify the facts. We hold that truth is more natural to men than untruth; and that a truth depending upon a simple definite fact of *yes* or *no*, would have been sure to have leaked out through some of the many confederates necessary to so great and complex a plot as this must necessarily have been, *had it been.*

Therefore silence is to be held a proof, and not a light one, against the claim for Bacon.

There are *no* contemporary or early suggestions of Bacon's authorship of poems, other than those he claimed.

There are many notices, however, of his high position in oratory and in prose writing, of which the most telling is in Ben Jonson's "Timber or Discoveries," because there he has carefully classified away the *poets illustrated by William Shakespeare;* before describing orators that were

also writers, *such as* Cicero.   He gives Viscount St. Albans
as the illustrative man.   The mere repetition of the phrase
of "insolent Greece and haughty Rome" is a phrase used
for mere rhetorical effect in both places; "filled up all
numbers" here has only to do with "eloquentia," as any
careful student of the following may see.

Ben says, speaking of *De Claris Oratoribus :* "I have
known many excellent men that would speak suddenly, to
the admiration of their hearers, who, upon study and pre-
meditation, have been forsaken by their own wits, and no
way answered their fame; their eloquence was greater
than their reading, and the things they uttered better than
those they knew; their fortune deserved better of them
than their care.   For men of present spirits and of greater
wits than study do please more in the things they invent
than in those they bring.   And I have heard some of them
compelled to speak, out of necessity, that have so infinitely
exceeded themselves, as it was better both for them and
their auditory that they were so surprised, not prepared.
Nor was it safe then to cross them, for their adversary,
their anger, made them more eloquent.   Yet these men I
could not but love and admire, that they returned to their
studies.   They left not diligence (as many do) when their
rashness prospered; for diligence is a great aid, even to
an indifferent wit; when we are not contented with the
examples of our own age, but would know the face of the
former.   Indeed, the more we confer with, the more we
profit, if the persons be chosen.

"*Dominus Verulamius.*—One, though he be excellent and
the chief, is not to be imitated alone : for no imitator ever
grew up to his author; likeness is always on this side
truth.   Yet there happened in my time one noble speaker,
who was full of gravity in his speaking.   His language
(when he could spare or pass by a jest) was nobly censo-
rious.   No man ever spake more neatly, more pressly,
more weightily, or suffered less emptiness, less idleness, in

what he uttered. No member of his speech but consisted of his own graces. His hearers could not cough or look aside from him without loss. He commanded where he spoke, and had his judges angry and pleased at his devotion. No man had their affections more in his power. The fear of every man that heard him was lest he should make an end.

"*Scriptorum Catalogus.*—Cicero is said to be the only wit that the people of Rome had, equalled to their empire. We have had many. . . . Lord Egerton, the Chancellor, a grave and great orator, and best when he was provoked. But his learned and able (though unfortunate) successor is he who hath filled up all numbers, and performed that in our tongue which may be compared or preferred either to insolent Greece or haughty Rome. In short, within his view and about his times were all the wits born that could honour a language or help study. Now things daily fall, wits grow downward and eloquence grows backwards, so that he may be named, and stand as the mark and ἀκμή of our language.

"*De Augmentis Scientiarum,* Julius Cæsar. Lord St. Alban: I have ever observed it to have been the office of a wise patriot among the greatest affairs of state to take care of the commonwealth of learning. For schools they are the seminaries of state, and nothing is worthier the study of a statesman than that part of the republic which we call the advancement of letters. Witness the care of Julius Cæsar, who, in the heat of the civil war, writ his books of analogy, and dedicated them to Tully. This made the late Lord St. Alban entitle his work *Novum Organum,* which, though by the most of superficial men, who cannot get beyond the title of nominals, it is not penetrated nor understood, it really openeth all defects of learning whatsoever, and is a book—

'Qui longum noto scriptori proroget ævum.' " [1]

---

[1] Horat. de Art. Poetica.

Edmund Bolton's *Hypercritica,* reprinted in Hazlewood's *Essays upon English Poets,* 1815.   Printed by Hall, 1722.

" Prime gardens for gathering English according to the true Gage or Standard of the tongue about 15 or 16 years ago." . . . "Most of all, there are Sir Francis Bacon's writings, which have the freshest and most savory form and aptest utterances, that (as I suppose) our tongue can hear.   These, next to his Majesties' own most Royal Style, are the principal *prose writers,* whom out of my present memory, I dare commend for the best garden-plots out of which to gather English Language.

"In *verse* there are Ed. Spenser's Hymns.   I cannot advise the allowance of other his poems, as for practick English, no more than I can do Jeff Chaucer, Lydgate, Pierce Ploughman, or Laureat Skelton."

Then he goes on to treat poets of the modern style, see *ante,* under date 1610.

If, therefore, his contemporaries did not even claim him to be a poet on the strength of the verses he acknowledged, none need claim him as *the poet* of poems he never owned.

Reading has only increased my conviction, not only that Bacon *did not* write the plays, but that he *could not,* and his editor Spedding thought the same.

CHAPTER VI.

THE HISTORY OF THE HERESY.

I HAVE presupposed hitherto that those who read this book must have understood the various doctrines of the heresy, and the history thereof. In case, however, that some may be ignorant of the bases of the various assaults, I shall go through a few of the chief statements. Since they have gained form various people have claimed priority.

Farmer, in 1789, was the first real anti-Shaksperean; and Horace Walpole's *Historic Doubts* have been ranked in the list. But this present contest was really first broached in *The Romance of Yachting*, a novel written in 1848 by Hart, New York.

In August 7, 1852, in *Chambers's Edinburgh Journal*, Mr. Jamieson wrote the anonymous article, " Who wrote Shakespeare ? " and suggested that he " kept a poet." [1]

Miss Delia Bacon's article on the *Philosophy of Shakespeare's Plays Unfolded* appeared in *Putnam's Magazine* for January 1856, and was afterwards reprinted. She held that the poet Shakspere kept was " Bacon," and that he had used these plays to unfold his new philosophy. She

---

[1] " Who wrote Shakespeare ? "—*Chambers's Edinburgh Journal*, Saturday, August 7, 1852. " Thus asks Mrs. Kitty in *High Life Below Stairs ;* to which his Grace, my lord Duke, gravely replies, ' Ben Jonson.' ' Oh, no,' quoth my Lady Bab ; ' Shakespeare was written by one Mr. Finis, for I saw his name at the end of the book.' " Though the author of this article laughs at these errors, he goes hastily through the subject, suggesting that Shakspere *kept a poet;* that when the poet died, the plays ceased to appear ; but Shakspere, as manager, retired rich.

was nevertheless so inconsistent as to dwell over every souvenir of Shakspere; to haunt the places where he had lived; to spend even a night in Stratford Church by his tomb; and to lose her reason in her perplexity. But she suggested the idea in America, where many subsequent writers took it up. Meanwhile in England Mr. William Henry Smith was working at it, and in 1857 he published his book *Bacon and Shakespeare, an Inquiry touching Players, Playhouses, and Playwriters in the days of Elizabeth.* This was said to have convinced Lord Palmerston.

Mr. William D. O'Connor, in a novel entitled *Harrington, a Story of True Love,* published in Boston, U.S., gave his strong support to Miss Delia Bacon's views, 1860.

The Hon. Nathaniel Holmes, called by Mr. Wyman, the bibliographer, "the apostle of Baconianism," in 1866 wrote a substantial book to prove that Bacon wrote the plays, and that he was known to be the author by some of his contemporaries. His *Authorship of Shakespeare,* written in two volumes, has reached the third edition. This is really the text-book of the Baconians proper, and gives all their strong "points." It sifts out a chronological order of production of the plays, and of the several writings of Bacon, and shows there can be no possibility of borrowing; and that the parallel or identical passages are incontestable proofs of Bacon's authorship, especially those in science and philosophy.

It represents much good work with a mistaken idea. It is much the best book on that side, and is certainly interesting to read as a psychological development.

The Australians next became interested in the question; and Dr. William Thompson of Melbourne in 1878 wrote a pamphlet entitled *The Political Purpose of the Renascence Drama: The Key of the Argument;* another in 1880, *Our Renascence Drama, or History made Visible,* in 1881 he added a continuation, *William Shakespeare in Romance and Reality;* in the same year *Bacon and Shakespeare;* and another pamphlet, *Bacon, not Shakespeare, on Vivisection.* In 1882 he published still another pamphlet, *The Political Allegories in the Renascence Drama of Francis Bacon.* In 1883 appeared *A Minute among the Amenities,* which he puts forth as answer to some Shaksperean critics, whom he thought had been severe on him.

Dr. Thompson, in *Bacon and Shakespeare on Vivisection,* says that Bacon was a vivisector; that Harvey caught his idea from him; and that the medicine in the plays agrees with Bacon's views; and that the examination of the murderers of Sir Thomas Overbury had taught Bacon the powers of poison, as shown in *Hamlet* and *King Lear.* He also in *The Renascence Drama* says that the division into five acts and many scenes was an alteration in the plays; that they were all originally written in trilogy, as may be seen by intelligent comparison; that W. H. of the sonnets is William Herbert, afterwards Earl of Pembroke, who supported Bacon twenty years after against the bitter attacks of Southampton in the House of Lords. There is no authority for Shakspere knowing Chapman, though *Troilus and Cressida* is taken from his Homer.

" Camden [1] never mentioned Shakespeare in his Annals; neither did Bacon." But Camden did mention Shakespeare. Bacon also forgot to mention Ben Jonson, Beaumont, Fletcher, and many others.

Meanwhile many short articles appeared on either side; but in his *Shakespearean Myth,* 1881, Mr. Appleton Morgan slightly varied the ground. He says in it that there are three Anti-Shakespearean Theories :—

1. The Delia Bacon, or Junta Theory.

2. The Baconian or Unitary Theory.

3. The New Theory.

It is a little difficult at first to grasp the distinction of the New Theory. He says that " experts have proved that the style of Bacon and Shakespeare are as far apart

[1] See Chap. iv.

as the poles.   Yet that internal evidence preponderates in favour of the Baconians.   The New Theory is, that all the learned parts are by a learned hand, but that Shakespeare put in all the clown business.   The New Theory and the Delia Bacon Theory agree in this, that William Shakespeare was fortunate in the manuscripts brought to him, and grew rich in making plays out of them.   A modern manager does the same.   Our gratitude is due to W. Shakespeare as editor, though not as author of the plays.   *The plays* could not have been popular then; therefore his own plays were of a different and popular class, but his name was at every one's service, and his own real plays are apparently lost. Among all the stage managers, only one, William Shakespeare, was able to retire as a landed gentleman, and purchase an Esquire."   Mr. Morgan has forgotten Alleyn, and the property Burbage at one time owned, and that without the help of *writing* plays.   "Bacon was daily writing under other names, and much of his handwriting is preserved.   None of Shakespeare's is left.   The 'unblotted' copies could only have been the stage parts.   The literature of the country had, up to the date of their appearance, failed to furnish, and has been utterly powerless since to produce, any type, likeness, or formative [1] trace of them. The history for a century on either side of their era discloses no resources upon which levy could have been made for their creation.   The death of the author [2] attracted no contemporary attention, and for many years afterwards the dramas remain unnoticed.   Mr. Manager Shakespeare produced them, but nobody cared to know the author.   To suppose he *wrote* the plays, was to suppose a miracle in London.   Is a Jack-of-all-trades about a theatre the ideal poet, philosopher, and seer?   There is no record of his plays in his will.   Grant that the circulation of the blood was a

---

[1] See Mr. Symonds' antecedent dramatic literature.
[2] See Chap. v.

familiar fact in the days of Shakespeare, that the *Menœ-chmus* of Plautus was translated; that Iago's speech in *Othello* and the stanza of Berni's *Orlando Innamorato* were mere coincidences; or better still, admit that there was an English version of the poem in Shakespeare's day; admit if required that the *Hamlet* of Saxo-Grammaticus had been translated.[1] The Stationers' Company records bear no trace of any such claimant as William Shakespeare."

It is wise occasionally to quote a few passages *in extenso.* Mr. Morgan is fairer than most anti-Shakespeareans. He does grant that though Hervey's "circulation of the blood was discovered in 1619, published 1628, that Servetus had taught it in 1553; Walter Warner spoke of it; Ricardus Columbus and Cisalpinus believed in it many years before Harvey wrote on it." But he does not seem aware that the *Menœchmus* of Plautus *was* translated at least before the play of the *Comedy of Errors;*[2] that the particular idea of Berni's, upon which Iago's speech must have been founded, *was* rendered in Thomas Wilson's *Art of Rhetoric,* which Shakspere more than likely studied at school; that Saxo-Grammaticus[3] *was* translated not only into Danish but into French, and through that into English; and that the

---

[1] See the whole of Chap. v.

[2] June 10, 1594, Thomas Creede entered for his "booke entituled Menæchmi, beinge a pleasant and fine conceeyted Comedye taken out of the most excellent wittie Poet Plautus, chosen purposely from out the rest as being least harmful and most delightful."—*The Stationers' Registers.*

The Comedy of Errors was not played until the end of December same year.

[3] Saxo-Grammaticus in the twelfth century wrote the *History of Denmark,* and in it of Hamblet. Bellforest, a French author, translates the tale, slightly altering it. On an English translation of this romance, called *The History of Hamblet,* Shakspere based his play. It is in black-letter, printed by Richard Bradocke for Thomas Pavier, 1560. Some suppose the modern story satirised modern characters. Burleigh, as old Polonius, gave his son similar advice before he set out on his travels in 1598. Sir Philip Sydney supposed to be the real Hamlet.

Stationers' Company records *do* bear several traces of William Shakspere as a claimant at his own date.

This shows that reasoning upon negatives is not so strong as on affirmatives, as it leaves more room for changing views with extending knowledge.

He says further that "Gravitation is mentioned in *Troilus and Cressida,* though Newton's book came out in 1642, and that in *Hamlet* the philosophy of Giordano Bruno (then Professor of Philosophy in Wittemberg) was taught." But Mr. Morgan forgets that Giordano Bruno was in Oxford, 1583–86, publicly lecturing against Aristotle and in support of the Copernican theory of the earth, which *Bacon disbelieved.*

He asserts that there is "*no proof* that Shakespeare knew Southampton;" yet further on he quotes a letter from Roland White to Sir Robert Sydney, October 11, 1599, saying, "My Lord Southampton and Lord Rutland come not to the Court, the one but very seldom; they pass away the time merely in going to plays every day;" therefore Southampton *must,* at least, have known Shakspere from afar on one side; as the dedications show, Shakspere must have known Southampton to a certain degree on the other. He also reminds us that Wotton, in a letter to Bacon, says that "the burning of the Globe destroyed only a little wood and straw, and a few forsaken cloaks." This, opposed to De Witt's evidence, makes one suspicious of Wotton, whose authority has more than once been proved insufficient. "The gaining arms to Shakespeare involved venality and falsehood in father, son, and two kings-at-arms, and did not escape protest."[1] If this were true, it would not be to the point; but it is not true, and three kings-at-arms would have been involved.

He repeats again, "The New Theory, that *various noblemen* wrote these plays, and that they used Shakespeare's name as a *nom de plume,* and that the printed plays are

[1] See Appendix, Note 9.

totally different from those acted and popular as his. Hemings and Condell only selected 25 out of the 42 plays credited to Shakespeare in life, and added nine *never before heard of.*" "The Shakespeareans take Jonson's verses, but are marvellously afraid to take his prose. Ben does not put Shakespeare among the wits, but among his personal acquaintance. Yet on Jonson's [1] uncorroborated lines they build his fame. Bacon, Raleigh, Matthew never heard of Shakespeare, or would have spoken of him." As Morgan does not confess to be a Baconian, it may be hoped that further reading may induce him to return to the "faith of his fathers."

In 1883 Mrs. Pott published a large volume called *Bacon's Promus of Formularies and Elegancies,* which she edited with voluminous notes, and parallel passages from various authors of the period, chiefly Shakspere, asserting that Bacon wrote his plays at least, if not those of several other dramatists.

The *Promus* had been noticed and condensed in Spedding's edition of Bacon's Life and Works, but Mrs. Pott thought it worthy of being printed *in extenso,* as a specimen of Bacon's literary workshop. It commences in 1594, and goes on for two or three years.

I do not think it proves much. The quotations were evidently not original; indeed most of them can be traced to older dates; and those that cannot, probably arose from remembrance of conversations.

In 1884 Mrs. Pott published a pamphlet called *Thirty-two Reasons for Believing that Bacon wrote Shakespeare.* As these contain the "reasons" of Judge Holmes and other Baconians in a condensed form, I treat them here as illustrating the general question.

I condense her statements :—

1. "That nothing in his life makes it impossible for Bacon to have written the plays."

---

[1] See Chapter v.

II. "That chronological order, dates, and other particulars coincide with facts in the life of Bacon."

III. "The hints given by the author's experiences applicable to Bacon and not to Shakspere."

IV. "That Bacon was a poet."

V. "That Bacon was addicted to the theatre, got up masques, and wrote *The Conference of Pleasure, The Gesta Grayorum, Masque of an Indian Prince.*" No person who *could* write the plays *would* have written these; but I have already said much on this point in the general question.

VI. "The Earls of Southampton and Pembroke are not shown to have any intimacy with Shakspere, but they had with Bacon." The "dedications" would have been all the more impossible to Bacon had they been written to an intimate.

The Baconians make so much use of tradition, that they also should remember the very persistent one that Southampton *gave* Shakspere the money to buy New Place as a present from himself for dedicating his poems to him.

VII. "Many of the wits and poets acknowledged Bacon their chief. For example—

The Great Assises of Parnassus." We have shown in Chap. v. how entirely the interior of this pamphlet, of which the title-page is quoted here, supports Shakspere in his true position as actor and dramatic poet, and leaves Bacon merely as scientist and Lord Chancellor.

VIII. "That Ben Jonson used the same words in addressing both." Only one similar phrase, and I show elsewhere how that might arise. "Ben Jonson does not put Shakspere among the sixteen greatest *wits* of the day." That has been accounted for. "Sir Henry Wotton does not mention him at all." As, however, he also omitted Spenser and other great poets, this is not so surprising.

IX. "That in the time of Bacon's poverty, 1623, Ben Jonson tried to push the sale of Shakspere's works." The conclusion desired does not follow. These were printed by

Isaac Jaggard and Edward Blount, at the charges of W. Jaggard, Ed. Blount, J. Smithweeke, and W. Apsley, and all profits were shared by these, with probably a commission to Ben Jonson, and no share to Bacon.

x. "That Bacon had some connexion with Shakspere." This is, however, only shown by the same clerk scribbling their names on the same sheet of paper in the Northumberland MS., explained in Chap. iv.

xi. "That he uses 'the alphabet,'" and that this means a secret cipher, whereas it really means the "Alphabet of the Sciences." See Chap. vii., and Spedding's *Bacon*.

xii. "That Sir Toby Matthew's letter from abroad adds: *P.S.*—The most prodigious wit that ever I knew of my nation *on this side of the sea* is of your Lordship's name, though he be known by another." This of course refers to his brother, Anthony Bacon; when on his secret-service missions abroad he used an alias. "This side of the sea" excludes the possibility of his meaning Francis Bacon, as Matthew did not meet him there, when in his extreme youth he was abroad. "That Bacon speaks of his inventions, meaning poems." "Invention" he repeatedly uses as the application of imagination to experiment so as to make discoveries.

xiii. "That he called himself a 'concealed poet' to Sir John Davies."[1] Unless it implied that Bacon had written Davies' *Nosce Teipsum* for him, how was Davies to know what he meant? If Bacon wrote Shakspere's plays and spoke of it, he would not be a 'concealed poet.' It really however refers to his parabolical writings. See his definitions of poetry referred to in Chapter iv.

xiv. and xv. "The knowledge in the plays is that of Bacon, as, for instance, in Law and Classics," &c. As Shakspere had a cousin and many friends lawyers; as he lived near the law courts, frequenting the same taverns; as his father had been in an office that required some legal

[1] See Appendix, Note 15.

knowledge; as all people of the period seemed to go through numerous petty litigations; and as most dramatic writers of the time used law phrases freely, it is not unnatural Shakspere should have done so. Shakspere for his classical stories used the translations then so abundant—North's rendering of *Plutarch's Lives,* published by Vautrollier; translations of Ovid and Cicero by the same; *Diana of Montemayor,* translated by Thomas Wilson; *The Menæchmi* of Plautus, translated earlier, and published in 1595; Montaigne's *Essays,* translated by Florio; Baudwin's *Collection of the Sayings of all the Wise,* 1547. Then there were Lilly's *Euphues,* Sidney's *Arcadia,* Greene's plays and novels, with those of Marlowe and others; histories, travels, essays, probably Bacon's among the number.

"Shakspere's library," or the books he has referred to, has been collected by Collier and Hazlitt. But Bacon's *knowledge* is much more extensive and thorough than that of the plays, and of a different nature.

The general science of the plays comes not from Bacon's mind. The flowers of Shakspere are those naturally observed by a poet born amid rich woodland and river scenery, and transported to the suburbs of a large city, where woods were still within walking distance, and where some plants not very common were found by Gerard in the very theatre-field. (See Gerard's *Historie of Plants,* 1597.)

XVI. "That the subjects which engross them are the same."

XVII. "That the observations on character are the same."

XVIII. "That the scientific *errors* are the same." That is very natural, and depends on the advancement of the times; the scientific *knowledge,* however, is different both in kind and in degree.

XIX. "Bacon's studies of any time introduced into plays of the same date;" and

XX. "In several editions of a play, Bacon's increased

knowledge shown in the later editions." There are different
means of accounting for the element of truth that lies in
these ; as well as in the fact that

xxi. " The vocabulary is very much the same."

xxiii. "Baconian ideas and groups of ideas appear in
the plays." I have shown elsewhere, however, that Bacon,
no less than Shakspere, read much and borrowed much.

xxiv. "Mrs. Cowden Clarke's ninety-five points of Shakspere's style common to Bacon."

xxv. " Shakspere grammar of Dr. Abbott serves for
Bacon."

xxvi. " Figures of speech frequently the same."

xxvii. "The Promus notes do not appear in Bacon's
works, but in Shakspere's plays." Very probably they
were taken from them, or from common sources. None of
them were original; but we see that many of the proverbs
and headings *do* appear in Bacon's works and not in Shakspere's : for instance, phrases regarding wine.

xxviii. " Superstitious and religious belief the same."

xxix. " Bacon's favourite authors Shakspere's also." But
we must remember Bacon's age was nearly the same as
Shakspere's, his period, his place of residence, his public,
his sovereign, some of his friends, and many of his circumstances. Is there no resemblance between other two writers
in the same period, or of Dryden's period, or Wordsworth's
period of a similar nature ?

xxx. " Striking *omissions* from the plays fit the character
and circumstances of Bacon. No village experiences, no
brewing, cider-making, or baking." We have shown that
just in these points Bacon was more interested than Shakspere, and more likely to mention them.

" No children are mentioned, therefore the childless
Bacon wrote them." I think Mrs. Pott trips here. Mac-
duff's feeling for his children could only be portrayed by
a father. Constance and Arthur, and other parents and
children appear, and boys are always called "sweet." But

N

the interests of the times were more centred in plays on
adult life, and Shakspere supplied the demand; and though
they enjoyed "children players," these generally performed
plays suitable for adults.

xxxi. "That the folio of 1623 included plays never before
heard of." That is to say, it included plays of which the
criticism by name has not come down to us in some way or
other. But these were very few, only two or three. And
they were preserved and collected by the proprietors of the
theatre to which he sold them; who had no interest in publishing the plays beyond their loving desire to "keep the
memory of their worthy fellow alive," even at the cost of their
copyright. "The folio was published two years after Bacon's
fall, when he was trying to publish everything on account
of poverty and failing health." But how, without a free
confession, could he get his hands into the manuscript chest
of the theatre, so as to select and reconstruct and cipher
the number he wished printed? How did he bribe so many
concerned—proprietors, printers, publishers, poets—Ben
Jonson in particular—not only to tell such wholesale lies,
but to stick to them? What profit could come to him, as
his proportion of the reprint, done at "the charges" of
other men? What cause, other than profit or honour, could
have tempted him so to spend his failing health in toils
that kept him away from the great work of his life?

xxxii. "That the difficulties which have to be explained
away are much less in the case of Bacon than of Shakspere."
I do not agree with this statement, or with any of the
above, or I should not have taken the trouble to write these
pages; and I think careful comparison would convince any
one that any appearance of truth they have is only superficial.

Mrs. Pott's other pamphlet, published in 1885, *Did
Francis Bacon write Shakespeare?* treats the same ideas in a
different way. But I cannot see how any one could consider
them either proofs or reasonings. The first PROOF brought

forward is, "Bacon's mother was a lady; Shakspere's mother, of a peasant family." Though this contrast is quite irrelevant to the subject in hand, genius being of a different sphere from social distinction, one cannot accept it. The family of the Ardens was very far above the rank of peasants; a comfortable well-to-do, well-connected family, farming their own lands,[1] and living in houses very much above the average of the times, having a memory of a higher past, and aspirations towards a higher future, *that could not have entered a peasant's brain.* It is very evident that Mary Arden was at once possessed of powers and charms. She was her father's favourite daughter, and his executor, and was most probably a methodical help-meet for her ambitious but unpractical husband. She lived long, had a handsome family; and if we judge by the traces of her in the female characters of the plays, must have been tender, pure, and noble. A happier and more healthy-minded mother was she certainly, in any case, for a great man, than the learned, ambitious, narrow, masterful Lady Bacon, whose mind preyed on itself until it went crazy.

"It will tax ingenuity to invent any satisfactory explanation of the facts that some of Shakspere's plays appeared during his lifetime without his name, and some did not appear till after his death, supposing William Shakspere to have been the author." The very simple and satisfactory explanation is, that the habits of these days in regard to publication were perfectly different from ours; that it was perfectly common for writers to publish even their own writings without name or signature, and to do so in some editions and not in others; that Shakspere wrote *for the stage,* and therefore for the proprietors, and it was not to their interest to publish; and in his later plays, when his name had been famous some time, were more likely to be more jealously guarded than the earlier. But the pirates were always about, and either put on names or no names

[1] See Appendix, Note 4.

on the title-page, to suit their own convenience.   Printing
and publishing was a difficult business in these days, as we
can see in the Stationers' Records.[1]   "After his retirement,"
the Rev. John Ward, Vicar of Stratford-on-Avon, in 1663
writes that " Shakspere wrote two plays every year for the
stage, for which he was so well paid, he could spend at the
rate of a thousand a year ; " and the Rev. J. Ward knew
Shakspere's daughter Judith.

I believe it was a sense that, being removed from the
sphere of pure poetry by the mercantile impulse towards
them, they fell so far short of his ideas of what they should
be, which prevented his caring to publish them.   Yet his
brain may have been full of plans of correction and publication when he died.   Various other queries and difficulties
are brought forward, all the *important* points of which
have been answered.   The parallelisms only show how well
the industry of Shakspere kept him abreast of the literature of the time.   But we could not go through each
trifling dispute in detail without writing a mighty volume.
Our ignorance of many facts is to be deplored ; but research daily reduces our ignorance.

The revolt against authority and custom of our awakened
and intelligent period, good to a certain degree, sometimes
goes too far.   It often deems the reasons it brings stronger
than the reasons it finds, merely because of bringing them.
It would destroy the carefully guarded, to replace it with
new forms, whose only value lies in novelty.   It should
base itself on Bacon's laws regarding antiquity and novelty,
and it would be at once more valuable and more practical.

Much has been said and proved, contested and disproved,
regarding the authorship of the fourth Gospel.   This attempt at disproving our *fifth* Gospel is another outcome of
the same destructive creed, but I consider that the laws
regarding the authenticity of testimony and credibility of
witnesses can be fully satisfied in this case, and the attack

[1] See Appendix, Note 18.

resisted. The *Daily Telegraph* committed a fallacy in using the question-begging epithet, " *Dethroning Shakspere,*" in the correspondence on this subject, reproduced in book-form. Without doubt, it was an *attempt* to do so. Success requires greater strength than that. The "attempt and not the deed confounds it."

Yet some good comes out of all evil. The good for us in this discussion is, that it sends us back from second-hand traditions and repeated errors, forgeries, misstatements, and misconstructions, to read anew the real authors, and their real friends and foes, in the living reality of time and space contemporary with them. The more one reads of them, the less it seems necessary to answer the Baconian statements ; the answers seem so simple and self-evident.

CHAPTER VII.

BACON'S CIPHER'S.

BACON sometimes, as in *Valerius Terminus*, wrote his doctrines in a purposely abrupt and obscure style, such as would "choose its reader." He did not give his philosophy in a form which "whoso runs may read," and was scornful of "the general reader." But there is not the slightest ground in his works for believing there was a cipher in them. Nay, rather, he apologised for introducing ciphers as a part of learning at all. His connection with Essex, with his brother Anthony, with so many treasonable and state affairs, must have taught him the value of thoroughly understanding the powers of concealment in writing;[1] and we are not surprised he considers ciphers

[1] In the examination of the Lopez treason, in his report Bacon writes: "It was not so safe to use the mediation of Manuel Louys, who had been made privy to the matter as some base carrier of letters; which letters should also be written in a cipher, not of alphabet, but of words, such as mought, if they were opened, import no vehement suspicion. . . . These letters were written obscurely (as was touched) in terms of merchandise; to which obscurity when Ferrera excepted, Lopez answered, they knew his meaning by that which had passed before. . . . Gomez was apprehended at his landing, and about him were found the letters aforesaid, written in jargon or verbal cipher, but yet somewhat suspicious, in these words: 'This bearer will tell you the price in which your pearls are esteemed, and in what resolution we rest about a little musk and amber, which I am determined to buy,' which was confessed to be meant to be deciphered as 'the allowance of pearls,' that they accepted the offer of Lopez to poison the Queen,' and 'the amber and musk' meant the destruction of the Queen's ships, a longer message than the cipher!"

in his general survey of learning. But he gives them no prominence.

In the 6th Book of *De Augmentis*, Chapter i., Bacon treats of ciphers and the method of deciphering. "Communications may either be written by the common alphabet (which is used by everybody), or by a secret or private one agreed upon by particular persons, called ciphers. There are many kinds, simple and mixed, those in two different letters; wheel-ciphers, key-ciphers, word-ciphers, and the like. There may be a double alphabet of significants and non-significants. The three merits of a cipher are: 1st, easy to write; 2nd, safe, or impossible to be deciphered without the key; 3rd, such as not to raise suspicion." "Now for this elusion of inquiry there is a new and useful contrivance for it, which, as I have it by me, why should I set it down among the desiderata, instead of propounding the thing itself? It is this—let a man have two alphabets, one of true letters, the other of non-significants, and let him unfold in them two letters at once, the one carrying the secret, the other such a letter as the writer would have been likely to send. Then if any one be strictly examined as to the cipher, let him offer the alphabet of non-significants for the true letters, and the alphabet of true letters for the non-significants. Thus the examiner will fall upon the exterior letter, which, finding probable, he will not suspect anything of another letter written." He then alludes to his own contrivance in his early youth in Paris (which he gives in full), and is the same as that mentioned in *Every Boy's Book*. "But for avoiding suspicion altogether, I will add another contrivance. The way to do it is thus—first let all the letters of the alphabet be resolved into transpositions of two letters only. For the transposition of two letters through five places will yield 32 differences, much more than 24, which is the number of letters in our alphabet."

Example of an alphabet in two letters :—

A	B	C	D	E	F
aaaaa	aaaab	aaaba	aaabb	aabaa	aabab
G	**H**	**I**	**K**	**L**	**M**
aabba	aabbb	abaaa	abaab	ababa	ababb
N	**O**	**P**	**Q**	**R**	**S**
abbaa	abbab	abbba	abbbb	baaaa	baaab
T	**V**	**W**	**X**	**Y**	**Z**
baaba	baabb	babaa	babab	babba	babbb

"Nor is it a slight thing which is thus by the way
effected. For hence we see how thoughts may be communicated at any distance of place by means of any objects
perceptible either to the eye or ear, provided only those
objects are capable of two differences. It was subject to
this condition that the infolding writing shall contain five
times as many letters as the writing infolded, and no other
condition or restriction is implied.

"When you prepare to write, you must reduce the interior epistle to this literal alphabet. Let the interior
epistle be

F L Y.

EXAMPLE OF REDUCTION.

F	L	Y
aabab	ababa	babba

Have by you at the same time another alphabet in two
forms; I mean one in which each of the letters of the
common alphabet, both capital and small, is exhibited in
two different forms—any forms that you find convenient.
Then take your interior epistle, reduced to the biliteral
shape, and adapt to it, letter by letter, your exterior epistle
in the bi-form character, then write it out. The exterior
epistle is ' Do not go till I come.'

EXAMPLE OF ADAPTATION.

F			L			Y	
aa	bab	ab	aba	b	a	bba
Do	not	go	till	I		come.

"The doctrine of cyphers carries with it another doctrine, which is its relative. This is the doctrine of deciphering, or of detecting ciphers, though one be quite ignorant of the alphabet used or the private understanding between the parties, a thing requiring both labour and ingenuity, and dedicated, as the other likewise is, to the secrets of princes. By skilful precaution indeed it may be made useless, though as things are it is of very great use; for if good and safe ciphers were introduced, there are very many of them which altogether elude and exclude the decipherer, and yet are sufficiently convenient and ready to read and write. But such is the rawness and unskilfulness of secretaries and clerks in the courts of kings, that the greatest matters are commonly trusted to weak and futile ciphers."

In paragraph 202 Bacon speaks of a cipher within a cipher: "You write in a common cipher, with an alphabet of eighteen letters, the cipher being such that the five vowels are used as nulls; then by the last cipher the five vowels are made significant and give the hidden sense." He seems to speak of this as his own. Mr. Ellis's notes to Spedding's *Bacon* say: "The earliest writer on ciphers, except Trithemius, whom he quotes, is John Baptist Porta, whose work *De Occultis Literarum Notis* was reprinted at Strasburg in 1606. The wheel-cipher is described in chapters 7, 8, and 9. The *Ciphra Clavis*, described by Porta, is a cipher of position. The cipher of words is worked at both by Trithemius and Porta. The *Traité des Chiffres, ou secrètes manières d'escrire,* par Blaise de Vigenère, Bourbonnais, Paris 1587, brings forward another cipher. The two authors whom he chiefly mentions are Trithemius and Porta. The key-cipher of which Porta speaks he ascribes to a certain Belasio, who employed it as early as 1549, Porta's book not being published until 1563: "Auquel il a inseré le chiffre sans faire mention dont il le tenoit." Porta's book, he goes on to say, was not "en vente" till 1568. The invention was ascribed to Belasio by the Grand Vicar of St. Peter's at Rome, who was a great scholar in ciphers. Vigenère gives an account of ciphers in which letters are represented by combinations of other letters, which Porta already had done. But he also gives the biliteral alphabet and the combinations above. The transition from this to Bacon's cipher is so easy, that the credit given to him must materially be reduced.

The Baconians have been driven to the desperate attempt of seeking and finding a cipher in the plays to prop up their otherwise unsupported conclusions.

"Tragedy and Comedy are of the same alphabet." Mrs. Pott and other Baconians anxiously taught the existence of one, basing their belief on this phrase that can be read simply enough, if we take it to mean that the same letters and words rearranged differently can tell of woes and death, or mirth and joy. This idea is supported by another sentence written to Sir Toby Matthew (1621). "Set the alphabet in a frame as *you* can very well do. My instauration I reserve for our conference; it sleeps not. Those works of the alphabet are, in my opinion, of less use to you where you are now, than at Paris" (Bacon to Matthew, 93rd). Even if this meant something more, it can be explained from the table of the Greek alphabet, under which Bacon classifies all the branches of his learning and works.

Bacon's "*Alphabet of Nature.*"

Earth . .	Greater masses $\tau \, \tau \, \tau \, \tau$ 67th inquiry.
Water . .	Greater masses $\upsilon \, \upsilon \, \upsilon \, \upsilon$ 68th inquiry.
Air . .	Greater masses $\phi \, \phi \, \phi \, \phi$ 69th inquiry.
Fire . .	Greater masses $\chi \, \chi \, \chi \, \chi$ 70th inquiry.
Heavens .	Greater masses $\psi \, \psi \, \psi \, \psi$ 71st inquiry.
Meteors . .	Greater masses $\omega \, \omega \, \omega \, \omega$ 72nd inquiry.

Conditions of Beings.

Existence and non-existence .	$a \, a \, a \, a$ 73rd inquiry.
Possibility and impossibility .	$\beta \, \beta \, \beta \, \beta$ 74th inquiry.
Much and little . . .	$\gamma \, \gamma \, \gamma \, \gamma$ 75th inquiry.
Durable and transitory . .	$\delta \, \delta \, \delta \, \delta$ 76th inquiry.
Natural and unnatural . .	$\epsilon \, \epsilon \, \epsilon \, \epsilon$ 77th inquiry.
Natural and artificial . .	$s \, s \, s \, s$ 78th inquiry, &c.

"The rule of the alphabet:—The alphabet is constructed
and directed in this manner. The history and experiments
occupy first place . . . Since these are deficient, crucial
instances form designed history . . . In case of any more
subtle experiment, the method is explained . . . Admo-
nitions and cautions likewise interspersed respecting the
fallacies of things. I attach my own observations . . .
Rules and imperfect axioms I set down provisionally . . .
Lastly, I sometimes make attempts at interpretation. For
the sake of clearness and order, some introductions to the
inquiries . . . For use, some reminders concerning practice
are suggested. To rouse human industry, a list of desiderata is proposed. The inquiries are so mixed up that
they fall under different titles . . . Such then is the rule
and plan of the alphabet. May God the Maker, the Pre-
server, the Renewer of the universe, of His love and com-
passion to man, protect and guide this work, both in its
ascent to His glory, and its descent to the good of man,
through His only Son, God with us."—*Spedding's Bacon.*

Complete ciphers have, however, been presented to us,
each supporting the wish of the translator. One point
worthy of consideration is, that *no cipher suggested is drawn
either from Bacon's works or from those of his instructors.*
More than one cipher-reader professes to find a different
cipher under different conditions in the same works, giving
the same chief conclusions, with different accessories.
How many ciphers can the same works enrol at the same
time is a new puzzle, more difficult to solve than the
authorship of Shakspere's plays.

Mrs. C. F. A. Windle, of San Francisco, has one pamphlet addressed to the New Shakspere Society in 1881, and
another to the Trustees of the British Museum in 1882,
*On the Discovery of the Cipher of Francis Bacon, Lord
Verulam, alike in his Prose Writings and the Shakspeare
Dramas, proving that he wrote the latter.* She quotes Bacon
on cipher :—" Writing in the received manner no way

obstructs the pronunciation, but leaves it free. . . . But to prevent all suspicion, we shall annex a cipher of our own which has the highest perfection of a cipher, that of signifying *omnia per omnia.*" Mrs Windle says, "There is not so much as a single line of all Bacon's prose works or letters, as he has, with omniscient security and provision transmitted them, without, as it now appears, its definite design of a final conjoinder with this great resurrection, and its assigned part in the fulfilment and proof of the predestined miracle." She claims Montaigne's *Essays* for him, and also adds:—"I have already hinted my belief that the marvellous psychological phenomenon of his future recognition by another mind was preconceived by Lord Verulam as a part of the value to the world of his anticipated resurrection. It stamps his work with the miracle of prophecy and fulfilment. . . . For myself, it were stupid and soulless in me not to have felt in this revelation, as it has come to me, a direction and inspiration something more than merely natural—a mysterious intercommunication with the spirit of this first of all the departed, as still existent, apart from, no less than in the immortal work, in which it has been mine, as the favoured human agent, to recover him to the world. . . . I feel the deepest responsibility resting on me to fulfil perfectly this duty, devolved on me from the unseen realm ; more especially as I realise that *if left to another the true exposition will never be made.*" One example given is from Cymbeline : "When at the time that a Posthumous fame, borne of a British Lion shall, unconsciously and without seeking, find itself embraced by the tender 'Ariel' of its own Book, *Ah, Rare one !* and when the branches of Bacon's poetry, philosophy, and virtue, which lopped from the stately Cedar of Britain's renown have been dead many years, shall afterwards revive, be jointed to the old stock, and freshly grow, then shall the misery of his delayed recognition terminate, Britain be fortunate and flourish in peace and plenty." " I am assure that the recognition of Bacon's title cannot be much longer delayed."

Mrs. Windle argues strongly against the possibility of a successor.

The *San Francisco Chronicle* of August 20, 1882, criticises her views, and adds : " As the work goes on, even the plays are not adhered to, and Holy Writ and Montaigne's Essays come in for an equal share of explanation. If by this time the value of Mrs. Windle's discovery is not apparent, it will need no further extracts to know that too close an application to a 'startling exemplification in philological science' has wrought its mischief, and unsettled a mind which, with proper use, might have produced something more valuable and less pitiable than a cipher."

In spite of her warning, a successor did appear to Mrs. Windle.

A great contrast to the slender bulk of her cryptogram are the mighty volumes of Mr. Donnelly's great cryptogram :—

" That the cipher is there; that I have found it out; that the narrative given is real, no man can doubt who reads this book to the end."

" A more brain-racking problem was never submitted to the intellect of man."

" I was often reminded of the Western story of the lost traveller whose highway changed into a waggon-road, his waggon-road disappeared in a bridle-path, his bridle-path merged into a cow-path, and his cow-path at last degenerated into a squirrel-track, which ran *up a tree !* "

I quote three of Mr. Donnelly's own sentences, with the *first* of which I disagree.

I have honestly done my duty, and have read the whole of these weighty volumes from beginning to end. There are some chapters in the work that possess interest and value ; for instance, those on the parallelisms and identities in thought, expression, constructions, and errors in Bacon and Shakspere. I respect the industry and perseverance that have led the author through labours equal to those of Hercules, and I only wish that more exactitude, honesty, fairness, learning, and common sense had been added to the industry, so that a book had been produced creditable alike to Mr. Donnelly and his country.

The work divides itself naturally into two parts—the resumé of what is called the Baconian theory proper; and Mr. Donnelly's own special contribution, which he calls the Great Cryptogram, to distinguish it from others. In regard to the general question, I consider that " the great assizes holden in Parnassus " would not permit Mr. Donnelly to be a judge, or even to be a juryman or witness in such a question, because he is—1st, Too violent a partisan. A personal "animus " against Shakspere is shown in every line, in every noun and adjective he flings at him. 2nd. He is illogical in the reasonings he brings to bear on facts. 3rd. He is inconsistent in the adducing of the facts he reasons from. 4th. He sometimes falsifies facts, either through ignorance or selection. He says of Shakspere's editors, "False in one point, false in all." But with, Gratiano, we may thank him for teaching us a word that sometimes so well applies to his work. 5th. The current of his faith in his idea, and of his imagination, carries him away. He was evidently intended to be an original poet.

Fortunately for us, the laws of authenticity of testimony and credibility of witnesses decide that the opinion of the large group of contemporaries who knew Shakspere and Bacon is more valid than that of a man born about 300 years after them, in another hemisphere, even when he is backed by a following of friends who think it would be more congruous to their own thought that Bacon should have written Shakspere.

The previous chapters have shown the weakness of the general case, the real points of difference in character, in the works of the men, and in the testimony for each; but there seem to be some few points worth noticing in this large work.

Mr. Donnelly is a master of bathos. "Here I would remark that it is sorrowful, nay pitiful, nay shameful, to read the fearful abuse which in sewer-rivers has deluged the fair memory of Francis Bacon within the last four months." I think Mr. Donnelly does not believe he is the worst sinner in this respect, nor does he imagine that the sentence might much more naturally be written of the Baconians in their abuse of Shakspere. They have dwelt upon unauthenticated *tradition* (when it is uncomplimentary), misjudged it, garbled it, and set it in opposition to well authenticated *writings*. Truly, as was once said of the Pharisees, "Ye have made the Scriptures of none effect through your tradition." And when Mr. Donnelly does judge from writings, he selects the unsavoury, dwells on them, magnifies them, and clouds therewith his style and reasoning, ignoring all points that tell against him, and attempting to make his readers do the same. What though Stratford was at times "unsavoury"? All towns of the period were and some of a much later date. Erasmus and De Witt speak strongly against the uncleanliness and coarse habits of the nation at the time. Great ladies carried sweet odoured balls "to smell to," when they became aware of the offensive. Can a poet not escape to the woodlands and the primrose banks? And after all, even though the whole question is utterly irrelevant, is open-air drainage more injurious to brain power than a drainage that gives a superficial tidiness and sends the deadly drain-poisoned airs through chink and cranny to suck the life out of body and soul like a vampire bat?

Mr. Donnelly says Shakspere had nearly every vice, and was disgraced in the eyes of men in every way; that he was coarse, vulgar, and ugly; was indeed the original of *Falstaff*, of crooked *Richard*, and of *Caliban!*

"In the greatest age of English literature the greatest

man of his species lives in London for nearly thirty years, and no man takes any note of his presence !" Has he not read Dr. Ingleby's *Centurie of Prayse ?* His superiority to "his fellows" and those who acted and wrote for the stage may be seen by the position he had taken towards them in seven years after his arrival in London.

"Compare the little we know of him, and the much we know of Ben Jonson." The men are different; Jonson is like Bacon, and wishes to let men know about him.

The most original thing that Mr. Donnelly says of him, though he means it as a crowning insult, *might* have been believed. He says: "I have *proved* he was a brewer." "We peep into the kitchen of New Place, Stratford, and we see the occupant brewing beer." Looking back to the early chapter that *proves this*, I find it really must be transcribed as a fine specimen of the style of Mr. Donnelly's "reasonings."

"Shakspere a brewer.

"He carried on brewing in New Place.

"It is very probable the alleged author of *Hamlet* carried on the business of brewing beer in his residence at New Place. He sued Philip Rogers in 1604 for several bushels of 'malt' sold him at various times between March 27 and the end of May of that year, amounting in all to the value of £1, 15s. 10d."

"The business of beer-making was not unusual among his townsmen.

"George Perrye, besides his glover's trade, useth buying and selling of wool and yarn and making of malte."

"Robert Butler, besides his glover's occupation, useth making of malte."

"Rychard Castell, Rother Market, useth his glover's occupation, his wife uttering weeklye by bruying ij strikes of malte."

"Mr. Persons for a long tyme used malting of malte and bruyinge to sell in his house."—(*Old MSS.,* 1595.)

(This is taken from the notes to Mr. Halliwell-Phillips's *Outlines of the Life of Shakespeare*, without the context.)

"Think of the author of *Hamlet* and of *Lear* brewing beer!"

But Mr. Donnelly mistakes. *It* is no *proof*, that he should hold malt, and that other men who held malt brewed beer to sell. Malt was often received as rent, often as tithes. Malting and brewing were carried on in *every* gentleman's house of the kingdom at that time; but the only home in which it is *proved* that the Head of the House *concerned* himself with the manufacture was *Bacon's;* because we have his experiments, written with his own hand.[1] Therefore, if Bacon did write *Hamlet* and *Lear*, we *must* "think of the author of these plays as brewing beer," though we have no authority that Shakspere did. But why should he not? Mortal men do not live the whole twenty-four hours on the Mount of Transfiguration.

"The identities of the question of temperance," I have illustrated as the strongest *contrast* in Chapter iii.

"It is a little surprising that a writer whose sympathies were always with the aristocracy should convert the finest house in Stratford, built by Sir Hugh Clopton, into a Brewery, and employ himself peddling out malt to his neighbours, and sueing them when they did not pay promptly. And taken in connection with the sale of malt, there is another curious fact that throws some light upon the character of the man of the household. In the Chamberlain's account of Stratford we find a charge in 1614 for 'one quart of sack and one quart of clarett wine given to a preacher at the New Place.' What manner of man must he have been who would require the town to pay for the wine he furnished his guests?" It seems to be forgotten that towns often gave handsome gifts to individuals; that in this case the smallness of the gift to the preacher who

---

[1] See Chap. iii.

had pleased them all depended on the knowledge that he had been liberally treated at the best house in the place. The choice of wine was not unusual for a gift.

Mr. Donnelly follows the well-known legal trick classed among the Logical Fallacies—" No case; abuse the plaintiff's attorney, or himself." So he abuses Warwickshire, Stratford,[1] the house where Shakspere was born; forgetful that for the period it was large and substantial enough for a man in a very good position. He abuses his name, his family and himself, and his supporters, in every possible way.

He (Donnelly) tries to suggest vile thoughts of Shakspere, and even that there " was something wrong in the breed," because Shakspere's first child appeared sooner than is usual after marriage. Pope's biography can prove that no explanation of this need be necessary, but we must further remember that the habits of the time were different from ours; that the pre-contract or betrothal had a more binding force than the engagement of our days, and was equivalent to a civil marriage. Surely in times when *the same thing* happened in the cases of Sir Walter Raleigh and Earl Southampton, at older age, without blame or disgrace, there is no need to annihilate a man so young for a fault that he repaired as fully as he could, if there were a fault *at all.* And we must clearly remember there is *no authority* for any suspicion of a further blot on his fair fame through life.

Mr. Donnelly, however, says Shakspere was a " usurer." I think that he was a man who had discovered the uses of adversity, and learned the lessons of experience, and that, seeing that his father had lost his fair chances for himself

---

[1] By the way, this was before he had seen it. When he went down this spring to Stratford, I have it on very good authority that he was surprised at the apparently respectable character of the " Birthplace." Further, he was surprised that the Stratfordians were not more angry with him and his book. One of their seniors mildly said, " It does not affect us in the least."

and family by carelessness in money matters, he had determined the value alike of exactitude and economy.

"He combined with others to oppress the poor, when an
attempt was made to enclose the public lands;" while the
fact remains on record that he opposed and prevented the
enclosures. The only certain utterance of Shakspere that
has come down to us is, "I cannot bear the enclosing of
Welcombe." "He was a mean peasant, and *lied* to beg a
coat of arms for his father."[1] Facts are against Mr. Donnelly here also. Shakspere's honour was unimpeached.
"The author of the plays was a profound scholar and labo-
rious student, and therefore must be Bacon." Most students
differ from Mr. Donnelly in the degree of *profundity* apparent, which would take a volume as large as his own to
contest, and he does not seem to be aware of the character
his fellow-dramatist, Webster, gave Shakspere for his "right
happy and copious industry;" nor of the opportunities he
had for education late in life, even if he had neglected his
school-tasks; nor of the numerous translations of foreign
authorities then extant.

Some questions are asked which all would like to be able
to answer. There are, of course, some extraordinary things
in connexion with him, or Mr. Donnelly would not have
had the chance of writing this book. Five-and-a-half
volumes of the large catalogues of names of books in the
British Museum are occupied by the titles of editions of
Shakspere, or books written about him. The chief difficulty
in studying him is this fact. But we must remember that
fires happened frequently then, and were often on the trail
of Shakspere; that the Globe was burned down in 1613;
that a great fire occurred in Stratford in 1614; that Ben
Jonson was in Stratford-on-Avon in 1616, at the time of
Shakspere's death; that probably he took some of Shakspere's papers to London with him; that Ben Jonson's
papers were destroyed by fire late in the same year. The

[1] Appendix, Note 9.

will of his son-in-law, Dr. Hall, who with his wife was his
residuary legatee in 1635, says: "Concerning my study of
bookes, I leave them to my sonn Nash, to dispose of them
as you see good. As for my manuscripts, I would have
given them to Mr. Boles if he had been here; but forasmuch as he is not here present, you may, son Nash, burn
them, or do with them what you please." Some of these
were original,[1] though some may have been Shakspere's.
There is a tradition that a grand-nephew of his had a large
box of his papers, which were destroyed in the great fire
at Warwick; and there is no doubt that the great fire of
London, 1668, destroyed many homes where many records
of Shakspere would have been preserved.

Mr. Donnelly having annihilated the possibilities of Shakspere having had anything to do with the plays, attempts
to put up Bacon in his place, and supports his case on
Carlyle, who, he says, makes this most significant speech:
"The wisdom displayed in Shakspere was equal in pro-
foundness to the great Lord Bacon's *Novum Organum.*"
Our edition of Carlyle says otherwise: "It is unexampled,
that calm creative perspicacity of Shakspere. . . . *Novum
Organum,* and all the intellect you will find in Bacon, is of
a quite secondary order—earthy, material, poor in comparison with this." [2]

Because Bacon writes a better hand than Shakspere he
was more likely to write the plays.

"The writer of the plays must have been in Scotland."
Bacon is not proved to have gone so far, while Burbage's

---

[1] "Select Observations on English Bodies, or Cures both Empericall
and Historicall performed upon very eminent persons in desperate diseases, first written in Latin by Mr. John Hall, Physician, living at
Stratford-on-Avon, in Warwickshire; where he was very famous, as
also in the counties adjacent, as appears by these Observations drawn
out of severall hundreds of his, as choysest; now put into English for
common benefit by James Cooke, Practitioner in Physick and Chirur-
gery," 1657.
[2] *Heroes and Hero-Worship.*

company played in Edinburgh in 1601, and it is more than probable Shakspere was with them. It is discovered that Ben Jonson uses the same phrase *once* in regard to Bacon and Shakspere. Of Shakspere, in 1623—

> " When thy socks are on
> Leave thee alone for the comparison
> Of all that insolent Greece or haughty Rome."

This phrase impressed Jonson as a good one, and, after the manner of his patron Bacon, he serves it up again *réchauffé* in his *Discoveries* when he placed Bacon among the great *Orators* that treated oratory as an art. It is possible he had thought of Mark Antony's oration when he applied that phrase to Shakspere, and by associated ideas quoted it for Bacon.

" Bacon's imagination is revealed in his works ; " for instance, " For as statues and pictures are dumb histories, so histories are speaking pictures." This, like many others of Mr. Donnelly's, is an unfortunate selection, as it is cribbed from Simonides without any acknowledgment—a common habit of Bacon's.

" Bacon took part in many plays." He wrote some Masques, which nobles played in, but he chiefly concerned himself with the decorative part of the getting up of others. " Why was it the fountain of Shakspere's song closed as soon as Bacon's necessities ended ? " asks Mr. Donnelly. Other Baconians insist that because they kept appearing after Shakspere's death Bacon wrote them.

Mr. Donnelly gives a Syllogism in Camestres to prove Shakspere could not have written the plays, because a lawyer must have done so.

> " The writer of the plays was a lawyer.
> Shakspere was not a lawyer.
> ∴ He did not write the plays."

He says afterwards, " Nothing is more conclusively proved

than that the author of the plays was a lawyer." Surely a logical syllogism, even if perfect in form, goes beyond its duty in proving the material truth of its premises. It is still to be proved that Shakspere was not a lawyer, and that a lawyer wrote the plays. And it strikes others that reasonings are more conclusive when based on true universals than on singulars. This would produce—

> All writers of plays are lawyers.
> No Shaksperes are lawyers.
> ∴ No Shaksperes are writers of plays.

Which, being converted into Celarent in the First Figure, would read—

> No lawyers are Shaksperes.
> All writers of plays are lawyers.
> ∴ No writers of plays are Shaksperes.
> ⤬ ∴ No Shaksperes are writers of plays.

But while we may allow the first premise, we must deny the second; and this syllogism would fall, as Mr. Donnelly's would, on the premises being proved untrue.

"Bacon is naturally given to secretiveness, and seeks a disguise." That may be true. In his *Essay on Truth* he says, "The admixture of a lie doth ever make truth more pleasant."

Mr. Donnelly quotes Mr. Watts, and agrees with him in taking as a support of this view Jonson's lines on Lord Bacon's birthday—

"Thou standst as if a mystery thou didst."

But this is another instance of the unwisdom of taking their authorities without the context. Because any ordinary person reading these lines would see that Jonson, impressed with the dignity of the ancestral home of his friend, addressed the *genius of that home*. It is wise to give it in full, that this may be once for all understood.

LORD BACON'S BIRTHDAY

(HIS SIXTIETH).

Hail, happy genius of this ancient pile !
How comes it all things so about thee smile ?
The fire, the wine, the men ! and in the midst
Thou standst as if some mystery thou didst.
Pardon, I read it in thy face, the day
For whose returns, and many, all these pray,
And so do I. This is the sixtieth year
Since Bacon and thy Lord was born, and here ;
Son to the grave, wise Keeper of the Seal,
Fame and foundation of the English weal.
What then his father was, that since is he.
Now with a title more to the degree ;
England's high Chancellor, the destined heir
In his soft cradle to his father's chair ;
Whose even thread the fates spin round and full
Out of their choicest and their whitest wool.
'Tis a brave cause of joy, let it be known,
For 'twere a narrow gladness, kept thine own.
Give me a deep-crowned bowl, that I may sing
In raising him, the wisdom of my King.

"If he had been known to have written plays and poems,
it would have been dangerous to his worldly success."
Why did poems not hinder the worldly advancement of
other men, Sackville, Spenser, Raleigh, Sir John Davies
even, to whom he wrote begging him to be good to "concealed poets"? I do indeed wonder that Mr. Donnelly did
not claim more for him when he was at it. If Bacon
wrote all his own works, all Shakspere's, all Montaigne's,
all Burton's, all Marlowe's and the minor Dramatists'
productions, all anonymous works (as he demands for him),
surely this sentence might have engulphed those of Sir
John Davies[1] also, who writes a philosophic work and
metrical translation of some Psalms. Mr. Donnelly proves
so much, that the same reasonings would prove much

[1] Appendix, Note 15.

more. "Burton's *Anatomy of Melancholy* is not at all unlike his style, therefore he wrote it." "When it was first attributed to Burton I do not know." The book was signed in the first edition of 1621 at the end; not signed in the second of 1624; in the third of 1628, nor in the fourth of 1632. But that it was *attributed* to him is proved in the "Stationers' Registers of 24° May 1622, when Michael Sparkes entered for his copies, under the hand of Master Knight, Warden, and by consent of Henry Crippes, all the estate that the said Henry Crippes hath in the three copies hereafter mentioned, viz., Burton's *Melancolie*, Goodwin's *Antiquities*, and A Sermon of Peter du Moulin." Mr. Donnelly also forgets that Bacon was a Cambridge man, and that Burton was an Oxford man; that the book was printed at Oxford by Henry Crippes throughout, but was probably sent to London for purposes of publication. He also forgets that Burton gives all his authorities, and discloses the exact range of his reading, which Bacon never does.

Mrs. Windle had suggested that Bacon wrote Montaigne; Mr. Donnelly clings to the idea. "We are brought face to face with this dilemma; either Francis Bacon wrote the *Essays* of Montaigne, or Francis Bacon stole many of his noblest thoughts and the whole scheme of his philosophy from Montaigne." The choice is fair, but there is no dilemma at all. Bacon invariably takes every good thing he finds in his reading, assimilates it, uses it, thanks God and himself for it, and says nothing of the debt to his ignorant public.

"The whole publication of the folio of 1623 is based on a fraudulent statement. . . . False in one thing, false in all." The MSS. of Heming and Condell were probably the playhouse copies, the earlier editions being pirated from eager listeners catching up the occasionally varied acting forms; and, as it is perfectly certain that Shakspere in acting would modify his phrases to his peculiar mood at the time, that quite accounts for the singular variations in the texts. " If the plays are not Shakspere's, then the whole make-up of the folio is a fraud, and the dedication and the introduction are probably both from the pen of Bacon "— which means, in short, if Shakspere wrote the plays, it was a fraud ; if Shakspere did not write the plays, it was a fraud ; but either Shakspere or Bacon wrote the plays, so in either case it was a fraud. Query, would the fraud be nobler if Bacon perpetrated it than if Heming and Condell did ? Would not the falseness affect *Bacon* in this case more radically than the loving-hearted slips of an actor who wished to commemorate his dead poet ?

We now come to the cipher. We cannot but remark the extraordinary manner in which the cipher supports, in a coarse, vulgar, pointless story, in un-Baconian language, the opinions of the Baconian Theory. Yet surely no insult to the dignity and character of Bacon, no insult to his knowledge and style, was ever offered by any one like to this. That HE could have invented and inserted Donnelly's cipher in the plays ! It crowns all.

The conclusions that *might* be drawn from this part are the following :—1st, Mr. Donnelly's, that Bacon wrote the plays and inserted the cipher. No man that had any notion of the dignity of poetry could so degrade it by making it a packhorse to bear a burden of mean prose-gossip. Were that supposition granted, his character would be stained, and he would be considered a liar, a hypocrite, and a plagiarist of no ordinary meanness. For besides all the dishonesty of the publications and dedications of the Folio, he would have to bear the odium of copying Plutarch, Tacitus, &c., and cribbing all other previous play-wrights' works, without having any right to do so. And we must remember that what in Shakspere—actor, manager, playwright as well as poet—was justified and justifiable, in Bacon would be gross plagiarism and contemptible literary robbery, and that Ben Jonson's epigram on *The Poet Ape* must then be applied to Bacon, and thereby intensified, and that his speeches and dedications to the Queen were not mere exaggerations, but hypocritical lies, which I for one do not believe.

2nd, " But another of those luminous intellects (whose existence is a subject of perpetual perplexity to those who reverence God) has made the further suggestion that, granted there is a cipher in the plays, Bacon put it there to cheat Shakspere out of his just rights and honours." There is much to be said in support of this " luminous intellect." If Bacon could crib from Montaigne enough to fix Mr. Donnelly between the two horns of a dilemma, why should he not do more ?   " False in one point, false in all." We thank thee for that word again.   We have seen that he at least borrowed many hints.   And the very cipher which Bacon claims, which suggested to Mr. Donnelly his years of patient labour, was cribbed from Vigenère's volume, and taken possession of *without acknowledgment.* If he stole the cipher, what was there to prevent him stealing the plays, think some.   We do not think so. Bacon only appropriated what he valued, and his own works prove that *he did not value the plays.*

3rd, A third conclusion has come to some, that Mr. Donnelly put there what he found there, or manipulated things to the obscuring of the senses, after the principles of Messrs. Maskelyne and Cooke.   As Mr. Donnelly assures us he did not, we accept his word, though we think it one of the most slipshod ciphers that ever has been found out, and one that Bacon would have been ashamed of.   In no case is any regularity of any method strictly adhered to, and the root-numbers are varied by the reader at will.   A cipher in such conditions is utterly valueless.   Cipher value at any time only lies in the certainty of transmitting exactly the writer's meaning.   But when numbers are used that vary, and when selections are made, sometimes of whole words, sometimes of syllables in words, in which the re-

maining syllables are either counted as a word or not, as
Mr. Donnelly pleases—it is evident that he must do it
intending to find what he did find. Certainly it is more
intricate and ingenious than that of Mrs. Windle, but she
had the advantage of priority, and of making no enthusiastic
pretence to exactitude. The tales she educes are also more
poetically told. Does "one nail not drive out another"
here?

4th, But there is a fourth possibility that I claim as
original. As men used to seek the *Sortes Virgilianœ*, many
have sought the *Sortes Shakspereanœ*. Is it not possible
that what materialists might call chance, fatalists fate, or
superstition-mongers the ministers of the black art, might
have arranged the words so as to have tempted Mr. Donnelly
to find a sequence in the unconnected and a story in chance
words? The style of the Cryptogram narrative is wonderfully like the *Oracular*. That these same powers generally
help a man to spell out what he wants to see is very well
known.

> " Black spirits and white,
> Red spirits and grey,
> Mingle, mingle, mingle,
> You that mingle may."

But the general experience is that the "mingling" is
neither profitable nor pleasant in the long-run. Macbeth
began "to doubt the equivocation of the fiend that lied
like truth," and concluded :—

> " Be these juggling fiends no more believed,
> That palter with us in a double sense ;
> That keep the word of promise to our ear
> And break it to our hope."

Though fiends and faith have alike gone out of fashion,
it is just possible that the "mingling" remains, and that
this is a specimen.

I could find a possible fifth conclusion, but will not
suggest it; so here is a Tetralemma, a more horned animal

even than the Montaigne Dilemma.   The worst of it is,
that each horn buffets somebody—either Bacon, whom we
reverence for what he has really done or been; or Mr.
Donnelly, whom we ought to reverence for what he wanted
to do.   None of them affect Shakspere at all.

Mr. Donnelly says Bacon was the original "Hamlet" and
"Prospero."   "Miranda" is "the Works of Alphabet;"
but that is worked out by the application of Mrs. Windle's
cipher.   Mr. Donnelly's is too intricate to give anything
so simple.   According to his own showing, the intricacies
of the cipher pressed as heavily upon Bacon as on himself.

"The cipher pressed him hard when he wrote such a
sentence as this : 'Thy horse[1] will sooner con an oration'"
(*Troilus and Cressida*, Act ii. sc. 1).   "As there is no
Francisco present or anywhere in the play, this is all
rambling nonsense, and the word is dragged in for a purpose."   "Are there any other plays in the world where
characters appear for an instant, and disappear in this
extraordinary fashion, saying nothing and doing nothing?"
"What was the purpose of this nonsensical scene, which, as
some one has said, is about on the par of a negro-minstrel
show ? . . . It enabled the author to bring in the name of
Francis twenty times in less than a column."   "The com-
plicated exigencies of the cipher compel Bacon to talk
nonsense."   And so Mr. Donnelly is content.   He fancies
that as he proves that the plays are too good to be written
by Shakspere, that Bacon wrote them; but that, at the same
time, they contain much "nonsense,"—a form of literature
specially unlikely to have been written by Bacon.   Be sure
that Mr. Donnelly could not prove that without talking
much nonsense himself.   "Let us examine this.   The

---

[1] I found in reading the old Stationers' Registers an interesting
history of the craft that gives some facts that might lend a double
meaning to this word :—" Every printing-house is called a chapel. . . .
The compositors are called galley-slaves ; and the press-men are jocosely
called *horses*, because of the hard labour they go through all day long."

word Bacon is an unusual word in literary work. . . . I undertake to say that the reader cannot find in any work of prose or poetry, not a biography of Bacon, in that age, or any subsequent age, where no reference was intended to be made to the man Bacon, such another collocation of Nicholas—Bacon—Bacon-fed—Bacons. I challenge the sceptical to undertake the task!" And I, the sceptical, accept the challenge. In *Gammer Gurton's Needle*,[1] printed 1575, Mr. Donnelly will find "Bacons" enough to prove that play written by Queen Elizabeth's little Lord Keeper at the age of thirteen, as his cipher applied to it would bring out the same conclusions.

Gammer Gurton's Needle was acted at Christ's College, Cambridge, before 1575; and though later than Nicholas Udall's *Ralph Roister Doister*, is by many considered the first English Comedy. I give a few selections :—

(First Act. First Scene.)

Diccon. Many a peece of bacon have I had out of their balkes, In roming over the countrie in long and wery walkes. . . . When I saw it booted not, out at doores I hied mee, And caught a slip of bacon, when I saw none spyed mee. Which I intend, not far hence, unless my purpose fayle, Shall serve for a shoeing horne to draw on two pots of ale.

2nd Act. The Song. "Back and side go bare," &c.

Diccon. Well done, by Gog's Malt, well sung and well sayde. . . . *Hodge.* A pestilence light on all ill luck, chad thought yet for all this, Of a morsel of bacon behinde the dore, at worst should not misse, But when I sought a slyp to cut, as I was wont to do— Gog's soul, Diccon, Gyp our cat, had eat the bacon too. (Which bacon Diccon stole, as is declared before.)

---

[1] "A right pithy, pleasant and merrie Comedy, intituled Gammer Gurton's Needle, played on Stage not longe ago in Christes Colledge in Cambridge. Made by Mr. S. Master of Art. Imprented at London, in Fleet street, benethe the Conduit, at the signe of St. John Evangelist, by Thomas Colwell, 1575."

Diccon. Ill luck, quod he? Mary swere it Hodge, this day the
    truth tel.
Thou rose not on thy right side, or els blest thee not wel,
Thy milk slopt up, thy bacon filched, that was too bad luck—Hodge !"

We can also read in Marlowe's *Jew of Malta,* 1594 :—

"Excellent ! He stands as if he were begging of Bacon."

"I am Gluttony ; my parents are all dead, and the devil a penny
have they left me but a small pension ; and that buys me thirty meals
a day and ten bevers, a small trifle to suffice nature. I come of a
Royal Pedigree ; my father was a Gammon of Bacon, and my mother
was a Hogshead of Claret Wine."—Marlowe : *Dr. Faustus,* ii. 2.

In the *Return from Pernassus,* 1597 :—

"*Studiosus.* That I shoulde fare no worse than their owne houshold
servantes did ; have breade and beere and Bacon enoughe, while my
Mistress Mincing Avaritia said, 'There was not suche an house within
forty miles.' "

Thomas Randolph, addressing Ben Jonson, says, 1632 :—

"Ben, do not leave the stage. . . .
    Wilt thou engross thy store
        Of wheat and pour no more,
    Because their BACON-brains have such a taste
        As more delight in mast ? . . ."

Since my first edition I am glad to find that the Rev.
Dr. Nicholson of St. Albans, Leamington, has mathe-
matically refuted the cipher, and proved the truth of the
fourth possibility I suggested regarding it, that "the equivocation of the fiend that lied like truth " need not be held
as the truth. For Dr. Nicholson finds that the same cipher
can be made to prove exactly the opposite facts ; not that
he thereby holds that he has proved the opposite, but that
neither reading nor rendering is worth anything, and that
the result is nil.

The Rev. Dr. Nicholson's little book is named, "No
Cipher in Shakespeare : a Refutation of the Hon. Ignatius
Donnelly's Great Cryptogram." He proves by the abstruse
workings of Mr. Donnelly's own root-numbers and modi-

fiers, that under five variations of modifiers the cipher produces, "Master William Shakspeare writ this play, and was engaged at the Curtain," and "I, William, son to John Shakespeare, got the honour of a herald's coat of arms, on a painted field, for the ancient services of mine house to King Henry, in King Richard's time in Warwickshire." This, then, should be held to be five times as strong. It is important to remark that this Shakespearean cipher is of a more Elizabethan style than Mr. Donnelly's. But of course, on this account, Dr. Nicholson does not prove that Shakspere inserted a cipher in the plays, but simply that there is none at all. The utterly unscientific nature of principle and process is clearly shown on the natural laws of figures, in a way that must *pose* Mr. Donnelly once and for ever. Dr. Nicholson shows how when a key does not fit the lock, it may be filed to fit it, or the wards may be tampered with. And this Mr. Donnelly has done. The words, "Sir, to amiss loose see look upon it as a bold plot," are said to mean " Sir Thomas Lucy," &c.

"Further, Mr. Donnelly gives himself the advantage of counting the words in any one of four different ways to suit his experiment. 1. Omitting both *b* and *h*. 2. Adding both *b* and *h*. 3. Adding *b* only. 4. Adding *h* only." That he may make a new mode of calculation, whenever required, by confounding together two counts of the same series, and forming the topsy-turvy principle. Hence, as the operation is not uniform, it is of no value as a cipher, even to *those who know what to expect.*

Dr. Nicholson's facts are :—

1. There is no key, or at least no reason to choose any of the five keys.

2. There is no fixed way of counting.

3. When each of the five keys have been applied in vain, then the filing must begin.

4. There is no rule to confine any of the modifiers to any particular key-number or root.

5. When the key is modified and converted, there is no rule to apply it to any page or column.
6. By means of these, any story desired can be got.
7. Either by Mr. Donnelly or his contradictors.
8. The law of combinations gives an incalculable number of chances to pick up the words desired.
9. The reservation of a secret master-number is a mere delusion.

Dr. Nicholson also alludes to the discredit it would have been to Bacon to have been associated in any way with the low person evoked by the Cryptogram cipher; and yet, low as he was, the ungrateful Bacon trusted his word, his faith, his silence, though at one time his life hung on the mercy of this player-mask, whose one tell-tale word would have cost Bacon his life, and brought in a rich harvest of reward.

The Cryptogram is indeed like a Frankenstein, which must produce fear and terror in its evoker.

I am truly glad that the Rev. Dr. Nicholson has taken the trouble to review this question as he does. It disposes at once of a strong argument the Baconians have often brought forward. "We would have had an answer given us were there any answer to bring." Now the answer has been brought, and it is sufficient. "False in one point, false in all." Habet!

Mr. Wyman of Cincinnati publishes a Bibliography of the publications on each side of the Bacon-Shakspere question. The bulk of these are in pamphlets, magazines, and newspapers, with the exceptions of the books I have mentioned.

" Bacon *versus* Shakespeare, a Plea for the Defendant," by Thomas King, Montreal, appeared in 1875, in answer to Judge Holmes. He denies the poetic faculty to Bacon, claims the author of the plays as a Warwickshire man, and gives a list of his authorities.

I have not been able to read or find this book, so cannot in any way criticise it.

Another book appeared since the publication of my first edition, and came to my notice after the second edition was in the press, which I have only had time to read—*Is there any Resemblance between Shakespeare and Bacon ?* by Charles F. Steel, an American gentleman. It is an exceedingly interesting and well-written book on the Shaksperean side.

With this I conclude the earnest labours of many months, begun at first simply for the purpose of self-education, afterwards for the purpose of publication. For I found that many had been confused by the specious arguments of the Baconians, in the absence of any answer more permanent than magazine or newspaper articles. For the sake of those chiefly who live too far from the British Museum to be able to verify the facts for themselves, I worked out and published my little book, and have now expanded it. A few have thought lightly of the need, and have suggested that I am merely "slaying the thrice slain." These should remember that Antæus regained life each time he touched his mother-earth. I am attempting to remove the question from its mother-earth in not leaving it " a place whereon to stand." The true philosophic spirit teaches us to " prove all things ; " so that it may be wise at times to pause and review even our most cherished beliefs ; but it also teaches us to believe those facts that satisfy the nature and needs of proof ; and such a proved fact I believe this to be—that Shakspere wrote the plays and poems that have always been attributed to him.

> " Our Shakespeare wrote, too, in an age as blest,
> The happiest poet of his time and best ;
> A gracious Prince's favour cheered his Muse,
> A constant favour he ne'er feared to lose.
> Therefore he wrote with fancy unconfined,
> And thoughts that were immortal as his mind ;
> And from the crop of his luxuriant pen
> E'er since succeeding poets humbly glean."
> (*The History and Fall of Caius Marius,*
> Otway, 1680.)

P

APPENDIX.

—••—

NOTE I.—WARWICKSHIRE.

IN Becon's *Jewell of Joye*, published 1560, dedicated to Elizabeth, he makes Philemon, Eusebius, Theophile, and Christopher talk together of the religious state of the kingdom. Philemon, who is evidently Becon himself, had been driven from town by persecutions of enemies. He first travelled into Derbyshire, where, at the Peak, he met one Christian gentleman, which he and his friends considered marvellous in so barbarous a region. Philemon went next to Stafford, Leicestershire, and Warwickshire, supporting himself everywhere he went by teaching. His testimony is important:—"I departed into Warwykeshere, where in lyke manner as afore I frelye enjoyed the lyberallytie of my most swete and deare frende John Olde, whych, impelled by urgent causes, departed into that country for to inhabite. There lykewise taught I divers gentlemen's sonnes, whyche I truste, if they live, shall be a beautie to the publique weale of England, both for the preferment of true religion, and for the mayntenance of justice.

Euse. Howe fancied you that countrye?

Phile. I travelled boeth in Darbyeshire in the Peke, in Staffordshire, and in Lecestershere; yet Warwykeshere was to me most dere and pleasant.

Chris. Howe so?

Phile. In Lecestershire (as I may pass over the other) I had familyarite only wyth one learned man, a countryman of oures called John Aylmer, a master of arte of the Universitie of Cambridge, but Warwykeshere mynistred unto me the acqueytaunce and frendshyppe of many learned men.

Chris. What are theyr names, I prey you?

Phile. Firste commeth to my remembrance a man worthy to be loved and reverenced of all Chrystene menne, not only for the puernes of hys lyfe, whyche hath alwayes before the world been innocent and blameles, but also for the synceritie and godlynes of hys Evangelique doctrine, whyche since the beginning of his preaching hath in all poyntes been so conformable to the teaching of Christe . . . Maister Latimer . . . sometime Bishop of Worcester." Philemon had been a child of 16 at Cambridge when he heard his sermons there, showing that the Scriptures ought to be read to the people. "With this true preacher of God's word I chaunced in Warwykeshire to be somewhat acquainted (which was to me of no small comforte), not with him only, but with divers others, whereof some were men of worship wel bente towards the Holy Scriptures, some were men very godly learned in the laws of the Most Highest, and professoures of ye same. So oft as I was in their companye, me thoughte I was clean delivered from Egypte and quietly placed in the newe gloriouse Jerusalem, which is descrybed in the revelacion of blessed John, so swete a thing is it to be in the company of godly learned men.

Euse. Travelled you into none other countrey afterwarde?

Phile. While I was trayning up of youth, and fashionyng their minds unto true godlynesse in this countreye, beholde, unlooked for, were letters sent unto me from my moste deare mother, in the whych she requyred me to returne into my native countrey, and to be a staffe of her old age, forasmuch as my father-in-lawe was departed from thys vale of myserye. In consyderyng my duetye, and the honoure whych I owe unto her by the manifeste commandemente of God, immediatelye after, not wythoute the frendly consente of my wel wyllers departed from Warwikeshere, and with all haste repaired home."

As to its warlike tendencies, even at other times than "The King Maker's," we read much. In Drayton's *Polyolbion*, Book xiii., there appears—

" Brave Warwick, that abroad so long advanced her ' Bear,'
By her illustrious earls renownèd everywhere,
Above her neighbouring shires which always bore her head."

In Fuller's *Worthies*, written some time before being printed by his son in 1662, he speaks of the various counties and their distinguished men.

His notice of Shakspere appears in Chapter v.

He says that John Rous died in 1491, who had been born in Warwick, educated at Oxford, and had retired to write his *Antiquities* to Guy's Cliff, near Warwick. " A most delicious place, so that a man in many miles' riding cannot meet so much variety as one furlong doth afford. A steep rock full of caves, in the Bowels thereof washed at the bottom with a Christall River, besides so many clear springs on the side thereof, all overshadowed with a stately grove, so that an ordinary Fancy may here find to itself Helicon, Parnassus, and what not ? " . . .

" Michael Drayton was born at Athelstan, within a few miles of William Shakespeare, his countryman, and buried within a fewer paces of Jeoffrey Chaucer and Edmund Spenser in Westminster Abbey."

He says in Song 13, p. 213 :—

> " My native country,
> If there be virtue yet remaining in thy earth,
> Or any good of thine thou breathest into my birth,
> Accept it as thine own, while now I sing of thee,
> Of all thy later brood th' unworthiest though I be."

Dugdale, author of the *Antiquities of Warwick*, was also a Warwickshire man.

NOTE 2.—STRATFORD.

The division between Arden and Feldon, by the Avon, in the county of Warwick, is well expressed by Shakspere in *King Lear*. Stratford had been called so from being the " ford " on the great street from Henley-in-Arden to London. Three hundred years before the Conquest, Stratford was a lordship belonging to the bishopric of Worcester. Two hundred years before the Conquest it had a bishop of its own. Early in the sixteenth century it had come into the possession of the Earls of Warwick, and was incorporated in 1553. Sir Hugh Clopton had built a handsome bridge, which brought much trade to the town. It had a yearly fair, lasting three days, and dedicated to the Holy Trinity. The Rother Market, or cattle-market, was an important feature in Stratford life, as most of the wealthier families engaged in farming. Speede's County Map of England was published in 1610. An order is extant, dated 1607, requesting all gentlemen and other residents in the county to assist him in his work. He draws the relative size and importance of the towns and villages by a condensed little group of buildings ; and in spite of scorn thrown now at " the peasant village of Stratford," it is sketched the same size as Warwick, and second only to Coventry in the county.

The parish of old Stratford was fifteen miles in circumference, and included Shottery, Clopton, Little Wilmcote, &c. It had a Holy Guild, the history of which can be found in Dugdale and French ; their " College " had been well endowed, and up to 1535 supported four priests at £5, 6s. 8d., and a schoolmaster at £10 salary ; so education was then honoured. At the dissolution of "the Holy

Guild " the town received the possessions together with the great tithes, to maintain a vicar, a curate, and a schoolmaster, to pay the almspeople, and repair the chapel, bridge, and other public buildings. Half of these tithes Shakspere bought at the suggestion of Abraham Sturley.

The Grammar-school had been founded by the Rev. Mr. Jolyffe in Henry VI.'s reign, but had got into difficulties in the reign of Henry VIII., which may account for the poor education of Shakspere's father. But the charter of Edward VI. guaranteed the schoolmaster an annual stipend of £20 a year and a free house, at a time when £10 was the ordinary salary. Thomas Hunt was the schoolmaster in Shakspere's time.

The disputes among the stationers of the time show that school-books were the most profitable patents at that time, and that in one case Roger Ward had infringed Day's patent "by printing 10,000 copies of the A B C, with the little Catechism appointed by her Highness' injunction for the instruction of children, with the patentee's name and trade-mark thereon, and sent them down to sell in the country." Professor Baynes gives the list of the books ordinarily used at the time in grammar-schools. For young children there were this A B C, Catechism, Psalter, New Testament, and Book of Common Prayer, in English.

The 1st form had the Accidence and Sententiæ Pueriles.

2nd. Lily's Grammar, Cato's Maxims, Pueriles Confabulatiunculæ, Colloquies of Corderius.

3rd. Grammar, Latin Testament, Æsop's Fables, Dialogues of Castilio and Eclogues of Mantuanus, Colloquies of Helvicus.

4th. Testament, Grammar, Elements of Rhetoric, Terence, Selected Epistles of Cicero, Ovid's de Tristibus and Metamorphoses, and Buchanan s Psalms.

5th. In addition to Rhetoric, Livy's Orations, Justin, Cæsar, Florus, Colloquies of Erasmus, and Virgil.

6th. Horace, Juvenal, Persius, Lucan, Plautus, Martial, Cicero's Orations, and Seneca's Tragedies.

A record of these as the usual books was drawn up by the Free Grammar-School of St. Bees in Cumberland in 1583.

Brinsley, headmaster of Ashby-de-la-Zouche, 1612, and Charles Hoole (born 1610), describe the master's method. Hoole suggests Butler's Rhetorick or Talaeus's Rhetorick, " Let them repeat part of the Elementa Rhetorica every Thursday." Alciat's Emblem-book was much used, and many schoolmasters preferred the Eclogues of Baptista Mantuanus to Virgil. It had many editions and one translation by Shakspere's time. He makes Holofernes speak of them (*Love's Labour's Lost*). In the *Taming of the Shrew* the heroic epistle from Penelope to Ulysses from Ovid is construed. " Titania " is taken from Ovid, meaning one of the Titans ; also Autolycus, as a name, comes direct from Ovid. A study of Professor Baynes' interesting articles suggests how much Latin and Greek the poet ought to have known, to have induced Ben Jonson's relative judgment of him.

The Rev. Mr. Ward was made Vicar of Stratford in 1662, and he states that fever prevailed much after the stream of Avon overflowed its banks—probably a low typhoid form, which prostrated Shakspere.

NOTE 3.—JOHN SHAKSPERE.

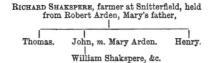

RICHARD SHAKSPERE, farmer at Snitterfield, held from Robert Arden, Mary's father,

Thomas. John, *m.* Mary Arden. Henry.

William Shakspere, &c.

The immediate family of Richard has not been distinguished. Many of the name of Shakspere are found on the list of the brothers and sisters of the Guild of St. Anna at Knoll, from 1407 till the dissolution of the fraternity in 1535, and these have the common names of the family — Joan, Thomas, Richard, Isabella, Alice, William.

Dugdale (ed. 1656) said "that a multitude of persons, whereof most were of good quality, nay, some of the great nobility in those days, had admittance of this guild."

In 28 Henry VIII., 1537, Thomas, Richard, and William Shakspere were mentioned as in the King's service; but the definite relationship has not yet been discovered.

Application for his coat of arms states that his antecessors rendered valiant service to Henry VII., probably at Bosworth.

But in Stratford, where John came in 1551, his own tenements, his wife's property, and his own capabilities, soon after his settlement, let him take a leading place in its life, until the losses in Shakspere's youth made him keep from going either to the Halls or the Church. He was elected Ale-taster, 1557; Constable, 1558; Chamberlain, 1560; Alderman, 1565; High Bailiff, 1568; Chief Alderman, 1571 till 1586.

NOTE 4.—MARY ARDEN.

It is well to remember the various family connections.

APPENDIX.

TABLE OF MARY ARDEN'S FAMILY.

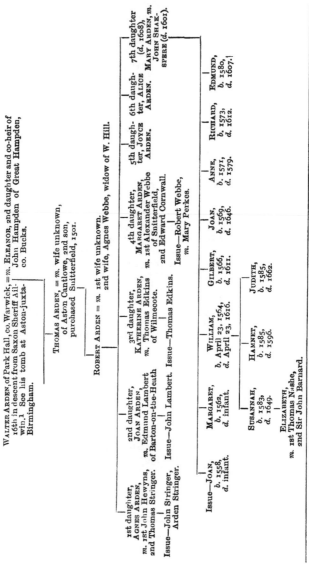

WALTER ARDEN, of Park Hall, co. Warwick, = m. ELEANOR, 2nd daughter and co-heir of 16th in descent from Saxon Sheriff Ail- John Hampden of Great Hampden, win.[1] See his tomb at Aston-juxta- co. Bucks. Birmingham.

THOMAS ARDEN, = m. wife unknown, of Aston Cantlowe, 2nd son, purchased Suitterfield, 1501.

ROBERT ARDEN = m. 1st wife unknown. 2nd wife, Agnes Webbe, widow of W. Hill.

1st daughter, AGNES ARDEN, m. 1st John Hewyns, and Thomas Stringer.
Issue—John Stringer, Arden Stringer.

2nd daughter, JOAN ARDEN, m. Edmund Lambert of Barton-on-the-Heath.
Issue—John Lambert.

3rd daughter, KATHERINE ARDEN, m. Thomas Edkins of Wilmecote.
Issue—Thomas Edkins.

4th daughter, MARGARET ARDEN, m. 1st Alexander Webbe of Snitterfield, 2nd Edward Cornwall.
Issue—Robert Webbe, m. Mary Perkes.

5th daugh-ter, JOYCE ARDEN.

6th daugh-ter, ALICE ARDEN.

7th daughter (d. 1608), MARY ARDEN, m. JOHN SHAK-SPERE (d. 1601).

Issue—JOAN, b. 1558, d. infant.

MARGARET, b. 1562, d. infant.

WILLIAM, b. April 23, 1564, d. April 23, 1616.

GILBERT, b. 1566, d. 1611.

JOAN, b. 1569, d. 1646.

ANNE, b. 1571, d. 1579.

RICHARD, b. 1573, d. 1612.

EDMUND, b. 1580, d. 1607.

SUSANNAH, b. 1583, d. 1649.

HAMNET, b. 1585, d. 1596.

JUDITH, b. 1585, d. 1662.

ELIZABETH, m. 1st Thomas Nashe, 2nd Sir John Barnard.

1 Reynburn was the son of Guy of Warwick mentioned in the tale. In the 5th generation from him is the Saxon Sheriff Ailwin, father of Turchill, titular Earl of Warwick, who on the Norman Conquest first took the name of De Arden.

In Drummond's *Noble British Families* it is noted "that there are few families in Europe, and fewer still in Britain, that can boast of a descent in uninterrupted male line so antient as this of Arden."

In Robert Arden's will Mary is mentioned first, and is to receive £6, 13s. 4d. before anything else is divided. This was probably money for wedding-clothes, already allowed to her married sisters. She was also to receive all the land at Wilmecote called Asbies. The property was to be divided into seven parts; but as Mary had the sixth part of the interest in Snitterfield, it is probable that her sister Joyce had died, as there is no future mention of her. Alice and Mary are made executors of the will, in preference to their stepmother and married sisters. Everything points to Mary being the most capable of the family. As there is no further mention of Alice, it is probable that Mary also inherited her share, as some papers show her to have been possessed of another property at Aston Cantlowe.

To his wife Robert Arden also left £6, 13s. 4d. if she allowed his daughter Ales to enjoy half his copyhold in Wilmecote during the time of her widowhood; and if she did not, then she was to have nothing but her jointure in Snitterfield. This stepmother married Robert Arden in 1550; he died shortly after.

She died in 1580, and her will was proved 1581. She left nothing to any of the Ardens, but Snitterfield reverted to them, though the rights in it had been bought up by the Webbes. The half-copyhold in Wilmecote also probably reverted to the family—apparently to Mary through Alice, as by some deeds she is shown to have been possessed of another property in Aston Cantlowe, also sacrificed to meet her husband's pressing wants.—French's *Genealogica Shakespeareana.*

Note 5.—Asbies and Snitterfield.

In 1579 Mary Shakspere and her husband sold the reversion of the share in Snitterfield which would have come to her on the death of her stepmother. This was bought by Robert Webbe, to which family the stepmother belonged, and it was the sixth, not the seventh part.

The property of Asbies in Wilmecote had been mortgaged to Lambert, Mary's brother-in-law, or rather John and Mary Shakspere had borrowed £40 on it from him. He had drawn the income of it for three or four years, and they offered to pay back the £40 and free it. He refused to do this until other sums due to him from John Shakspere were paid. Apparently he had the title-deeds, and refused to part with them; though it is evident there was some wrong somewhere. Mary's sixth *share* of Snitterfield, which (as a whole) was of less value than Asbies, sold for £40. They agreed in 1587 to lend them £20 more on it.

When Shakspere made some money, his first effort, in 1597, was to regain possession of Asbies, proved by a case heard before Sir Thomas Egerton; but apparently the arrangements had been too loose and verbal; his uncle had died; his cousin was in possession; and we hear no more of Asbies, or even of a decree. See French's *Genealogica Shakespeareana.*

NOTE 6.—THEATRES OF LONDON.

" Early in Elizabeth's reign, the established players of London began to act in temporary theatres in the yards of inns."

In the time of Shakspere were seven theatres; three private houses—viz., Blackfriars, Whitefriars, the Cockpit or Phœnix in Drury Lane; and four public theatres. The Globe on the Bank Side; the Curtain in Shoreditch; the Red Bull at the upper end of St. John Street; and the Fortune in Whitecross Street (Waldron's *Shaksperean Miscellany*).

It is the fashion to decry these theatres as rude, after Sir Henry Wotton's manner, but the papers of De Witt, who had visited London in 1596, say that by that time they were the finest he had seen; that they were able to accommodate 3000 spectators, and he gives particulars of their decoration. He mentions the *Rose* theatre, the *Globe,* and the *Swan,* the *Theatre* founded 1576, and the *Curtain,* 1577, north of Bishopsgate. The drawing of the Swan is circular, in three tiers; the upper called Porticus; the second, Sedilia; the third, Orchestra; the Mimorum Aedes, behind the stage; and the whole "planetries sive arena" open. "Ex observationibus Londinensibus Johannis de Witt. Nach einer in Utrecht befindlichen Handzeichnung vom Jahre 1596, edited by Karl Theodor Gaedertz." The effect of theatrical performance on habits and education is well illustrated in Dekkar's *Gul's Hornbook,* 1609.

Chap. vi. shows "How a young gallant should behave himself in a play-house."

"The theatre is your Poet's Royal Exchange, on which their muses (they are now turned to merchants) meeting, barter away that light commodity of words, for a lighter ware than words, Plaudities and the Breath of the Great Beast, which (like the threatening of two cowards), vanish all into the aire. Seat yourself on the very rushes where the Commedy is to dance. For do but cast up a reckoning what large commings in are pursed up by sitting on the stage, first a conspicuous eminence is gotten, by which means the best and most essentiall parts of a gallant (good cloaths and a proportionable legge, white hands, the Persian lock, and a tolerable beard) are perfectly revealed. By sitting on the stage you have a signed patent to engross the whole commodity of censure, may lawfully presume to be a girder, stand at the helme to steere the passage of scenes, yet no man shall once offer to hinder you from obtaining the title of an insolent over-weening coxcombe.

" By sitting on the stage you may (without travelling for it) at the very next doore aske whose play it is ; and by that Quest of Inquiry, the Law warrants you to avoid much mistaking : if you know not ye Author, you may raile against him ; and peradventure so behave yourselfe, that you may enforce the Author to know you. . . . By spreading your body on the stage, and by being a Justice in examining of plaies, you shall put yourselfe into such true scænical authority, that some Poet shall not dare to present his Muse rudely upon your eyes, without having first unmaskt her, rifled her, and discovered all her bare and most mysticall parts before you at a taverne, when you most Knightly shall for his paines pay for both the suppers.

" By sitting on the stage you may (with small cost) purchase the deere acquaintance of the boyes ; have a good stool for sixpence ; at any time know what particular part any of the infants present ; get your match lighted, examine the play-suits lace, and perhaps win wagers upon laying 'tis copper, &c. And to conclude, of what stamp soever you be, current or counterfeit, the Stage, like time, will bring you to most perfect light, and lay you open : neither are you to be hunted from thence, though the scarecrows in the yard hoot at you, hisse at you, spit at you, yea, throw dust even in your teeth : 'tis most gentlemanlike patience to endure all this, and to laugh at the silly animals : but if the Rabble, with a full throat cry, Away with the foole, you were worse than a madman to tarry by it ; for the gentleman and the fool should never sit on the stage.

" Present not yourself on the Stage (especially at a new Play) until the quaking Prologue hath (by rubbing) got culor into his cheekes, and is ready to give the trumpets their Cue, that hees upon point to enter : for then it is time, as though you were one of the *properties*, or that you dropt out of the hangings, to creepe from behind the Arras, with your Tripos or three-footed stoole in one hand, and a Teston mounted betweene a forefinger and a thumbe in the other ; for if you should bestowe your person upon the vulgar when the house is but half-fulle, your apparell is quite eaten up, the fashion lost, and the proportion of your body in more danger

to be devoured than if it were served up in the Counter amongst
the Poultry: avoid that as you would the Bastome. It shall
crown you with rich commendation, to laugh aloud in the
middest of the most serious and saddest scene of the terriblest
Tragedy ; and to let that clapper (your tongue) be tost so high that
all the House may ring of it : your Lords use it : your Knights are apes
to the Lords, and do so too ; your Inne-a-court-man is Zany to the
Knights, and (mary very scurvily) comes likewise limping after it ;
bee thou a beagle to them all, and never lieve snuffing till you have
scented them ; for by talking and laughing (like a ploughman in a
Morris) you heap Pelion upon Ossa, glory upon glory : As first, all
the eyes in the galleries will leave walking after the Players and
onely follow you ; the simplest dolt in the house snatches up your
name, and when he meetes you in the streete, or that you fall into
his hands in the middle of a watch, his word shall be taken for you:
heele cry, *Hees such a gallant*, and you passe. Secondly, you publish
your temperance to the world, in that you seeme not to resort thither
to taste vaine pleasures with a hungry appetite ; but onely as a
Gentleman to spende a foolish houre or two, because you can doe
nothing else. Thirdly, you mightily disrelish the Audience, and
disgrace the Author. Marry, you take up (though it be at the worst
hand) a strong opinion of your owne judgment, and inforce the
Poet to take pity of your weaknesse, and by some dedicated sonnet,
to bring you into a better paradice, onely to stop your mouth. Provide yourselfe a lodging by the Waterside ; . . . it adds a kind of
state to you to be carried from thence to the stairs of your Playhouse ; hate a sculler (remember that) worse than to be acquainted
with one o' the Scullery. No, your Oares are your only sea-crabs. . . .
Before the Play begins, fall to cardes. . . . Now, sir, if the writer be
a fellow that hath either epigrammed you, or hath had a flirt at
your mistress, or hath brought either your feather, or your red-
beard, or your little legs &c. on the stage, you shall disgrace him
worse then by tossing him in a blancket, or giving him the Bastinado
in a Taverne ; if, in the middle of his play (bee it Pastoral or Comedy,
Morall or Tragedie) you rise with a screwed and discontented face
from your stoole to be gone ; no matter whether the Scenes be good
or no ; the better they are, the worse do you distaste them ; and
beeing on your feete, sneake not away like a cowarde, but salute all
your gentle acquaintances that are sprede either on the rushes, or
on stooles about you, and draw what troope you can from the stage
after you ; the Mimickes are beholden to you, for allowing them
elbow roome ; their Poet cries, perhaps, a pox go with you, but care
not for that, theres no musick without frets.

   " Mary, if either the company or the indisposition of the weather
binde you to sit it out, my counsell is then that you turn plain Ape,

take up a rushe, and tickle the earnest eares of your fellow gallants, to make other fooles fall a laughing ; mewe at passionate speeches, blare at merrie, finde faulte with the musicke, whew at the children's action, whistle at the songs, and above all curse the Sharers, that whereas the same day you had bestowed forty shillings on an embroidered felt and feather (Scotch fashion) for your mistris in the Court, within two houres after you encounter with the very same block on the stage, when the Haberdasher swore to you the impression was extant but that morning.

" To conclude, hoord up the finest play-scraps you can get upon which your leane witte may most savourly feede, for want of other stuffe, when the Arcadian and Euphuis'd gentlewomen have their tongues sharpened to set on you ; that quality (next to your shittle-cocke) is the only furniture to a courtier that is but a new beginner and is but in his A.B.C of complement."

The law-courts gave them motives for domestic drama, and were well attended by dramatists; and we can see from Heywood's Prologue the various kind of plays that must have come before Shakspere at times to judge.

> " To give content to this most curious age
> The gods themselves we've brought down to the stage,
> And figured them in planets ; made even Hell
> Deliver up the Furies, by no spell
> Saving the Muses' rapture.   Further we
> Have trafficked by their help, no history
> We've left unrified ; our pens have been dipped
> As well in opening each hid manuscript
> As tracts more vulgar, whether read or sung
> In our domestic or more foreign tongue.
> Of fairy elves, nymphs of the sea or land,
> The lawns and groves, no number can be scanned
> Which we've not given feet to ; nay, 'tis known
> That when our chronicles have barren grown
> Of story, we have all invention stretched,
> Dived low as to the centre, and then reached
> Unto the *Primum Mobile* above,
> Nor 'scaped things intermediate, for your love."

NOTE 7.—GERARD.

At this time Gerard lived in Holburn, and was studying the natures and habitats of plants with reverent love.   He tried to plant them in his spacious garden, and records those that thrive and those that do not. He must have had a large garden, as a large proportion of the plants of temperate climates he mentions as growing there. His friends sent him news of foreign and far-away plants; he himself is always making excursions in the neighbourhood of London, and recording those he found. I went through his *Historie of Plants* to see what flowers Shakspere would be likely to find when he took the country strolls he must have loved, to Hampstead Heath on the north, and Gipsy Hill and Norwood on the south. He put forth his *Historie of Plants*, "From my house in Holburne in the Suburbs of London. John Gerard, 1597."

The woods by Southfleete, near Gravesend, are a rich treasury: Buckthorne, Wild Hempe, Pimpernel, Wild Thyme, Starwort, Speedwell or *Fluellen*, Herbe Ivy, Canterbury Bells, Mullett, Blue English Harebells, Mustard, Rocket, Tway blade, Venus' Looking-Glass, the Butterfly Orchis, Sciatica cresses, Trichomanes and other ferns, Sea-Lavender, Sea Starwort, grow there.

Hampstead Heath produced also most of these plants, and the Royal Fern, Rough Spleenwort, Carduus Benedictus or Blessed Thistle, singular good against all poisons, ulcers, forgetfulness, deafness.

Adder's Tongue groweth in a meadow by the Preaching Spittle, adjoining to London.

The Arrowheads or Water Archers "doe grow in the watery ditches by Saint George his Field, neere unto London; and in the Tower ditche at London."

The Harteshorne plantains grow in barren plains and sandy grounds, as in Tonthill fielde, near unto Westminster.

Willow Herbe grows in the meadows as you go from Lambeth to Battersey, near London. A rare Orchis in a village near London called Stepney.

"Moneywort" found right against the Queen's Palace of Whitehall.

Pennyroyal grows in the common near London called Mile's end.

Wild Clarie grows in the fields of Holburne neere unto Graies Inne, and at the ende of Chelsey next to London.

Mullein grows in Blackheath. Saxifrage groweth in the great field of Islington. Vervaine Mallowe groweth by the ditch-sides on the left hand of the place of execution by London, called Tyborne; likewise among the bushes and hedges as you go from London to a bathing-place called the old Forde; and in the bushes as you go to Hackney, a village by London in the closes next the towne.

"The second kind of Crowfoot (*Ranunculus surrectis cauliculis*) is like unto the precedent, saving that his leaves are fatter, thicker, and greener, and his small twiggie stalks stand upright; of which kinde it chanced that walking in the field next unto the *Theatre* by London, in company of a worshipful merchant of London named Master Nicholas Seton, I founde one of this kinde there with double flowers, which before that time I had not seen."

Note 8.—Field and Vautrollier.

From Stationers' Registers.

J. Vautrollier became a freeman on 2d October 1564.

A note of J. Vautrollier's Priviledges :—

8th July 1578.—He hath one privilege granted to Ludovik Lloid on 15 Anno Elizabeth for viij yeres, of Plutarch de vitis imperatorum translated. He hath another priviledge for 10 years of these 2 bookes following Gia. Silva, Nor. Giordina, Cosmographica Continuato de B. Sylva.—18 April 1573.

Item ,, Paræ elegantes linguæ Latinæ phrases olim ab Aldo Manutio Paulo filio conscriptæ iam nero in ordinem alphabeticum redactæ et in Anglicum sermonem Conversæ.

Item ,, Another priviledge for x. yeres of Novum Testamentum Bezæ cum annotationibus et sive annotationibus.

Summæ Scripturæ thesaurus in locos communus digestus ex Augustine Marlorati adversariis Guglielmi Feuquercei Opera in Tabulas.

Biblia Latina ex versione Sancti Paginæ.

Synonymorum sylva Pelegronis ex Germania in Latium conversa.

Ovidii Nasonis Opera Omnia.

Ciceronis Opera omnia ex Lambini et doctissimorum virorum annotationibus simul et separatim.

Dialectica Rami illustrata per Makilmanum.

" He hath libertie to retain in the printing of these bookes above mentioned 6 Frenchmen or Dutchmen, or such like."

Thomas Vautrollier, 1578.—A right comfortable treatise containing xiij. poyntes of Consolation for them that labour and are laden, iiij^d and a copie.

1579.—Geffrey Fenton's Translation of ye History of Guicciardini of the Low Countries. "The Latin in 1567."

A Boke in English called Plutarch's Lives (*i.e.*, from the French of Amyott, Englished by Sir Thomas North. Folio).

Luther's Sermons in English.

Luther's Consolations in English.

Eusebius' Historie in English.

10th August 1579.—Richard Feilde, sonne of Henry Fielde of Stratford upon Avon in the county of Warwick, Tanner, Hath put himself Apprentis to George Byshop, citizen and Stationer of London for vij yeres from Michaelmas next. ij^s. vi^d.

29th Sept. 1579.—It is agreed yat this Apprentis shall serve ye first vj yeres of his Apprentiseship with ye said Vautrollier to learne ye arte of printing and ye vijth yere with ye said Byshop.

Richard Feild became a freeman 6th February 1587.

18th Sept.—Thomas Vautrollier. Licensed unto him under the handes of the bishop of London and both the Wardens. " Claudii a Sanctu vinculo de pronunciatione lingua e galleiæ libri duo." iiij^d.

15th Jan. 1582.—Thomas Vautrollier. Receaved of him for his licence for printing these ij books, viz., paraphrases, aliquot psalmorum Davidis, Carmina heroica, Scipio Gentilis aucthore. And Le Jardin de Vertu et bonnes mœurs par J. B. gentlehomme (*i.e.* Jacques Bellot) Cadomois xij^d and copies.

Thomas Vautrollier, 20th Feb. 1587. —La Main Chretienne aux touches.

1587.—The treasons of the Scottish Queen, sentence at Fotheringay. A poem intituled Sir William Herbertes Sidney. An excellent ditty of general rejoicing for cutting off of the Scotch Queen.

From the publications themselves we know that Vautrollier published :—

The Institution of the Christian Religion, written in Latin by Mr. John Calvine, and translated into English by Thomas Norton, 1578.

A Treatise on French Verbs. A most easie, perfect, and absolute way to learn the French tongue, 1581.

An Italian Grammar, written in Latin by M. Scipio Lentulo, and turned into English by Henry Grantham, 1578 and 1587.

Claude de Sainliens, the French Littleton, &c. Campo di Fior, or else the flourie field of foure languages, for the furtherance of the learners in the Latine, French, English, but chiefly of the Italian tongues, 1583.

An Astrological Catechism, Englished by Turner. Leowitz.

A Brief Introduction to Music. Collected by Paul de la Motte, a Frenchman. Licensed. London, 8vo, 1574.

De Beau Chesne. Translated by John Baildon.

A book containing divers sorts of hands, etc.

In Herbert's *Typographical Antiquities* there is another list of Vautrollier's publications.

Discursus Cantiones ; quæ ab argumento sacræ vocantur quinque et sex partuum. Autoribus Thomæ Tallisio et Gulielmo Birdo. Cum privilegio. London, oblong 4to, 1575.

Gaspard de Coligny, Admiral of France. The Lyfe of the most godly, valeant, and noble capteine and maintener of the trew Christian Religion in France, &c.

Field, we saw, became a freeman in 1587, and on Vautrollier's death soon after, married his widow and succeeded him.

24th Dec. 1588.—Richard Feilde entred for his copie a booke in French intituled Le politique reformé, qui est une apologie pour les Princes Reformez contre les Calomnies de la Ligue. Entered for his copie the same booke, being translated into English.

26th May 1589.—Master Feild entered for his copie, as well in French as English, The Declarations of the Frenche Kinge, and the Kinge of Navarre, upon the truce concluded between yer Majesties together with the King of Navarre's Declaration at his passage over the Ryver of Loire ; Master Hartwell's hand being to these copies. xij^d.

Richard Ffield, 2nd June, David's Faith and Repentance. Daniell, expounde by Scriptures in Hebrue, Greeke, and English.

9th June.—Vray Discours sur la Diffaicte des Duc D'Aumalle et Sieur de Battagny avec leurs troupes, par le Duc de Longueville et autres seigneurs, &c.

Lettre d'un gentilhomme de Beausse a un sien aux Bourgeois de Paris. Lettre du Roy de Navarre a Messieurs d'Orleans Du 22 Maij 1589, a Banquenay. xvj^d.

The following book was entered shortly, that I have expanded from the title 1589 :—

Puttenham's Arte of English Poesie. Contrived into three Bookes ; the first of Poets and Poesie, the second of Proportion, the third of Ornament. Dedicated by Puttenham to the Queen, and by Field to Lord Burleigh. It expresses strong objection to rhymed plays, and teaches that vice should be reproved in comedy.

Richard Ffeild, 16th June 1689.—Entred for his copie to be prynted in Frenche and Englisshe a booke entituled Discours brief mais tressolide, monstrant clairement qu'il est loisible, honneste, utile et necessaire au Roy de s'allier au Roy de Navarre.

7th August 1589.—Le vray Agnus Dei pour desarmer le peuple François Escrit pour Le Roy tres chrestien Henrie iij Roy de Fraunce et de Pologne sur le point de son Massacre. Dedie au Roy treschrestien Henry iiijme Roy de Navarre.

Richard Feild.—A booke intituled The furious, translated by James the Sixte, Kinge of Scotland, with the "Lepanto" of the same Kinge.

1st Dec. 1589.—A briefe discourse of the Spanishe State, with a Dyalogue intituled Philobasites.

13th March 1590.—The Method of Phisicke. Phillip Barroughe aucthore.

16th May 1590.—A sovereigne salve for a sicke soule, teachinge the righte use of a patient bearinge the crosse.

16th May 1590.—Richard Field: A brief discourse dialoge wyse shewinge how false and dangerous their reportes are which affirme the Spanyardes intendid invasion is for reestablishment of the Romishe Religion; her Majesties alliance with the Netherlands, &c., by Sir Francis Drake's enterprise three years past into the West Indies.

25th June.—Allowed unto him for his copie. The French Lyttleton, sette forthe by Holiband, and printed by Vautrollier.

Allowed also unto him.

The Treatise of Christian Righteousness, which was Thomas Vautrollier's copie.

Stat. Reg. 7 Feb. 1591.—Jasper Field, son of Henry Feild of Statford upon Avon, in the County of Warwick, Tanner, hath put himselfe an apprentice to Richard Feild, citizen and stationer of London for seven yeres from the date hereof (7 Feb. 1591) ij^s. via.

26th February 1591.—A book entituled John Harington's Orlando Furioso of Ludovico Ariosto.

6th Dec. 1591.—Parti prima Delle Reni Dimonstrationi et precetté utilissimi de Diversi propositi morali politici et Iconomisi Da Petruccio Ubaldino Cittadini Fiorentino.

1st July 1592.—A booke entituled The Frenche Alphabet, together with the treasure of the French tonge.

5th Feb. 1593.—A briefe discourse of man's transgression and of his Redemption by Christ, with a particular survey of Romysch religion and Rome itself.

5th March 1593.—A brief apologie of certain new invençons, compiled by Master H. Plot.

(Walter Bigg's: "A summary and true discourse of Sir F. Drake's West Indian Voyage," &c.

Thomas Cogan: "The haven of health, chiefly made for the use of students."

David Hume of Godscroft: "Daphnis-Amarylis.")

18th April 1593.—Richard Field entered for his copie under the handes of the Archbishop of Canterbury and Master Warden Stirrup, a booke intituled Venus and Adonis. v^d.

(Assigned over to Master Harrison, senior, 25th June.)

11th Dec. 1593.—Entered for his copye a booke intituled The Pearle of Practise or Practisers Pearle of Phisick and Chirurgie.

31st Dec.—A discription of the properties of all the principalleste mineralles.

Richard Ffeilde, 14th January 1594.—Assigned unto him the printing of Tullies Orations in 16mo for the Companye, and he to allowe upon every impression vj^d in the pound to the use of the poore of the Company, according to the order in yat behalf. Mem.

That this entrance is onely of Tullies orations, in decimo sexto in 3 volumes.

Richard Ffeilde assigned unto him in like sort the printing of Tully's Offices in decimo sexto only. Allowing vi^d in the pound uppon every impression, to the use of the poore.

1st May 1594.—Master Feilde, The Holy Historie of our Lord and Saviour Jesus Christus, Nativitie, Life, Acts, Miracles, Doctrine, Deathe, Passion, Resurrection, and Ascension, gathered into English meeter by R. H. Holland, Master of Artes.

Richard Field, 7th May 1594.—Assigned over to him for his copye from Master Bonham Norton, by consent of a court holden this day, The history of Guicciardini, conteyning the warres of Italy, &c., and also the argumentes with a table, &c., reduced into English by Geoffrey Fenton.

   „   „   Assigned unto him from Master Harrison th' elder (Lyacropedius de conscribendis epistolis).

25th June 1594.—Master Harrison, senior, assigned over unto him from Richard Field in open court holden this day, a book called Venus and Adonis, the which was before entered to Richard Field.

Master Harrison, senior, and Richard Field, a booke entituled Phrases Manutii.—2 Dec. 1594.

Observations on the Arte of English Poesie, by Thomas Campion, 1594. (1602. Field, Thoma Campiona. Poema.)

30th Oct. 1596.—Richard Fielde. Entered for his copy intituled A newe discourse of a stale subject called The Metamorphosis of Ajax, with the Anatomy and Apologie of the same, wrytten by Mysacmos to his frend and Cozen Philostilpnos.

6th March 1599.—Richard Feilde. The Sacred Shield of all Christian Souldyours, &c.

Richard Field payd x.lb. for exemption from Rentership on 26th March 1604.

Master Field, Warden, 1605.

(Saluste du Bartas. " The Divine Weeks and Works."

Giordano de Bruno's Philosophy.

Cicero's Orations (ad imprimendum solum).

Timothy Bright. A Treatise on Melancholy, containing the causes thereof, and reasons of the strange effects it worketh in our minds and bodies. 1586.

Jacques Bellot. Le Jardin de Vertus et bonnes mœurs.

Many editions of the Bible. Sir Thomas Chaloner De Rep. Anglorum instauranda Libri Decem.)

Note 9.—Shakspere's Coat of Arms.

Of the grant of arms to John Shakspere, 1596, two drafts are preserved in the College of Arms, MS. Vincent, 157, Art. 23 and Art. 24, stating that the reasons that John Shakspere should bear a coat of arms and hand it down to posterity are these :—" His parents and late antecessors were advanced by King Henry VII. for valiant services ; that they continued in good reputation and credit in the same parts ; that John had married Mary, daughter and co-heir of Robert Arden of Wilmcote, in the said county, esquire." William Dethick, Garter king-of-arms, granted a shield or cote of arms, viz., Gould on a bend sables, a speare of the first, steeled argent ; and for his crest or cognizance a falcon, his wings displayed argent, standing on a wrethe of his coullers, supporting a speare, gould set upon a helmett with mantelles and tasselles as hath been accustomed." His motto, " Non sans droict."

There were memoranda below this draft. "This John showeth a patierne thereof under the Clarent Cooke's hand in paper xx. yeares past. Had been Q. officer and cheffe of the towne (Justice of the Peace), was a Baylife of Stratford on Avon, xx. or xxi. yeares past. That he hath lands and tenements of good wealth and substance, £500. That he married a daughter of Arden, a gentleman of worship." There was an objection made that the arms selected too much resembled those of Lord Manley ; but the answer to the objection made was that the spear on the bend was a patible difference.

In 1599 there was a further request to be allowed to impale the arms of Arden, which was granted by William Camden, now Clarencieux king-at-arms, going through the previous grant, and adding (MS. Coll. of Arm, R. 21): "And we have lykewise uppon another escucheon impaled the same with the auncyent arms of the said Arden of Wellingcote, signifying thereby that it maye and shalbe lawfull for the said John Shakespeare gent. to beare and use the same shields of armes single or impaled as aforesaid, during his natural lyfe, and that it shalbe lawful for his children, issue, and posterity to beare, use, and quarter, and shewe for the same with their dewe difference in all lawfull warlyke feates and civill use. The arms of Arden were, "Ermine a fesse chequy, or and azure. Crest, on a chapeau azure turned up ermine a boar passant, or. Motto, Quo me cunque vocat patria." Therefore three successive kings-at-arms allowed this coat of arms, *i.e.* Cooke, Dethick, Camden. —From Mr. Russel French's *Genealogica Shakespeareana.*

A. W. C. Hallen's Pedigree of Shakspere's Family:—

In the draft of the grant of arms, John Shakspere is styled gentleman, and his great-grandfather referred to as having rendered faithful and valiant service to Henry VII. A facsimile of the grant of arms by Sir William Dethick, Garter, 20th October 1596, also of the assignment of arms to Mary Arden, his wife, in 1599, appeared in *Miscellanea Genealogica* and *Heraldica*, 3rd series, July 1884, p. 109.

There is also a manuscript in the Heralds' Office, marked W. 2, p. 276, where notice is taken of this coat, and that the person to whom it was granted had borne magistracy at Stratford-on-Avon. —Waldron's *Shakespearean Miscellany*.

The Shakespeare arms, not impaled with the Ardens, are placed over William's tomb in Stratford Church, probably through the choice of his surviving relatives. It has often been represented that he was buried in the chancel, only because he owned the tithes. I think not. In the Stratford Registers are notices of the extra fees to be paid for those that are buried in the church and the chancel. And in the *Returne from Pernassus*, "Perceval" is made to say of his father, " Marrie I coulde be contente to be at coste to burie him in the churche, but that I will not bringe up new customes ; he shall lie with his posteritie in the churchyard."

NOTE 10.—BACON'S GREAT WORK.

While Bacon was still at the University, his revolt against Aristotle took shape, and he conceived the first sketch of his great work, calling it " Partus Temporis Maximus," or " The Greatest Birth of Time." His legal studies prevented him from following this out either as fully or as rapidly as he would have wished. Yet his life-thought ever turned towards it, and it came out in parts.

" Francis of Verulam reasoned thus with himself, and judged it to be for the interest of the present and future generations that they should be made acquainted with his thoughts." And future generations have found it to be so. The plan of the great work was not strictly adhered to, and never completed.

Instauratio Magna.

It was in six parts.

1. The Division of the Sciences.
2. The New Organon, or Directions concerning the Interpretation of Nature.

3. The Phenomena of the Universe, or a Natural and Experimental History for the Foundation of Philosophy.

4. The Ladder of the Intellect.

5. The Forerunners or Anticipators of the New Philosophy.

6. The New Philosophy or Active Science. The first part of the *Instauration,* The *Advancement of Learning* he published in 1605 and dedicated to James I. The second part of the *Instauration* or *New Organon* appeared in 1620, incomplete, because "he numbered his days, and would have it saved." Various other works, published or designed for publication by him as parts of the *Instauratio Magna,* are—

Natural and Experimental History of the Winds.
History of Heavy and Light.
History of Sympathy and Antipathy.
History of Sulphur, Mercury, and Salt.
Fragment of Abecedarium Naturæ.
History of Life and Death.
History of Dense and Rare.
Sylva Sylvarum, or Natural History.
Inquiry respecting the Magnet.
Inquiry respecting Light and Luminous Matter.
Catalogue of Particular Histories.

Other works connected, but not meant to be included in the
Instauratio Magna.

Thoughts on the Nature of Things.
On the Ebb and Flow of the Sea.
New Atlantis.
On Principles and Origins.
Magnalia Naturæ.

Works intended to be included, but superseded, are

Description of the Intellectual Globe.
Theory of the Heavens.
Valerius Terminus. Filum Labyrinthi.
Cogitata et Visa. De Motu. Calor et Frigus.
Historia Soni et Auditus. Phænomena Universi.
Physiological and Medical Remains.

The *Instauratio* was published in 1623.

Note 11.—The Opinion of Contemporaries.

In *Fragmenta Regalia, or Observations on the late Queen Eliza-beth, her Times and Favourites*, written by Sir Robert Naunton, Master of the Court of Wards, 1653, Sir Nicholas Bacon is mentioned on p. 38. " He was father to that refined wit, which since hath acted a disastrous part on the publique stage, and of late sate in his father's room as Lord Chancellor. Those that lived in his age, and from whence I have taken this little model of him, give him a lively character, and they decipher him for another Solon, and the Synon of those times, such a one as Oedipus was in dissolving of riddles. Doubtless he was as able an instrument ; and it was his commendation, that his Head was the Mawl, (for it was a great one), and therein he kept the wedge that entered the knotty pieces that came to the Table."

Ben Jonson on Bacon—*Timber :*—" My conceit of his person was never increased towards him by his place or honours, but I have and do reverence him for the greatness that was only proper to himself, in that he seemed to me ever, by his work, one of the greatest men, and most worthy of admiration, that had been in many ages. In his adversity, I ever prayed that God would give him strength ; for greatness he could not want. Neither could I condole in a word or syllable for him, as knowing no accident could do harm to virtue, but rather help to make it manifest." Jonson's opinion of his talents is mentioned in Chapters iv. and v.

In State Trials, vol. ii., I find in the arraignment of Bacon, " The person against whom it is alleged is no less than the Lord Chancellor, a man so endued with all parts, both of nature and art, as that I will say no more of him, being not able to say enough. The matter is *corruption.*"

Bacon acknowledged this, and pled guilty, but he was very mildly treated by all. He said that though the censure was just, yet he had been the justest judge they had for long. Peter Bömer, his domestic apothecary, suggested that a statue should be erected to his memory in acknowledgment of his moral virtues. "Therefore it is a thing to be wished (he having died on the 9th of April 1626, aged 62 years) that a statue in honour of him may be erected in his country, as a memorable example to all of virtue, kindness, peacefulness, patience."

Those who saw him nearest in life gave him the best character : those who criticised him in parts, admired him as a whole.

Sir Henry Wotton wrote to Bacon on receiving three copies of his great work :—" Your Lordship hath done a great and everlasting benefit to all the children of Nature, and to Nature herself in her utmost extent of latitude, who never before had so noble and so true an interpreter, never so inward a secretary of her cabinet."

There is no doubt that he *might* have outlived his technical disgrace, and gained a new dignity among his contemporaries as a philosopher and man of science, as he has with his successors ; for he left his memory to the next ages, and they have forgot the politician and remembered only the author of the great work that founded the new school of thought we have named " The Baconian Philosophy."

NOTE 12.—BACON'S ESSAYS.

Bacon's Essays appeared in very small octavo, 1597, dedicated to his only brother, Anthony. In the Preface he says :—" I do now, like some that have an orchard ill-neighboured, that gather their fruit before it is ripe to prevent stealing." This points to the common habit of lending about works in manuscript ; and though it suggests that some one meant to rob him, it also seems that Bacon was able to forestall him. The Stationers' Registers show how.

24th Jan. 1597.—Richard Serger entered for his copie under the hand of Master Warden Dawson, a book entituled Essayes of Master Francis Bacon, with the prayers of his Sovereigne, vj^d.

Cancellatur ista intratio per curiam tentam 7 February. See correct entry below.

Humphrey Hooper entered for his copie under the handes of Master Francis Bacon, Master Doctor Stanhope, Master Barlowe, and Master Warden Dawson, A booke intituled Essaies, Religious Meditationes, Places of Perswasion and Disswasion by Master Frauncis Bacon vj^d. 7th February.

The first is evidently the pirated edition he alludes to. Here Bacon is treated as " Censor " of his own book. " Under the handes " is the phrase of permission.

Montaigne's *Essays*, published in French, 1580, translated by Florio, 1603, were probably introduced to Bacon's notice by his brother Anthony, who knew Montaigne while wandering on the Continent between 1579 and 1592. His endless rambling from the subject must have been distasteful to Bacon's more methodical spirit, yet the novelty of the form attracted him, and he began to write down his own ideas in his own way in this new essay form ; so that when published in 1597, he was able to say they had passed long ago from his pen. Yet he utterly ignored his guide, and in his second edition of 1612 he refers Prince Henry in the dedication to Seneca's Epistles to Lucullus as the prototype of the modern essay. Not only, however, was Montaigne his predecessor, but a small book of essays appeared in 1596 called *Anonymous, his Remedies against Discontent*, which discourses are 1. Howe wee ought to prepare ourselves against passion. 2. Of the choice of affaires. 3. Of foresight. 4. Of the vocation of every man. 5. How wee ought to rule our life. 6. Of the diversitie of men's actions. 7. Of the choice of friends. 8. Of dissembling. 9. Of vanitie. 10. Of prosperitie. 11. A comparison of our owne estate, with the fortune of other men. 12. Of adversitie. 13. Of sorrow. 14. Of the affection of good men. 15. Of other men's faults. 16. Of injuries, wrongs, and disgraces. 17. Of povertie. 18. Of death. So that though Bacon established this form, he was not quite the first English Essayist. See Arber's Reprints.

Machiavelli's Discourses upon Livy's First Decade was a favourite book with Bacon, and he must have owed the suggestion of his essay on the Vicissitude of Things to Chap. v. Book ii. of Machiavelli. Rawley said that when he had occasion to use other men's words, he had a use and a faculty to dress them in better vestments and apparel than they had before; hence, perhaps, he did not acknowledge them.

Note 13.—Conference of Pleasure.

Mr. James Spedding edits a "Conference of Pleasure" (called "Mr Francis Bacon of Tribute or giving what is dew"), composed for some festive occasion about 1592 by Francis Bacon, and found in a MS. belonging to the Duke of Northumberland. In a supplement to Stephen's second collection of smaller pieces of Lord Bacon were two pieces—"Mr. Bacon in Praise of his Sovereign," and "Mr. Bacon in Praise of Knowledge," which are found to be parts of this whole. Four friends meet. A presides; B gives an oration in praise of Fortitude, the noblest virtue; C, in praise of Love, the noblest affection; D, in praise of Knowledge, the noblest power; A, in praise of his sovereign, the noblest person, who combines all these qualities. The style is utterly unlike that of Shakspere. It is copied by a scribe in a folio paper book of twenty-two sheets. 1st. comes the Conference of Pleasure in full. Then 2nd. comes an Essay on Magnanimity, afterwards merged in the advancement of learning. 3rd. An advertisement touching private censure. 4th. An advertisement touching the controversies of the Church of England. 5th. A letter to a French gentlemen—the middle sheet, where some may have been lost. 6th. The Hermit's first speech. 7th. The Hermit's second speech. 8th. The Soldier's speech. 9th. The Secretarie's speech. 10th. The Squyre's speech, written for a device, 1595, presented by the Earl of Essex on the Queen's day. 11th. For the Earl of Sussex at ye . . tilt, An: 96. 12th. A letter like Cabala. 13th. A copy of Leicester's Commonwealth.

On the back, among various scribblings, are written these titles in a list.

Below in another column—

Richard the Second.

Richard the Third.

Asmund and Cornelia.

Isle of Dogs poem ? by Thomas Nash and inferior players. These are not in this volume.

All over the page scribbled William Shakespeare, Francis Bacon. *Ne vele velis,* &c.

There is no trace of Bacon's own handwriting.

It is supposed to have lain since Bishop Percy's time in two black boxes awaiting investigation.

The printed form of Shakspere's name is used.

NOTE 14.—BEN JONSON'S PURGE.

During Shakspere's early London days an attempt at an Aristophanic revival had checked the advance of the Drama, and had brought in laws against the Players.

Ben Jonson not only differed from Shakspere upon Dramatic Rules and the treatment of the Unities, as we saw in *Every Man in his Humour,* but he differed from him in regard to the use that may be made of the stage in satirising persons directly. Not only had he satirised known persons and habits in *Cynthia's Revels,* but in the *Poetaster* he produced what has been called an Aristophanic play, of which he gave the key in his ordinary conversation. He represented himself as Horace, and Marston and Dekker as Crispinus and Demetrius. Horace is immeasurably bored by the platitudes, pertinacity, and long words of Crispinus ; and finally gives him a dose that makes him vomit the most objectionable words, some of them sticking in his throat. We may notice that some of these words are now used in our familiar speech, and others have never entered it : Poet. Act v. sc. 1. He is also supposed to have satirised other known contemporaries, and to have ridiculed Shakspere's coat of arms. He certainly ridicules Players in general in the persons of the sneaking informers Histrio and Æsop, and in the remarks put into the mouth of Lupus about the whole profession, "These players are an idle

generation, and do much harm in a state . . . besides they will rob
us magistrates of our respect, bringing us upon the stage, and making
us ridiculous to plebeians." Deckar answers this in his *Satiro-Mastix*,
in which he castigates Jonson severely. He retains the same
characters, and represents Shakspere as "William Rufus" presid-
ing at "the untrussing of the Humourous Poet;" and uses the phrase
"Hamlet-Revenge." It is this play of Deckar's that is supposed
to be alluded to in the *Return from Pernassus*, Part II.; though
Shakspere's answer to Ben Jonson to which Chapman alludes,
appears in the "Malvolio" of *The Twelfth Night*, and "Thersites
and Achilles" of *Troilus and Cressida.* Shakspere's satiric vein is,
however, mild and gentle, and consistent with the dramatic action
of the other characters. "Malvolio," the "cross-gartered gull,"
however, stuck to Ben a while, and may have purged him of his
Humours.

Note 15.—John Davies.

John Davies, of Hereford, 1563–1618, was a writing-master. He
writes *The Scourge of Folly, Microcosmus, Witte's Pilgrimage, The Muse's
Sacrifice,* and many minor poems; as well as versified translations
of the Psalms. He writes praises of Shakspere, as our English
Terence, &c., and in one poem says—

> " Good wine doth need no bush, Lord, who can telle
> How ofte this old-said saw hath praised new books ?"

We mention this because the proverb is one of the identities given
by the Baconians.

Sir John Davies, a lawyer and friend of Bacon's, 1569–1626,
publishes *Orchestra,* 1596; *Hymns to Astræa* (Elizabeth), 1599;
Metrical Psalms, Nosce Teipsum, 1599. Went to Scotland to "welcome" King James in 1601. Bacon asked him then to be good to
"conceled poets," and he doubtless was so, as we find James ready
to receive Bacon when he came to England. Query, Whether did
Bacon write his *Orchestra, Psalms,* or *Nosce Teipsum,* or all three?

It is well to notice these similar names so near the same date, and
avoid confusion.

Note 16.—List of Actors.

The chief actors in the plays mentioned in the 1623 edition are :—

William Shakspere, 1564–1616.—For life see "Outlines" by J. Halliwell-Phillips. He had chief charge of the King's Players until 1604; and they got into trouble when he left them. He evidently acted the young lovers in his youth, but gradually retiring as he wrote and managed more, latterly played stately parts, like the ghost in *Hamlet* and Adam in *As you Like it*.

Richard Burbage, 1567–1619.—Three years younger than Shakspere, he seemed to have been trained to take Shakspere's parts, and succeeded so well as to allow Shakspere to retire gradually. He took all principal parts; especially *Hamlet*. That he grew fat, the different editions of the play show. In the early editions the age is reckoned different. It keeps pace with Burbage's age, and the later edition says, "He's fat, and scant of breath." His grandfather, John Burbage, was bailiff of Stratford in 1555; his father, James Burbage, was first a joiner, then a first player in Earl Leicester's company; in May 1574 he "was authorised to act." When he went to London, he "became the chief builder of playhouses." Richard had a daughter named Juliet, 1602–1608; a son William, 1616; and he himself died in 1619 at the same age as Shakspere.

> " Dick Burbage that most famous man,
>   That actor without peer,
>   With this same part his course began,
>   And kept it many a year.
>   Shakespeare was fortunate I trow
>   That such an actor had ;
>   If we had but his equal now,
>   For one I should be glad."

—Manuscript of time of Charles I. Collier's Memoirs of the Principal Actors.

John Hemming, probably a Warwickshire man, born 1556, was an important actor in 1599. He relinquished the active duties of his profession at the time of bringing out the folio edition, the printing of which must have taken a year.

Augustine Philipps, first heard of as acting in 1588, was in early youth a comic actor, became more serious later, and died May 1605.

Samuel Gilbarne.

Robert Arnim, also a pamphleteer of London. Tarleton made Arnim his adopted son; probably born in 1570.

William Ostler was one of the "children" in the Queen's Chapel in 1601, and was married before 1612, but little is known of him.

Nathan Field was born in 1587, the same year his father, a Puritan preacher, died. He became a good actor and successor to Burbage.

William Kemp, the author of *Kempe's Jig*, succeeded Richard Tarleton as Comedian in 1589, and was the original Dogberry, and Peter, Gravedigger, &c. He was a finished actor. He left the company in 1592 to join Alleyn. He visited Rome; and then lived in Southwark. He "expanded plays," as is alluded to in *Hamlet;* and was dead before 1609, when Dekker wrote the *Gul's Hornbook.*

Thomas Poope, probably a Warwickshire man, first mentioned in 1588. Supposed to have sold his shares to Shakspere. Died in 1603.

George Bryan acted in Tarleton's *Dance of the Seven Deadly Sins.* He had a son 17th February 1599, but no record of his birth or death has been found.

Henry Condell was not mentioned in the players' lists of 1587. In 1598 he acted in Ben Jonson's *Every Man in His Humour* (see ed. 1616), and played in most of the dramas of Beaumont and Fletcher with Burbage. Died 1627.

William Slye, a common name in Warwickshire; he lived in Norman's Rents, Southwark, in 1858, and acted in 2nd part of Tarleton's *Seven Deadly Sins.* Died 16th August 1608.

Richard Cowley appears also in Tarleton's *Dance*, he acted Verges, and died 1618.

John Lowine, son of Richard Lowine, born in St. Giles, Cripplegate, 1576; acted in *Sejanus* along with Shakspere; wrote a book on *Dances.* Died in 1668.

Samuel Crosse, probably a Blackfriars man.

Alexander Cooke, one of a numerous family, joined the company young, and acted as a woman in *Sejanus* and *The Fox.*

John Underwood.	Nicholas Tooley.
William Ecclestone.	Joseph Taylor.
Robert Benfield.	Robert Goughe.
Richard Robinson.	John Shancke.
John Rice.	

Besides these players mentioned we have also notice of *Lawrence Fletcher*, who died in 1608, and was buried in St. Saviour's, Southwark.

Gabriel Spenser, the man slain by Ben Johnson, 24th September 1598, in Hogesden Fields.

Edmund Shakspere, "a player buried in the church with a forenoon [1] knell of the great bell 20ˢ." Books of St. Saviour's, Southwark.

---

[1] I think this is probably owing to the Players being accustomed to act in the afternoon they would take the forenoon for their funeral rites.

NOTE 17.—BAUDWIN.

William Baudwin, author of the *Myrrour for Magistrates*, has a poem on Richard II. and on Richard III. 1571.

He is the compiler of a "Treatise on Morall Philosophy, contayning the sayings of the wyse wherein you maye see the worthie and wittie sayings of the Philosophers, Emperors, Kynges and Orators, of their lyves, their aunswers, of what linage they come of ; of what countrie they were, whose worthy and notable precepts, counsailes, parables and semblables, doe hereafter followe." The editions of 1547, 1567, 1575, 1584, 1587, 1591, 1596, 1610, 1620, 1630, are in the British Museum.

His 1st Book is—
  Of Lives and Aunswers.
2nd. Of Philosophical Theologie.
3rd. Of Kynges and Rulers, and of Lawe.
4th. Of Sorrow and Lamentation.
5th. Of Mental Powers and Virtues.
6th. An admonition to avoid all kinds of vices.

This has been a rich field for readers and writers of the period, and one can trace much of Shakspere's knowledge and philosophy to it.

NOTE 18.—PRINTERS.

Through the difficulties of books patented for a certain number of years or for life, great troubles arose among the printers, some of whom could not support themselves. A Commission was appointed on 1st June 1583. The Bishop of London wrote—" I was enformed that printinge of laufull bookes, and suche as be nott otherwise appointed by her Majestie's graunter, is not matter sufficient to mainteigne anye man withoute his losse." The wardens of the Stationers' Company told him that the patentees had eaten up the trade. Robert Bourne, on 3rd February 1586, pleading before the Star Chamber, said that he had been an apprentice printer for eight years, and was now free, with no other means of livelihood, " having no other trade whereby to lyve and maintene himself and his family then the arte of printinge, doth think it no lesse unreasonable to prohibit him from all labour, than to prohibit him from printing in his lawful trade which, although by theirs and such other like priviledges to other particular persons graunted some for printing of lawe books, some for psalm books, some for grammar bokes, schoole bookes, Latyne Hebrewe and Greke bokes, almanner of praier books, Bibles and Service bookes, there is almost no liberty lefte for printinge but for ballettes and toyes and such like, which might with better reason be prohibited then the rest, and which will not suffice to maintaine the printers not priveledged and their families (this defendant verly thinketh), with bread and water." Hence arose pirated editions. Roger Ward printed 10,000 copies of the "A B C with the little catechism appointed by her Highness' injunctions for the Instruction of Children," with the patentees Day's name and trade-mark thereon, out of which rose the Star-Chamber case. The patentees were reasonable, and gave workes for "the reliefe of the poore of the Company," and the Master and Wardens gained the right of imposing sixpence in the pound for registration. School-books were the most lucrative of "patents" then.

In 1583.—The Stationers' Company of London also had a conflict with the University of Cambridge about printing ; and in 1586 there were great disputes among them about the powers of the Company. The Sweeping Star Chamber decree of 23rd June 1586 finally concluded this agitation, and confirmed the power of the Company in the hands of the Master, Wardens, and Assistants; and of such as by co-optation should succeed them.

25th Dec. 1598.—The later rule they formulated was this:[1] "Whereas several members of this Company have great part of their estates in Copies; and by ancient usage of the Company, when any book or copy is duly entered in the Register Book of this Company to any member or members of this Company, such person to whom such entry is made is, and always hath been reputed and taken to be the Proprietor of such book or copie, and ought to have the sole printing thereof, which privilege and interest is now of late often violated and abused. It is therefore ordained, That where any Entry or Entries is, or are, or hereafter shall be duly made of any Book or Copy in the said Register-Book of this Company, by, or for any Member or Members of this Company, that in such case, if any other Member or Members of this Company, for whom such Entry is duly made in the Register-Book of this Company, or his or their Assignee or Assigns, Print, or cause to be Printed, Import or cause to be Imported from beyond seas, or elsewhere, any such Copy or Copies, Book or Books, or any part of such Copy or Copies, Book or Books, or shall sell, bind, stitch, or expose the same, or any part or parts thereof to sale, That then such Member or Members so offending, shall forfeit to

[1] An Act made 19th year, King Henry VII. renewed in 33d Charles II.

the Master and Keepers or Wardens and Commonalty of the Mystery or Art of Stationers of the City of London, the sum of Twelve Pence for every such Copy or Copies, Book or Books, or any part of such Copy or Copies, Book or Books Imprinted, Imported, sold, bound, stitcht, and exposed to sale contrary hereunto." The Master and Wardens had also the privilege of searching any Warehouse suspected of evading this order, and of imposing a penalty of Ten Pounds on refusal.

INDEX.

—✦—

THE END.

PRINTED BY BALLANTYNE, HANSON AND CO.
EDINBURGH AND LONDON.

SHORT SELECTIONS

SOME OPINIONS OF THE PRESS.

FIRST EDITION.

———◆◇◆———

"Mr. C. Stopes, a sound Shaksperean, takes occasion to consider the matter from a novel point of view. His inquiry is intelligently ordered, and his results are curious and entertaining. The tendency of the whole argument is, of course, to show the different habits of mind of the two men, and the several interests by which they were animated in their treatment of the question. Shakspere's point of view was, it need hardly be said, purely moral and psychological, while Bacon's (we need scarcely remark) was absolutely scientific. That the Baconian (so called) should fail to grasp these differences is no more surprising than that the Gladstonian should Gladstonise, or the Wagnerite date the origins of Opera and the beginnings of Melody from the production of *Tristran*. Mr. Stopes, however, has done well to bring them out once more, and that upon a point so trivial and so significant as the one he has chosen; and as his book contains besides a statement of the whole historical argument, it may be cordially recommended."—*Saturday Review*, Sept. 1st.

"If we turn from this overwhelming mass of evidence to Bacon, and consider his writings apart from the moral weakness of their author, the calm philosophy, the rigid reasoning, the science, and careful elaboration, we wonder, and with Mr. Stopes conclude, that surely no insult to the character and knowledge, the style and dignity of his work, was ever like to this: 'that *he* could have invented and inserted Mr. Donnelly's cipher in the plays. It crowns all.' It does, indeed!"—*The Spectator*, Oct. 13th.

"An admirable piece of work."—*Truth*, Nov. 15th.

"The vast majority of Englishmen, and, it may be added, Americans, do not need to be convinced that Shakspere wrote the plays of Shakspere. If any one doubts that he did so, and believes that these great poems are the work of Bacon, he cannot do better than read Mr. C. Stopes's little book. It is seldom that we have read with so great pleasure a book on a subject which may at first sight appear to have an interest only for the student and the

scholar. Mr. Stopes has written a lucid, logical, and able *exposé* of
the fallacies of the Baconians. His answer to Mrs. Pott and Mr.
Ignatius Donnelly is complete and effective. The plan of the work
under notice is marvellously simple. The author divides his answer
into four groups: 1st, the probability from the known character
and education of the writer of the plays; 2nd, internal evidence
gained by comparing the plays with Bacon's works; 3rd, the
external evidence of most of the poems and plays being at some
time claimed by Shakspere, and *never* by Bacon; and 4th, the
external evidence of the writings of contemporaries, some of whom
personally knew both Shakspere and Bacon. Proceeding on these
lines, Mr. Stopes gives his idea of the character of the country-bred
Shakspere, and contrasts it with Bacon's. He says:—'Turn to
Bacon, full of ambitions, with no personal duty to others to raise
and purify them. Essentially a city youth, a university student, a
classic critic, an observant traveller, a man of the world, a statesman born and bred, a lawyer, a member of Parliament, an essayist,
a scientist, a philosopher—in short, the author of *The greatest
birth of Time.*' Bacon, the polished man of letters, would have
despised the plays, with their neglect of scholarship and their
neglect of the unities. Mr. Stopes's argument on the internal
evidence of the plays of Shakspere and Bacon's books is a very
strong one. Nothing could be more dissimilar than the passionate
Venus and Adonis and the *Novum Organum.* The external evidence is even stronger. With amazing industry Mr. Stopes has
collected every allusion to Shakspere by his contemporaries, and
shows conclusively that they at least who knew him in the flesh,
and saw him act on the stage, believed him to be the author—and
never is there a contemporary allusion to Bacon as claiming any of
the works attributed to Shakspere. Even Ben Jonson, the friend
of Bacon, the man who thought himself *the* dramatist of the
time, condescends to pen verses to the great genius of Stratford-
on-Avon. It was left for cranks two and a half centuries later to
discover that Bacon, and not Shakspere, was the true author. To
our mind this argument is conclusive; but Mr. Stopes has not
stopped at this. He takes Mrs. Pott's thirty-two reasons, and shows
their want of reason. Nor does he neglect Mr. Donnelly, as befits
the bigness of his book. Mr. Stopes's task was an easy one so far
as the sympathy of the public goes, but he has certainly performed
it in a manner leaving nothing to be desired, and we fancy that the
Baconian Society will not get over the hard remarks he deals their
theories by ignoring them altogether, for to answer them seems
impossible."—*The Evening Post* (Leading Article), Aug. 20th.

"The controversy which has arisen on the bizarre contention that

Shakspere's plays and poems were not written by Shakspere at all, but by Francis Bacon, has not been without at least one profitable result, inasmuch as it has, in this studiously-prepared and most interesting volume, received a contribution in which are collected the sayings and the sentiments which our great national, and not yet disenthroned, poet gives to many of his characters, when the ways and usages of his countrymen in the matter of beer, wine, and drinking chance to come in view. It at the same time states very fully and very fairly, and examines very carefully, the main arguments adduced on both sides of the controversy, and, as it appears to us, utterly refutes the claim set up for Bacon. We may leave it to the attentive perusal of all who feel an interest in the subject, promising them that they will find in its pages much pleasant reading of a very instructive kind."—*The Morning Advertiser,* Sept. 1st.

"Written in a clear and interesting style."—*Scotsman,* Aug. 20th.

"To the Bacon-Shakspere controversy Mr. C. Stopes has made a curious and interesting contribution. Whilst preparing some articles on stimulants, Mr. Stopes was struck by the manner in which intoxicants are referred to by Bacon and by Shakspere. This is an ingenious line of proof, and it has been ably carried out. Mr. Stopes does not restrict himself to this evidence, but although he argues the general 'Bacon-Shakspere question,' this is the most original and telling part of his work. Bacon, he says, was a scientist, and trade facts and processes were gathered and criticised by him. He wrote about wine-making and about brewing, gave recipes for preserving and doctoring, set forth the annals of the taxation of alehouses, composed a *Natural History of Drunkenness,* and indicated hints for avoiding the physical effects of inebriety. But 'the moral question never touched him; not even in his *Colours of Good and Evil* does he consider drink in relation to character. The physiological effect is treated only physiologically. Man to him is but a means of experimenting upon the various effects of spirit in wine.' This is very well said."—*Manchester Guardian* (Leading Article), Aug. 18th.

"The author of this book is perhaps better known in Glasgow as Miss Charlotte Carmichael than as Mrs. Stopes. She takes up a curious phase of the inquiry, which is a remarkably interesting one, as throwing light on the habits and ideas of modern writers. The book is able and interesting, and is certainly an important contribution to the great literary controversy."—*Glasgow Herald,* Aug. 30th.

"The controversy receives a fresh elucidation from this work by C. Stopes. His is a remarkably quaint collection of curious matter which ought to be examined by persons on both sides."—*The Publishers' Circular,* Aug. 15th.

"Although the Bacon controversy has begun already to show signs of flagging, there is quite enough vitality in it left to ensure Mr. Stopes' essay all due consideration."—*The Bookseller*, Sept. 5th.

"Differing in every single particular from the innumerable other treatises lately published upon the matter, Mr. Stopes' volume, by reason of its originality and the careful and painstaking manner in which it has been compiled, deserves to receive the undivided attention of all taking any interest in the controversy."—*The City Press*, Sept. 3rd.

"To those interested in this discussion a happier and more conclusive answer will not be found than this clever and scholarly volume of Mr. Stopes."—*The Citizen*, Aug. 25th.

"Except for the reason that what is left unanswered may be deemed by some persons to be unanswerable, it was hardly worth while for lovers of Shakspere to defend the bard's memory from the attacks of the American and other unfortunates afflicted with the Baconian mania. In a volume by Mr. C. Stopes are collected many interesting facts bearing on the problem, and this contribution to the 'Bacon-Shakspere Question' will be certain to find many readers. Altogether Mr. Stopes makes the Baconians seem very ridiculous though laboriously industrious persons."—*Liverpool Courier*, Oct. 17th.

"The cryptogrammic nut of Mr. Donnelly has been cracked, pulverised, and utterly dissipated by a sledge-hammer blow from Mr. C. Stopes."—*The Norwich Mercury*, Sept. 5th.

"Mrs. Stopes has her contrasts of Bacon and Shakspere ingeniously developed, and her arguments are ingenious and novel and cleverly worked out. The authoress, who is a Scotchwoman, deserves an honourable place among the women who have devoted their time, talents, and learning to Shaksperean studies. We congratulate her upon her work, which, we trust, will receive the careful attention to which its merits entitle it."—*The Queen*, Sept. 22nd.

"Mrs. Stopes is to be commended for her decision to bring the evidence on the matter within the reach of the reading public. It is only just to testify that her book shows adequate and patient study of the subject, presenting as it does, in careful detail, the historico-literary evidences which so completely discountenance the Baconian hypothesis."—*The Scottish Leader*, Sept. 27th.

"The little volume on this question, to which we referred on Wednesday as eminently suitable for sea-side reading, gives a great variety of information, which will be appreciated by all who value Shakspere's works. The book is well arranged for reference, and no lover of Shakspere will regret the possession of the varied stores of information it contains."—*Southport Guardian*, Aug. 25.

"This book is unquestionably valuable, and deserves to be placed among the best literary works of modern times."—*The National Guardian*, Nov. 14th.

"In this volume Mr. Stopes seems to have struck upon a hitherto unworked vein in this literary mine. . . . He deserves credit for his diligence, and his treatment of a novel phase of this vexed question entitles him to be heard as a witness for the defendant in Bacon *v.* Shakspere."—*The English Churchman*, Oct. 4th.

"The Bacon-Shakspere question by C. Stopes is the first serious attempt we have seen to answer Mr. Donnelly."—*Weekly Times*, Sept. 2nd.

"Mr. Stopes has done a very useful public work by placing within the reach of the people of this country a clear and decisive statement of the proofs upon which pretty nearly all English litterateurs rely in vindication of the unparalleled genius. He shows the utter absurdity of Mr. Donnelly's wild contention that the philosophic Bacon wrote the works of the 'immortal bard.' Mr. Stopes effectually refutes Mr. Donnelly's childish arguments, and places Shakspere once more upon the seat from which Mr. Donnelly endeavoured to dethrone him."—*England*, Sept. 15th.

"Mr. Stopes, an enthusiastic Shaksperean, has carefully collected the arguments pro and con, together with many personal facts connected with the two men. Mr. Stopes' arguments remove the uneasy doubts raised by Mr. Donnelly. Those who have taken it up find the book very interesting."—*The Bucks Advertiser*, Aug. 18th.

"After a long review no one can rise from the perusal of Mr. Stopes' volume without having learned much from its wealth of illustration and its sound common sense, and we are glad to know that a cheaper issue at a shilling is also on sale. Original and well put as the argument is, we hope to meet its author in other branches of literature at no distant date."—*The Printer and Stationer*, Aug. 20th.

"Mr. Stopes has much to say, says it ably, temperately, and to our thinking, speaking unofficially, says it conclusively; speaking *ex-cathedra*, we advise the reader to go through these pages carefully. This is a book to be read and studied."—*The Metropolitan*, Sept. 1st.

"If all Shaksperean critics do their work as well as Mr. Stopes has performed his task, the public will not have reason to complain. Certainly, if any doubt ever existed in the brain of a sane individual that Shakspere wrote the plays which bear his name, this work will surely dispel any further scepticism in the matter. Every authority, tradition, and incident, having any bearing on Shakspere, is dealt with so exhaustively, thoroughly, and we may add ably, that he must be an unbelieving Thomas indeed who any longer refuses to acknowledge Shakspere as the writer of all the dramatic and other works usually ascribed to him."—*The American Traveller*, Aug. 25.

"The Bacon-Shakspere question by C. Stopes, in addition to pricking Donnelly's 'gas bag,' the great cryptogram, contains a vast amount of curious as well as valuable information ; it will well repay perusal, and readers who are not fortunate enough to possess such works as Dr. Ingleby's *Shakspere Allusion-Book*, cannot do better than read very carefully the fourth chapter of this reply."—*Blackburn Standard*, Sept. 1st.

"An able vindication of the right of Shakspere to the honour of having written Shakspere's works. Mr. Stopes has managed to perform his task in a manner that renders his book very agreeable and interesting reading. His mastery of the subject is shown on every page."—*Printers' Register*, Sept. 6th.

"Mrs. Stopes is a scholarly Shaksperean student, and the ridiculous hypothesis of the so-called 'Baconians' does not merit demolition at the hands of such a champion ; but as the giving a quietus has been the occasion for the production of an interesting book, the result at least is not to be regretted."—*Westminster Gazette,* Sept. 1st.

"One result is that the public as well as the bibliopole have now within easy reach such a collection of Shakspearean notabilia as must hereafter prove very valuable."—*The Birkenhead Advertiser*, Aug. 23rd.

"It is sufficient to signal the appearance of an interesting and erudite contribution to the study of Shakspere."—*Medical Press*, Oct. 3rd.

"Mr. Stopes has compiled a most interesting and readable book, and one that will gain him an honourable place among Shaksperean students and lovers."—*The British Mail*, Sept. 1888.

"We can heartily congratulate Mr. Stopes on the result of his reading."—*Temperance Record*, Aug. 23rd.

"By his method of working out his argument the author has established his right to be reckoned with in the settlement of this controversy."—*The Literary World*, Aug. 31st.

"What with suppressing this and falsifying that, in the ardour of his bigotry, Professor Donnelly's 'Argument' is a sustained and vigorous indictment, which, to whose who are not something of literary students, is likely to carry conviction. It is, therefore, well to have the other side, not piecemeal in the pages of reviews and periodicals, but adequately in that book form which can alone do justice to a large subject. Mr. Stopes's answer is, we need not say, very complete and most ably developed. Into the ample and conclusive consideration of these divisions of his subject we cannot of course follow Mr. Stopes ; but in the second one there is an original argument advanced that ought to receive more attention than we can give it here. This is a strange turn to give to a learned controversy, but it is none the less a skilful one. Mr.

Stopes displays great skill in dealing with this portion of his task, which affords fresh evidence of an extremely novel kind. It is welcome as an additional proof, though the case which Mr. Stopes has so admirably prepared is in itself a perfect vindication of Shakspere's authorship of the plays and poems." — *The Stage*, Aug. 24.

"This is a cleverly-written volume, in which the author brings forward numerous proofs to show the illogical position occupied by those who would dethrone Shakspere from the high estate he has held for so many centuries. The work will be cordially welcomed by believers in Shakspere."—*The Northern Whig* (Belfast), Sept. 5th.

"This is an interesting, intelligent, and suggestive little book on the Bacon-Shakspere question. The spirit of the work is good."— *Life*, Sept. 27th.

"The author of this little book is a specialist. The success of Mr. Donnelly's work is adequately tested, with the result that it may be laughed out of existence. Mr. Stopes displays a full and accurate acquaintanceship with the character and writings of both Bacon and Shakspere. His method is happy, and convincing to all reasonable minds. The treatise winds up with the interesting examination of Bacon's ciphers. To those interested in the question a happier or more conclusive answer will not easily be found than this clever and scholarly volume of Mr. C. Stopes."—*The Hawick Advertiser*, Aug. 27th.

"This book is neither uncalled for nor untimely. It should be bought and studied by all for whom it is meant—admirers of Shakspere who have not the time at their disposal sufficient to thoroughly investigate the points round which so much controversy has raged of late."—*Border Advertiser*, Aug. 29th.

"We heartily welcome Mr. C. Stopes' contribution to this very important question, which ought to find a place in every library." —*Durham Daily Advertiser*, Sept. 7th.

"Mr. Stopes modestly opens an exceedingly able little work upon the question of Shakspere's authorship of the works attributed to him. It has often been asked, What reason is there to care very much who really was the author, provided he was an Englishman? Bacon or Shakspere, the heritage is equally glorious, our appreciation equally keen. We hold there is a very great reason to care. Mr. Stopes commences his argument on the psychological side of the question, compares the works of each writer, and records the notice of contemporaries. Suffice it to say, that it is treated with exceedingly great accuracy, and a force of argument which perhaps cannot be wholly attributed to Mr. Stopes, as the subject lends itself to such powerful argument."—*The Tablet*, Sept. 1st.

8   THE BACON-SHAKSPERE QUESTION.

" The answers are well and forcibly put, and ought to be read far and wide. It is a very ably written book."—*Stationer, Printer, and Fancy Trades Register*, Sept. 7th.

"Mr. Stopes has produced some very interesting and curious matter, and his work should find a ready sale amongst those who have been *au courant* in the controversy on this subject."—*Freeman's Journal*, Sept. 7th.

" In support of his opinions Mr. Stopes gives us the result of his studies on the subject of the authenticity of Shakspere's plays during two years; and, in a word, evolves from a vast amount of matter, cleverly collated, a crushing reply to Mr. Donnelly and his cipher.'' *Public Opinion*, Sept. 14th.

" If anything could kill the apparently exhaustless Shakspere-Baconian theory, this scholarly volume of Mrs. Stopes might be expected to do it."—*Englishwoman's Review*, Sept. 15th.

" This book has been very extensively and also flatteringly reviewed, and we have been exceedingly amused by the unanimity with which every critic we have seen has blundered respecting the sex of the writer. Mrs. Stopes has produced a rich mine of information, in which the student who lacks time and opportunity for the original research she has given to the subject, may find to his hand treasures of knowledge that he may amplify and retail. We can truly say that Mrs. Stopes has exhausted this phase of the controversy by the careful and painstaking way in which she has found and dealt with all reference thereto."—*Norwood Review*, Sept. 22nd.

" The recent attempt to revive a suggestion about Shakspere having palmed off Bacon's plays as his own has ignominiously failed to excite mankind except to rouse universal scorn on the vendor of so ignorant a slander. But, perhaps, it is well that some one should seriously treat the subject for the sake of future generations, and logically unmask the foolish vanity of the intruder by minute investigation of a critical and searching character. This is done in the elaborate and conclusive book before us, which must have cost a prodigious amount of labour, applied with consummate skill, by a process of scientific reasoning that gives its author a high position in Shaksperean literature. We will not criticise nor describe the skilful method adopted by Mrs. Stopes in her adroit choice of tests by which the relative works of Bacon and Shakspere are tested, save to say that it cannot be confuted."—*Croydon Guardian*, Sept. 8th.

" This work is an able, temperate answer to those whom the author dubs ' The Baconians.' "—*Newcastle Daily Chronicle*, Aug. 14th.

For EU product safety concerns, contact us at Calle de José Abascal, 56–1°, 28003 Madrid, Spain or eugpsr@cambridge.org.

www.ingramcontent.com/pod-product-compliance
Ingram Content Group UK Ltd.
Pitfield, Milton Keynes, MK11 3LW, UK
UKHW010347140625
459647UK00010B/888